FOUL LUCK & OUTRAGEOUS FORTUNE

A candid tell-all by a larrikin legend of racing

RICK HORE-LACY

CHAPTER ONE

When I started out as a trainer in country Victoria, it didn't take me long to realise that I was been regarded as a bit of an outsider by the other racehorse trainers. I hadn't grown up in a family of horse owners, trainers or jockeys, or served the apprenticeship that most trainers had served. And worse, in the eyes of the others, I wasn't a working-class knockabout like the rest of them, but from a wealthy background. 'The Silvertail' was one of the politer terms I heard muttered behind my back.

This reputation only became stronger after I had some success. The privileged background, the university education, the fact that I came from one of Tasmania's wealthier families, all became part of the 'angle' journalists used when they wrote up their articles about me.

There's a fair element of truth in this portrait of me — my family has been fortunate enough to have enjoyed some prosperity for several generations, making (and losing) fortunes on the way, and I certainly never remember having to go without when I was growing up. However, it really only tells part of the story of my family background. In fact, one side of the family tree couldn't have come from humbler beginnings — the convict stock.

The first of my direct descendants to set a foot on Australian soil possibly had a ball and chain tied to it at the time. William Bond was my mother's grandfather's grandfather, so that would be five generations ago. He was transported to Tasmania, or Van Diemen's Land as it was then called, in the first half of the nineteenth century. The exact crime for which he was sentenced is unknown. The version of events passed down through the family, a version started by William Bond himself, is that he was, more or less, an innocent victim of circumstances. He had been employed as a clerk in some London firm, and one fateful fortnight, had found himself a bit short of cash before payday. And so young William had 'borrowed' a few bob from the company to tide him over. I can only say he couldn't have been too popular with his employers because their reaction was to have him charged and thrown in gaol. He doesn't appear to have been a popular son either, for from that point his family washed their hands of him.

In those days, justice was summary and brutal, you didn't have clever defence lawyers pleading their client has ADD, or was given too much red cordial as a child, and that's why he does these bad things, but is now sincerely remorseful, Your Honour. So instead of getting a slap on the wrist and a good behaviour bond, William was sentenced to a six-month journey on a leaking, scurvy-ridden boat to the other side of the world, to the notorious penal colony of Van Diemen's Land.

William Bond would have been in the minority of transported convicts in that he had received some education, had learned his letters and numbers. Armed with this small advantage, he made himself useful to the other prisoners, writing letters and petitions for them. While still serving his time, he was given the position of 'Time Keeper Clerk.' I can shed no light on what that job might have entailed, one of those occupations that has since gone the way of the candlestick maker, town crier and so on, into the dustbin of obsolete professions.

It doesn't sound like it might have been a particularly fascinating job, but no doubt it kept William on the path of rehabilitation. He eventually earned his ticket of leave, a kind of parole that convicts were given after doing their time. It required them to report on a regular basis to the authorities and keep out of further trouble. Although ex-convicts would never have the same social status, or even political and economic rights of the free settlers who were arriving in Tasmania in growing numbers, once they had their ticket of leave, they were essentially free men and women.

Renounced by his own family, William Bond probably had little inclination to return to England. Instead he set himself up as a shoemaker in Hobart, and turned his thoughts to starting a family of his own. The woman who caught his fancy was a pretty English housemaid, whom he described in later accounts to his daughter — no doubt while his wife happened to be in earshot — as a 'vision of charming womanhood in that garden of thorns and briars' — that was Van Diemen's Land at the time.

As well as being a vision of loveliness, William's intended bride was also at least one step further up the social ladder than ex-con William. Apparently, his early attempts at courtship were all snubbed, with the housemaid wanting nothing to do with him. Perhaps he hadn't used the 'vision of charming womanhood' line yet. However, William had set his sights on the maid and was not to be denied. With a stubborn persistence, he kept up the pursuit, and here I recognise traces of myself in William — and not just in terms of bedding a pretty young woman. Eventually, and we don't know if it was out of genuine affection, or more like an exhausted rabbit brought down by its prey, she succumbed to his charms and became his wife.

Nineteenth century Tasmania has earned a pretty harsh and brutal reputation in the history books, by some accounts a kind of South Pacific gulag. Yet it was also a land of unbounded opportunity for those with a bit of resourcefulness and what we might now label as entrepreneurial spirit. My great-great-great-great grandfather William Bond saw his opportunity in northern Tasmania. He and his new bride settled in the West Tamar river valley just north of Launceston and with a small plot of land started a farm.

With the passing of time William Bond became more or less a respectable member of the community, eventually shedding his convict history. He was so successful in erasing his past that his own grandson, Frank Bond, who was to become a wealthy businessman and political figure, had no idea he was of convict stock until he started researching his family tree.

* * *

It was my great-grandfather, Frank Bond, who brought wealth to the Bond family. His business career had just about the humblest beginning you could imagine — he got his start collecting kindling for lighting fires from the sides of the road then selling them to passers- by, in their horse and carriages. There must have been some kind of market for it, because he quickly began to amass a fortune. One of his obituaries described him as a 'keen speculator' as a young man. Through this winning combination of bark and speculation he was able to accumulate enough capital to diversify into property, cattle and sheep trading, mines, railways and what was to become one of Tasmania's biggest tanneries. He had sheep and cattle stations as far afield as Queensland, and owned Tasmania's North Mount Farrell silver and lead mine. He had a finger in so many business pies that the same obituary recalled, 'it was difficult to remember even one company of which he was not a director in those days.'

A political career eventually beckoned, and at 46 years of age he was elected to the Tasmanian State House of Assembly as the member for Hobart. After the voters turfed him out an election later, he simply moved to the other house, the Legislative Council, where he served from 1909 to 1921. He had his fair share of legal stoushes — a bit like myself actually — during his business and political career. He tried, unsuccessfully, to get the result of one election overturned, by accusing his opponent of fraud and bribing constituents. He sued the Federal Steam Navigation Company for allegedly damaging his shipment of apples, and again was unsuccessful. He also took on Tasmania's leading newspaper *The Mercury*, bringing a defamation case against it after the paper accused him of some nefarious activities involving strike-breaking. This case he won, but it was a Pyrrhic victory — the jury awarded him damages of one penny, considerably less than the amount he was after.

Frank Bond became a well-known figure in Hobart not just for his achievements in business and public life, but also because of his size. As *The Mercury* described him, 'Not a tall man by any means, he turned the scales at over 22 stone and, it can easily be imagined, suffered a severe physical disability on account of his excessive weight.' This was in the early 1920s and his doctor gave him the standard 'either lose weight or die' lecture. Frank took the words to heart, for he lost 8 stone in twelve months, then told his story to *The Mercury*, an early forerunner to the celebrity miracle diet articles you read in the women's magazines today.

Frank's interview with *The Mercury* begins like the opening address to an Overeaters Anonymous meeting. 'On January 1, 1923, I weighed 22 stone 2 pounds, and I could not walk 50 yards without resting.' Frank's diet was the essence of logic — he would more or less starve himself. 'From January 1 to May 1923 I took only half a meal a day, during which time I lost three stone.' The half meal consisted of 'a little fried fish, a small wing of a fowl, a small quantity of vegetables, and a savoury.' The meal was supplemented by large amounts of water and nothing stronger.

He lost two pounds in that time, but found his weight levels then plateaued at 19 stone, so he ramped up the diet to half a meal, every two days. By the beginning of July his weight loss had plateaued again, at 17 stone. No problem — his diet now became a single half meal, every three days. By October he had lost 7 stone. He relaxed his Spartan eating regime a little, back to a meal every one or two days, and dropped another couple of stone. 'In measurements, I have lost 20 inches around the waist and there have been proportional reductions in the other parts of my body. Now I can walk any distance with ease and feel a new man... I am now convinced that many people would be greatly benefited if they ate less.' If Frank had lived in today's age, he'd be a pin-up boy for Jenny Craig.

Not surprisingly, Frank Bond was a man of determination. Referring to his diet, he noted, 'It is no use attempting to carry out such a treatment without a strong resolution.' I suspect that the strong resolution also came in good stead in his business dealings too. The diet was to buy Frank Bond another eight years of life before he passed away in his bed in the early hours of a December morning, 1931. He was seventy-six years old.

In common with many a family business, the Bond fortune started to wane almost immediately, through the efforts, or lack thereof, of the next generation. Frank Bond had four sons, my grandfather George, who was born in 1883, was the eldest. One son met an untimely death, and none of the others had their father's entrepreneurial flair and nose for business. George Bond did serve with distinction in the First World War — he was at Gallipoli and then went to France, via Egypt, and was awarded a Military Cross. He also injured his leg in a fall and, according to the Army medical records, suffered chronic laryngitis. The Army obviously decided he had done more than his bit for the cause, and so he eventually received a discharge from active service in 1917 and returned to Tasmania.

For whatever reason, he was never able to make the adjustment back to civilian life. He became a permanent fixture at the local pub — my mother who was a teenager at the time, was often given the job of bringing him back home as he was too drunk to make it on his own. When he died, his death certificate didn't sugar coat the facts. Cause of death was written down simply as... alcoholic poisoning.

* * *

On my father's side, the first to arrive in Australia was a great-grandfather, Dyson Lacy. Born in Nottinghamshire, England, he made the journey to the other side of the world when he was a young man, seeking his fortune. He arrived in Brisbane just in time to witness the birth of the new Queensland colony. Queensland's first governor came up from Sydney to preside over the opening of the new parliament at the same time.

In those days, large tracts of land were up for grabs all over Australia. You could literally find some suitable grazing or farming area that no other white person had taken, and claim it as your own. This is what Dyson Lacy did, setting off to north Queensland with a partner and their team of horses. En-route they bought around 5,000 sheep and were allowed to squat for twelve months around Isaacs/Burdekin. After the first shearing season, their funds boosted by the wool income, they headed further north and found suitable land around 400 miles inland from Rockhampton. There the squatters set up camp, naming their future sheep station 'Aramac.'

Their first shipment of wool to London wasn't a great success — when it eventually arrived about a year after leaving the station, it turned out they hadn't packed it properly and the wool was 'belted.' Dyson and his partner, though, soon got the hang of the wool exporting caper, and despite floods, disease, and the occasional outbreak of industrial unrest amongst the workers, plus the deprivations brought on by their isolation, despite all this the sheep station prospered. In 1873, Dyson paid a return to visit to England. Something romantic must have happened on that trip because later that year, back in Queensland, he was married to an English woman, my great-grandmother, Frances Irwin. She was from what used to be termed 'a good family' — her father, Captain Joseph Irwin, was Inspecting Commander of the Irish Coastguard for forty years, a prestigious military and political position. Captain Irwin also had had a distinguished career in the British Navy.

Frances and Dyson had their first child, my grandmother Emily Lacy, in 1874. As was the custom of the time, wealthy families would send their children to Europe to finishing school — which is exactly what Dyson and Frances did with Emily, sixteen years old, and her thirteen year-old sister, May. In late February 1890, the two schoolgirls boarded their transport, the *RMS Quetta*, at Rockhampton, accompanied by their uncle and chaperone, the Reverend Thomas Hall. The *Quetta* made its last mainland pick up at Mackay and with 292 people on board, including 101 passengers, chugged its way on to the next scheduled stop at Thursday Island.

The evening of February 28 was a typically balmy tropical night. Many of the passengers chose to sit or stroll around on the outside deck to enjoy the cooling evening breeze. May was downstairs in the cabin preparing for bed, while Emily was in the saloon. Although just a few days parted from her family, she was already writing a letter to them, no doubt sharing her impressions, her hopes and expectations of the future that was lying ahead of her in Europe. She would have had no idea, however, what a calamitous turn the future was about to take.

The *Quetta* was on its twelfth voyage from Brisbane to London. Along with the passengers, it carried a diverse cargo due to be delivered in three stages: flour, biscuits and seeds to Batavia, hides to be unloaded at Port Said, and wool, sugar, whiskey and tallow for London. It also served as a vital communications link between England and the colonies, carrying the all-important mail.

The *Quetta*'s captain steered the vessel around Cape York at the top point of Queensland and into the Adolphus Channel. Although the channel was notorious for its dangerous reefs, most had been chartered through the hundreds of voyages made in the past. Unfortunately, the *Quetta* was to discover one of the few unchartered ones, a rock that when the *Quetta* hit, ripped a hole from the bow and down along the side. Immediately the Adolphus Channel waters came flooding in, and in minutes the ship was under water.

There was little panic amongst the passengers after the rock struck. Emily in the saloon had the time, foresight and courage to go below and look for her sister. Then she and May, now in her nightgown, together made their way back to the deck where they were reunited with their uncle. The *Quetta* was now angling forward, its bow sinking under the water. The Captain ordered everyone to make their way to the stern. The deck had become a steep and slippery hill that passengers and crew were forced to climb. They were still if not exactly calm at least not in blind panic. However, a sudden lurch changed everything — it was the jolt of understanding that made everyone realise their lives were in jeopardy. Chaos reigned.

Realising that the sinking *Quetta* would suck them down as it went under, Emily, May and Thomas Hall decided to jump into the water and take their chances there. Dozens of fellow passengers were doing the same, and in the water Emily 'got several blows on the head from people's boots. I was nearly suffocated. Every second I thought it would be the last in this life.'

Lifeboats had been untied and set in the water, but most of them sunk under the weight of the many people clamouring aboard. Emily, who had survived the initial crush of bodies underwater, made it to the surface. She quickly realised that the heavy cumbersome clothing that was the young woman's fashion of the time, was becoming a waterlogged weight that would pull her down to the seabed, so removed her dress, petticoat, corset, shoes and stockings. She could see May manage to make it to an upright lifeboat, and felt relief. She then had to watch in horror as dozens more people tried to get on board it. The lifeboat rocked, turned and flipped over.

Emily was powerless to help May, but was in turn helped by the ship's purser, a man by the name of William Curvan. He had been able to put on a lifebelt and was clinging to a ship's grating. He called out to Emily who grabbed a cord of the lifebelt and with this tenuous thread clung for dear life. Another makeshift raft reached them, this one carrying the *Quetta*'s Chief Officer, name of Gray, and a couple of other survivors. The two fragile rafts were tied together to make something slightly sturdier.

Worried that the 'raft' would not last much longer, or perhaps in the throes of panic, Emily abandoned it and swam for a lifeboat she could see a little way off. Unfortunately for Emily, chivalry appeared to have died along with the *Quetta*. Those in the lifeboat, mostly crew members, kicked and pushed the schoolgirl away when she tried to clamour aboard. She returned to Purser Curvan and Chief Officer Gray and their makeshift raft. Together they floated for hours throughout the night, hoping that somebody would come to their rescue. Then the weather took a turn for the worse.

The breeze that had provided relief to the passengers earlier that evening had picked up, strengthening into a wind that chopped up the sea's surface. The swells and waves caused

Curvan to become seasick, while Emily battled with continuous cramping. For a second time, she tried to improve her chances by swimming for a larger and sturdier looking raft. Again, she was pushed back by those already on the raft, scared that the additional body would capsize it. Again, she had to swim back to her original scrap of wreckage that Curvan, Gray and the others were clinging to.

The increasingly rough seas eventually tore apart the two rafts, and Emily and Curvan were on their own again. Curvan was in a bad way from sea-sickness, so it was up to Emily to try and row the raft to shore, wherever that might be. Again, they saw a lifeboat and Emily swam over for assistance. Instead she received violent threats from those on board and she had to turn back. Unfortunately, now Curvan and the raft were nowhere to be seen. Emily was on her own. Worse, she had nothing to cling to — she would have to swim, tread water, swim some more, and hope for some kind of miracle. By this time it was mid-afternoon of the day after the sinking. Emily had been in the water for over 18 hours.

The authorities had been alerted to the *Quetta*'s sinking several hours earlier, and the rescue effort was coordinated from the nearest settlement, Thursday Island. The island was hardly equipped to deal with a major maritime disaster, but did the best it could. All available boats were sent out to look for and pick up any survivors. Fortunately, a large number of people had made it through the ordeal. The majority of them, including the ship's Captain, managed to reach land and were taken back to Thursday Island for treatment. Purser Curvan was one of them, found washed up on a beach, barely alive.

The rescue mission continued on through the afternoon and early evening. However, as night fell the flotilla of boats were forced to make their way back to Thursday Island. Finding any further survivors now seemed a forlorn hope. In total, they had brought back 157 passengers and crew alive. Emily Lacy, however, was not amongst them — she was still in the Adolphus Channel, still swimming, still treading water.

One of the boats involved in the rescue mission was a small and weather-beaten government steamer called the *Albatross*. The next morning it again headed out into the seas on the remote chance that someone might still be found alive. As they scanned the horizons one of the crew spotted what looked like a coconut bobbing in the water. The *Albatross* pulled up closer to investigate — the coconut was my grandmother. After thirty-six hours in the water, she was dehydrated, badly sunburnt, suffering from sunstroke, and exhausted — only some hidden reserve of will-power keeping her afloat. She was also delirious, initially trying to kick and push her rescuers away. The *Albatross* crew members managed to drag her aboard, and she announced to them that she'd come 'from a hotel at the bottom of the sea,' then passed out.

She was the last of the survivors to be rescued, and her heroic, improbable feat of survival made headlines not just in newspapers in Australia, but also across the world in England. In all, 134 people had died in the shipwreck, and it remains one of Australia's worst maritime disasters. Of the 158 survivors only three were female — Emily, a young woman named Anna Nicklin, and a toddler. Unfortunately, Emily's sister May didn't make it.

I think that if I had survived a shipwreck I'd never want to set foot on a boat again. Emily Lacy, however, was back on a ship a few months later, her European trip merely postponed as she sailed there on a French liner, this time accompanied by her parents.

I didn't have very much to do with my grandmother. When I was growing up she, then an elderly widow, lived in Moss Vale in the picturesque Southern Highlands of New South Wales. She only visited Hobart on the rare occasion. My impression of her was of a formidable woman, but also cold and intimidating — to be honest I was more than a little afraid of her. That steely determination and strong will that made it difficult for me to warm to her was, however, no doubt a major factor in her surviving thirty-six hours in the sea.

* * *

Leslie Fraser Standish Hore, a young man with an adventurous spirit that stretched as long as his name, travelled to Australia from England in the early 1890s to see what might turn up. He was from a wealthy family — his parents owned and ran a plantation in India where he was born. He was sent to England to be educated, and appears to have had little to do with his parents from that point on. Responsibility for rearing him was given to an aunt. After completing his schooling, instead of joining his parents in India, he continued even further south. He wound up in Brisbane, armed with a £10,000 endowment from his aunt (a considerable amount of money in those days) and a letter of introduction to a very distant relative. This relative happened to be Dyson Lacy, who was not long returned from Europe with his wife and daughter, Emily. Leslie headed out to the remote sheep station, Aramac, to help lend a hand. He also fell in love with Emily, and they were married in 1896.

The newlyweds spent time in London and from there moved to Hobart — apparently north Queensland's tropical weather didn't appeal. In Hobart Leslie worked as a solicitor and then a barrister. Along the way they had three children. My father Basil was the youngest, born in 1901.

It was around this time that my family also acquired its double-barrelled surname. It was one of the conditions Dyson Lacy had placed on Leslie Hore in return for his daughter's hand in marriage. Dyson didn't want to see the Lacy name die out, at least on his branch of the family tree, but with no son to carry on the family name the responsibility fell to his only surviving child, Emily. And so Emily Lacy became Emily Hore-Lacy, the children also picked up the hyphenated name, and Dyson Lacy could die happy that his name would live on after him. It seems an old-fashioned concept now, but they were different times, different mores and conventions.

When the First World War broke out, Leslie, like many Australian men, was eager to enlist and go off to defend the Empire, even though he was in his mid-forties. It now became Leslie's turn to face death, just as his wife had done fifteen years earlier. Leslie's first tour of duty, in April 1915, was to Gallipoli. He was part of the landing force that was to take the peninsula from the Turks and in doing so turn the tide of war — or so the theory went.

Leslie survived the landing and was to spend the next several months bunkered there as the fighting descended into a stalemate. To relieve the monotony and occupy the hours, Leslie began to sketch, drawing his surroundings, the Mediterranean landscape, and the daily rituals of a soldier's life. These sketches have been preserved and you can see them in the Australian War Memorial in Canberra.

Leslie's regiment was the 8th Light Horse Regiment, part of the 3rd Light Horse Brigade, in which he was a Captain. In August 1915, in an effort to break the stalemate, the Allied commanders decided on an audacious — some might say foolhardy, and others might even say criminally irresponsible — attack on the Turks. In the early hours of the morning of August 7, my grandfather took part in what was to be known as the Charge of the 3rd Light Horse Brigade at the Nek. It was to be one of the last great battles at Gallipoli. Those who have seen the movie Gallipoli might remember the climactic scene, with Bill Hunter leading his troops up and over the edge. The film used that assault, the Charge of the 3rd Light Horse Brigade, to symbolise everything that was heroic and futile about the Gallipoli campaign. It was also depicted in a famous painting by George Lambert; that too can be seen in the Australian War Memorial.

The Charge of the 3rd Light Horse Brigade was a suicide mission, and many of the soldiers knew it at the time. In total 234 Australian Light Horsemen were killed in that battle, a further 138 injured, including my grandfather. Most of them charged barely a few yards before they were cut down by Turkish machine gun fire. Leslie got a bit further than that, a bullet grazing the side of his face as he advanced, then a bullet to the leg as he, realising the futility of the attack, made his retreat. He was distraught at the loss of so much life and the destruction of his regiment, his feelings expressed in one of his letters, 'The 8th Light Horse Regiment is gone, it is no more!'

After he had recovered from his injuries Leslie was sent to France. He continued his battlefield sketching and, in fact, was asked by his commanders to draw the enemy positions — I guess a kind of low-tech espionage in a time before pilotless drones and satellites. Like my other grandfather, he was also awarded a Military Cross.

Just as an aside, it seems to me one of those remarkable coincidences that both my grandfathers were at Gallipoli, and both then served on the Western Front where both won Military Crosses. As far as I am aware they didn't form any acquaintanceship and may not have even met each other. They certainly would have no inkling that they would one day become relatives through the marriage of their then teenaged children.

At war's end Leslie Hore returned to Hobart, but not for long. As if the drama and danger of Gallipoli and the Western Front had not been enough, his thirst for adventure apparently remained unquenched for he now packed his family off to New Guinea. The German colony was a remote and inhospitable wilderness now under Australian jurisdiction, a spoil of war and reward for Australia's faithful service in the war. As well as the dangers, it no doubt offered opportunities for an adventurous type like Leslie Fraser Standish Hore.

Leslie, who seemed to have forgotten his dislike for tropical climes, had applied for and been appointed a judge in the town of Rabaul. One of his virtues was that he was a man of principle. A weakness, however, was that he appeared to be a poor political operator. Foolishly he gave a judgement against the powerful Production Control Board; not long after he found that his services as a judge were no longer required. It wasn't just his political masters he was to get offside by allowing principles to cloud his judgements. On an earlier occasion, he had proved himself conscientious enough to put justice ahead of family, jailing one of his nephews, Uncle Dyson, for six months for receiving a stolen pig.

My grandfather was able to make a relatively seamless career transition from the courts to business, taking over a formerly German-owned plantation at Kavieng in 1928. During his plantation boss days, he encountered a fellow Tasmanian there, Errol Flynn. Flynn was on his way to Hollywood, by a very Flynn-like means of transport — a sailing yacht. His reputation as an incorrigible womaniser was well-earned, and in evidence even in his pre-fame days. While in Kavieng he took a fancy to one of the European women there, who happened to be the wife of a German plantation owner. Errol was not to be denied by a small obstacle like a marriage vow, however, and had his way with the woman, a willing accomplice. Unfortunately for Errol, the plantation owner, a violent-tempered man, discovered the affair and came after Errol with a sword.

Errol Flynn might have been one of the finest swashbuckling

swordsmen on the big screen, but in real life he was no match for an enraged and cuckolded husband, and had his stomach sliced open. My father, who was a young man at the time, would tell the story in graphic detail, of how when Errol arrived on his doorstep for help, his intestines were almost spilling from his stomach. Strangely, Errol never mentioned the incident in his autobiography, while shamelessly admitting to murders, slave-trading, and numerous adulterous affairs. Perhaps my father was Errol's match when it came to the telling of tall stories.

Leslie Fraser Standish Hore survived Turkish and German bullets in the First World War, but was defeated by the New Guinean mosquitoes. He contracted malaria and died there in 1934 at the age of 64. He was buried on his plantation with full military honours.

His widow Emily Lacy died in 1951 — on dry land — at the ripe old age of seventy-seven.

CHAPTER 2

I am an optimist at heart, and whatever life throws at me — and believe me, it's thrown a lot of things my way during the course of the years — I've always managed to bounce back quickly. This temperament was something I was born with. My parents didn't drag me off to resilience workshops or whatever parents do nowadays — it was just an attitude that seemed to be with me from day one. Even now, I always think back on my childhood as a happy, carefree time. It's really only now that I realise that, for a more sensitive child, my childhood could have been quite traumatic.

As a child, I was a mother's boy. I thought the world of my mother, partially due to the fact that I was cross-eyed and saw everything in stereo, disorientating for a young child. And so I would cling to my mother's skirt everywhere we went, cementing the bond between us, so to speak.

In return, I was clearly my mother's favourite of her five children, no doubt to the irritation of my siblings. I was the eldest boy, and so in an immediate position of favour. But I also believe I was the most obvious in showing my love towards her, and Mum, being human, responded in kind. As many parents will know, there are few things more rewarding than a child's unconditional love.

My mother, Barbara Bond, granddaughter of the wealthy Frank Bond, was a beautiful, glamorous and vivacious woman. There's a portrait of her, now hanging in my home, which was painted when she was in her early forties, and she looks like a movie star. In her youth, with her good looks and inherited wealth, she was a fixture in what passed as a social scene in Hobart at the time. Although not exactly the Paris Hilton of her time and place, she was still someone that commanded attention, a regular in the social pages of the local newspapers. When she was a young woman she would zip around Hobart in a silver Alvis, an expensive sports car given to her by her doting grandfather. These were the days when most of Tasmania's few cars came in a colour choice of black or maroon. That Alvis instantly made her the centre of attention; she might just as well have got around town with a leopard on a leash. I think it's fair to say Mum enjoyed being in the spotlight.

Her striking good looks led to an offer to enter the inaugural Miss Australia Quest. The Miss Australia Quest was an idea thought up and organised by a company called Smith's Newspapers, owned and run by R C Packer, the father of Sir Frank Packer. The Miss Australia Quest was heavily promoted by two Packer publications, *Smith's Weekly* magazine and the recently launched but struggling newspaper, the *Daily Guardian*. *Smith's Weekly* later changed its name to *Woman's Weekly* and the *Daily Guardian* was to merge with the *Daily Telegraph*, both becoming flagship publications in the Packers' media portfolio.

The Packers also happened to be cousins of the Bonds; my mother's mother and Frank Packer's mother were sisters. My mother was keen to enter, even if just for the experience. Now, I don't know how much nepotism is a factor in beauty contests, but I don't think it would have hurt her chances to have her great-uncle running the show. In a tight contest it might have just proved the difference that brings home the winner's tiara. We'll never know, however, if Mum could have been our first Miss Australia, for her mother put a stop to the whole thing, forbidding her to enter. One of the components of the Quest, even in those early days, was the bathing suit section which would have been considered quite shocking. As far as my grandmother was concerned, beauty contests weren't the kind of things 'respectable' young ladies got involved in.

This first Miss Australia Quest incidentally was an unqualified success. That contest alone, conducted in a blaze of publicity, managed to more than double the *Daily Guardian's* circulation and provided a lucrative boost to its advertising revenue. The eventual winner, a nineteen-year-old Western Australian girl called Beryl Mills became an instant celebrity, and the following year went on a three-month promotional tour, organised by Smith's Newspapers, to the United States. There she was feted by business leaders, politicians and movie stars. On her return to Australia, she earned a tidy amount of money on the lecture circuit and ended up marrying a *Daily Guardian* journalist. My mother's destiny was to be entirely different.

My grandmother also played a big hand in my mother's marriage, to a man named Ray Robertson. Robertson came from a good family, was polite and well-mannered, and held the well-regarded profession of stockbroker. In other words, he was every mother's ideal son-in-law. I don't think my mother had the same high regard for him as her mother did. In those days, however, marriages were regularly entered into for reasons other than love, parental pressure often being one of them.

Perhaps my mother also felt that she might grow to love Ray Robertson over time, and they were married when my mother was just 18 years old. A daughter, Sally, soon followed but then the marriage quickly foundered. Mum was to later say that she left Ray because he was a disappointment in the love-making department. I guess she was a kind of forerunner of the liberated women of later decades, in that she would not endure a passionless marriage. It also says something about her personality. As well as being a bit of a sensualist, she was not afraid to risk society's and her parents' disapproval for the sake of her own happiness.

And society did disapprove, especially with the arrival of my father on the scene, out of the jungles of New Guinea. When the two hooked up it became a scandal in the fishbowl world of Hobart high society. The local *Truth* newspaper ran a story on the marriage breakup and Mum and Dad's affair with the salacious headline: 'No Bonds on Barbara.' So much for my grandmother's efforts to protect her daughter's respectability.

My father, Basil Hore-Lacy had grown up in New Guinea, though he had also spent several years in England where he attended Harrow. When his father died he left Basil and his brother, my uncle Dyson, a half share each in the New Guinea plantation. My father, however, sold his share to Uncle Dyson for £10,000, and returned to the more temperate climes of Tasmania.

Dad was twelve years older than Mum, had travelled to a lot of places, seen and done a lot of things, and was no doubt a real man of the world in her eyes. He and my mother fell in love. However, they were unable to get married straight away. Basically, a divorce in those days required some kind of grounds for annulment. In the case of my mother's marriage with Ray Robertson the grounds were desertion, but the period of desertion had to be at least three years. And so my parents left for Sydney, to make sure the courts would be in no doubt that Ray had been deserted.

Eventually they were married in 1938, and I was their first child, born in Hobart in 1939, just before the outbreak of the Second World War. My father then joined the Navy and went off to fight the Japanese. He may have even been in the British Navy — my father was never the sort of man to regale people with old war stories. The subject barely came up in our household, so much of his war career remains a mystery to me. He was out of sight for most of the early years of my life, though obviously many other children of my generation experienced the same thing with the war on. Nevertheless, it set the pattern for what I guess would be the text-book case study of an absent father.

In the war, he and his brother, Uncle Dyson, served together around New Guinea where their local knowledge was considered valuable by the Navy. My father must have made a couple of return trips to Tasmania because in 1941 my mother gave birth to her second son, Dyson, and in 1944 to another son, Nigel. Then Dad returned from the war permanently, even though the fighting still raged to the north. I never did find out the reason for his premature exit from the war. Perhaps he had a good reason, perhaps he just went AWOL. I suspect he may have simply missed my mother. I do remember our family receiving a white feather — the universal symbol for cowardice — in the mail one day. Obviously, someone else had firm ideas on why my father had returned early.

There were probably few places in the world more remote from the war than the outer regions of Hobart where I grew up. For the first years of the war, we lived at a family property of 1200 acres called Carrington at Campania, it is situated about 25 miles south east of Hobart, then at Kingston. In 1944 my mother used part of her inheritance, together with my father's share from the sale of his New Guinea holding, to purchase a property called Craigow for £26,000.

Craigow had belonged to a family named Murdoch. One of the early Murdochs was an officer in the Tasmania Police and was instrumental in capturing the bushranger, Martin Cash, and Craigow was his reward from the grateful citizens of Tasmania. It was a sizeable holding of land (2000 acres), set in the idyllic Tasmania countryside about six miles south east of the town of Richmond, with fruit orchards and paddocks for cattle and sheep. It was, however badly neglected, and my mother set herself the

Herculean task of making it productive again. She did a hell of a good job with the aid of the Department of Agriculture and Mum got herself a new lover. She had a soft spot for 'delightful gentlemen.' At least one of them was a radio announcer.

We lived in a sandstone homestead that was built in the nineteenth century. As our family grew we had to add extensions to the sandstone cottage. Clearly the new owners in recent times did not think our handiwork was historically significant because they tore down the extensions so that just the original homestead was standing.

There were four children in the Hore-Lacy family: myself, then Dyson, Nigel, and finally our little sister, Harriet, born in the first year of post-war Australia, 1946. There was also our older half-sister Sally, but for much of my childhood she lived with her father, the jilted Ray Robertson.

Despite being the closest to me in age, Dyson and I never really got along; in fact, we fought like lion cubs. The rivalry between us has continued throughout our lives, even to the present day. At one time, we didn't speak for thirty years, and I think the rift between us is partially because of the resentment Dyson harboured over my most-favoured-son status. The fact that my mother and I would jokingly refer to him as 'the Mistake.' wouldn't have helped endear us to him.

We loved Craigow when we were children. In my child's eyes, it was a self-contained universe where we could find everything we needed to keep us happy and amused. I have wonderful memories of running through the orchards, riding the horses, or swimming in the dam. Even doing farm chores like feeding the animals never seemed like work to me.

I also have fond memories of my mother at that time — her gaiety and optimism, and her hearty, sometimes raucous, laughter. We children loved making her laugh, partly because we knew that if we could get Mum laughing we could escape the punishment she was about to dish out. One day she said, 'now you know, Richard, what you will get if you tell a lie.' 'Yes, Mum, but what will I get if I 'tell the truth'?' This broke her up, especially coming from a four year old and has remained a family chestnut ever since. And her punishment was definitely something to be avoided — she had a backhander that could make you see stars. But our mother's laugh also had the magical effect of reassuring us that all was well with the world. Unfortunately, that laughter's magic was not enough to ward off the dark events that were about to intrude on our idyllic world.

Marriage was losing its lustre for my parents, and arguments between them became increasingly frequent. The verbal stoushes would sometimes spiral out of control, with slaps and punches thrown by both of them. Naturally I sided with my mother, though being just a boy there was little I could do to help her. Then in 1947, less than a year after Harriet was born, my mother decided she'd had enough of married life and kicked Dad out, leaving Mum a single mother of four.

For a short time, my mother embraced single life again. There seemed to be a steady stream of gentleman guests, lawyers and politicians most of them, arriving at Craigow in their cars at night. As soon as one of these male visitors appeared I would be banished to my bedroom by my mother with the abrupt order, 'Richard, go to bed.' I guess it was my mother's way of dealing with the marriage break-up. She wasn't going to wallow in self-pity, but continue to enjoy life and what it had to offer. Unfortunately, life still had a couple more blows to give her.

In contrast to my tempestuous relationship with Dyson, I thought the world of my younger brother, Nigel. Despite the five year age difference between us, we went everywhere together, and I was always looking out for him. Except for the day that I didn't, and that changed everything.

It was the 21st day of November in 1948, a beautiful spring day. Dyson, Nigel and I were down at one of the property dams near the cherry orchard, about a mile from the house. Dyson and I were trying to catch frogs while four-year old Nigel was somewhere nearby, amusing himself. The frogs provided a bit of sport, quick and agile leapers who were surprisingly difficult to catch. The frog pursuit led us further and further away from Nigel, but eventually we grew tired of it and left the frogs in peace, returning to the house for lunch.

Dyson and I entered the house, and Mum probably told us to go wash before eating. It was all very normal; I don't recall any dark sense of foreboding, that something was not quite right. Then Mum asked, 'Where's Nigel?'

I just shrugged and replied, 'I'm not sure. Last time we saw him he was down at the dam.' What was I to know, why would I think anything was wrong — I was just a kid. But my mother's expression altered in a flash, she headed straight out the door, striding down to the dam, breaking into a run.

She found Nigel, floating face down and lifeless in the water. There was nothing to be done for him. His all too brief life was over, drowned in Craigow's dam.

First the marriage break-up with my father, now the death of a toddler son. For Mum, it was a succession of blows from which she would never recover. This time she had a new defence mechanism. Instead of embracing life as she had done when my father left, she now tried to shut the world out, barricading herself indoors and rarely venturing outside the house. She would sit for hours in the drawing room, the curtains drawn, playing Patience, a card game for one.

I missed my father, though I was glad to see the end of his fighting with Mum. I certainly missed Nigel — and still do to this day, sixty-seven years on. But perhaps most of all I missed my mother's laughter, a sound that for years virtually vanished from our household.

* * *

My early schooling was at the Hutchins School, which was the Church of England Boys Grammar School in Hobart. Founded in 1846, it is Australia's second oldest public school. I was a day student there, before moving to Launceston Grammar where I was a boarder. The experience was nothing much out of the ordinary for much of the time there. I couldn't say I loved boarding school, but I certainly didn't hate it. However, one day, when I was just twelve years old, I had an experience that was again to give me a glimpse of another much darker side of life.

I was lying in bed in the dormitory one morning. Teachers would from time to time patrol the dormitory, generally keeping a supervisory eye on the boys. On this occasion one of our teachers, Peter Nixon, was on watch and had sat down on my bed. I no longer recall what he was talking to me about, but I'll never forget his hand sneaking its way under my blanket. I was trying to squirm my way out of his reach but that failed to give him the message. I jumped out of bed I took off, heading to the lavatory, but he followed me. I locked myself in one of the cubicles and sat there, quite shaken up, listening to Mr Nixon's footsteps coming closer. Thankfully, after some time he gave up and went away.

At that age, I probably didn't understand the full implications of what had occurred, only that it had made me feel very uncomfortable and scared. It continued to prey on my mind, so I decided to tell one of the prefect, Robert Firth. I guess I thought that would be the end of the matter, little realising that I had sparked off an increasingly serious chain of events. The prefect informed our Housemaster, Mr 'Tadpole' Sorrel (he had an enormous pot and we nicknamed him 'tadpole') of the incident, and not long after the police arrived.

I was called into the Headmaster's office and asked to recount the incident to the Headmaster and two police officers present. I can still remember the policeman asking, 'And he interfered with your person, did he?' I thought that was an odd way to refer to my dick, 'my person.' Again, after the interview, I went back to the classroom thinking that was the end of it.

Mr Nixon, like several other of the teachers, lived on campus, and in the same building as our dormitory. His lodgings were on a mezzanine floor below ours, and as I went up the stairs that evening I could hear him inside his room crying. It was strange to hear a grown man crying like that. A pitiful sound, except that I felt no sympathy for him, after what he had tried to do to me.

The next morning something was clearly up, because there were several police cars parked at the school. Instead of going to class, all the boys were asked to make their way to the other end of the school grounds, down to the swimming pool. I remember standing there with the other boys for a long time, and we could see that several teachers looked shocked and ashen-faced. Eventually word began to filter through. Mr Nixon was dead. The previous night he had put a gun to the roof of his mouth and blown his head off.

* * *

I was never the scholar in our family; that honour belonged to my brother Dyson. I was more of the outdoors type who liked his sports, especially cricket. Study held no interest for me, and I guess my early grades reflected that. So initially my mother wanted Dyson to attend Geelong Grammar, one of Australia's most prestigious (and most expensive) private schools. For whatever reason Dyson declared that he didn't want to go. Mum then, in an offhand kind of way, asked me if I wanted to attend instead, and I accepted. Perversely, Dyson then saw this as yet another occasion where I had received the Golden Boy preferential treatment.

I guess I said yes to my mother's offer as it seemed like an adventurous thing to do. Besides I was understandably keen to get away from Launceston Grammar after my experience there. Unfortunately, it wouldn't be the last time that I would make a decision I would quickly regret.

Geelong Grammar has educated some of Australia's best known public figures, including a former Prime Minister (Sir John Gorton), a Victorian Premier (Sir Rupert Hamer), business tycoons like Hugh Morgan, and more than a couple of media barons (Rupert Murdoch, James Fairfax and Kerry Packer). No doubt there are many Old Geelong Grammarians who attribute some of their success to the education I, however, hated the place. I was just so sick of prefects belting me on the arse.

I was never popular with my classmates. I have always had a lot of confidence in my own abilities (some people might describe it in different terms). And I have never been hesitant in expressing my opinions, and not always diplomatically. Not surprisingly, this did not endear me to many of my schoolmates. There's no doubt also that in the eyes of the teachers I was a difficult child. I came from a broken home, had grown up watching my parents stand toe-to-toe and slug things out, and I had lost a younger brother in tragic circumstances. All of which added up to a volatile combination of resentment and anger that inevitably got me offside with many of the teachers.

Countless books have been written about the boarding school experience — some of them make the places sound worse than prison, pubescent hells. My experiences were never as dramatic as that. I resented the discipline and strict regime we were forced to follow. I particularly hated been ordered out of bed so early every morning, especially so as thee managing director was invariably at full stretch! Kind of ironic then that I would choose horse training as a career where every day starts at 3:30 in the morning.

There was some petty bullying from the other boys, nothing too traumatic. Most of it was water off a duck's back for me. And we had the usual sprinkling of sadistic teachers, some of whom could put the fear of God into you. However, I mainly remember feeling bored and, even more painful, sexually frustrated. Like most teenage boys I was beginning to develop an interest in the opposite sex — the only problem was that at a boarding school there was very little of the opposite sex around. There was Matron Collins, a thirty something, quite attractive matron, but she was shared by the Housemaster, Mr Tunbridge, and my second cousin, Kerry Packer! The only other females that we had regular contact with were the maids. Newly arrived migrants, they appeared to know only one word in English, 'No,' and they could all run a hundred metres in ten seconds!

Actually, we schoolboys always felt some of the teaching staff were having more success with the maids than we were. I distinctly remember one school morning returning to my dormitory when everyone else was in class. I arrived in time to see a pretty young maid leaving the room of one of the Housemasters, straightening her uniform as she did so. Behind her I could see the Housemaster, and I'm sure I detected a smile of satisfaction, that is until he noticed me. A little more flustered and less commanding that his usual self he yelled at me, 'Hore-Lacy! What are you doing out of class? Get back to your classroom immediately!' Of course, she may have only been dusting his room.

My first House at Geelong Grammar was Barwon House. Initially I was a poor student with little interest in study. However,

I developed a friendship with the Housemaster there, Doug Fraser, who was a beaut bloke. He took me aside one day and he said, 'Look, I want to have a talk with you. You're a leader, and the other boys copy you. If you wanted to change your attitude you could do really well.'

I doubt if anybody apart from my mother had shown such confidence in my abilities before. It was just the sort of wise encouragement I needed, and for a time I took his advice on board. I started listening to the teachers in class, doing my homework, and, lo and behold, my grades dramatically improved. The next term I came first in four subjects. They were what were considered 'wet' subjects: English, History, Economics and Social Studies. (The really bright kids always excelled in Maths and Science). Nevertheless, I felt enormously proud of my achievements.

Our Economics teacher was a Mr Westcott. He had twelve children so naturally we students nicknamed him Sexy Westcott. He was actually very myopic, with Coke bottle thick glasses and had to hold the book right up to his eyes when reading — which, of course, kids being kids, we all ridiculed him about. I was one of his chief tormentors, until one day he had finally had enough and told me, 'Get out of my class and don't come back.'

As I was actually interested in Economics, and at that stage still determined to do well in my studies, I decided that I wasn't going to let the slight hurdle of being permanently banned from class deter me. I sought to continue my Economics education by eavesdropping on the lessons. I knew of a good vantage point on the mezzanine level above the classroom where, crouched under the stairwell, I could peer down into the class and hear every word spoken. From there I would listen intently to every lesson taking notes. At the end of term, Sexy Westcott had some of the boys to help him mark the examination papers — each question had 10 points the student had to mention — at the end all the points were added up and one of the boys told me he couldn't stop blinking when Hore-Lacy came out on top — he was absolutely incredulous.

After Barwon House I attended Timbertop, a campus located in the Victorian Alps. Timbertop was then only a recent addition to the school, and the facilities were still very rough and ready, not to say absolutely freezing in winter. Without Doug Fraser's benign influence around, my attitude towards study quickly deteriorated again. Eventually I was expelled from Timbertop. For the first time, but not I might add for the last, a woman was to get me into trouble.

The nearest town to Timbertop was Mansfield. In Mansfield, there was a cake shop on the main street. The best thing about the cake shop in my eyes was not the cakes but the pretty girl who served them. I don't think I ever knew her name, but she still made a big impression on me. One day, it was towards the end of Term 3, a late spring day, and I raced into Mansfield after telling the school that I was going on a bivouac on the Howqua River. My sole intention was to visit the cake shop and get to know the pretty girl a little better.

I thought myself quite the smooth operator that afternoon, and bought a stack of cakes from her to really win her heart. But then I made the colossal blunder of trying to cash a cheque for £100, which Mum had sent me as pocket money for the summer holidays. The suspicious cake shop owner called the school, and my truancy was discovered.

The Headmaster at Timbertop, Basher Montgomery, was almost gleeful when I walked into his office. 'Ha, I've been waiting to get you all year, Hore-Lacy.' He gave me six of the best, and expelled me.

To be honest, I felt relieved that my Geelong Grammar days

were over. I returned to Hobart and told my mother I'd been expelled. 'We'll see about that,' was all she said.

In the new year I returned to Geelong, this time accompanied by Mum. She went to see the school's long-standing and much revered Headmaster, James Darling. I don't know what Mum said to him while I waited outside the office, but when she came out she had a big smile on her face and announced, 'You're back in.' I can't say that I shared Mum's happiness.

I spent my final year at Geelong Grammar in Perry House. Also at Perry, a year ahead of me, was a cousin of mine, a boy by the name of Kerry Packer. I don't what happened to him — I expect he never amounted to much as he spent his entire time there reading Zane Grey westerns in class instead of studying. He was dyslexic and never passed an exam in his life!

Kerry Packer was my second cousin, although our family didn't have a lot to do with the Packers. Kerry's grandfather, Robert Clyde Packer, was Tasmanian born and bred, but had moved to Sydney at the turn of the century when his ambitions became too big for provincial Hobart to contain. Both Kerry and his father, Frank Packer, lived in Sydney for most of their lives, though I do remember them visiting Hobart once or twice for family occasions.

Likewise, I didn't mix much with Kerry at Geelong Grammar even though we were in the same House. My memory of him in those days was of a big lump of a lad who took not the slightest interest in school whatsoever. He would stick his paperback westerns inside his exercise books and read them in class, or gaze out the window daydreaming, perhaps of how he would one day make and break governments. The school made a couple of half-hearted efforts to get him to apply himself, but eventually I think the teachers just got sick of asking him questions, and left him to his own devices.

I remember one morning looking at the Job List Board and a

chap named, Sam Legge, whose family were well known in New Guinea, had given Kerry 3 black list jobs — 'Packer couldn't get up, Packer couldn't get up, Packer couldn't get up' — it was pretty obvious why Kerry didn't want to get out of bed! I once punched Kerry Packer in the face — something I doubt many other people have done, though I expect a few would have liked to. The punch was a beauty too, right on the jaw. It was in the boxing ring at the school gymnasium — boxing being one of the sports offered by the school, and one I quite enjoyed. Though perhaps not so much after I had hit Kerry.

We were a contrast in body types. Kerry, as I mentioned, was a big lad — he was later to become school heavyweight champion. I instead was relatively small in stature (5 foot 8 and a half inches a welterweight at best. He seemed to tower over me, and I can still remember the look in his eyes when I got him a beauty right on the nose. First they registered a momentary mild surprise, then they narrowed with fury, and I thought, 'Oh gawd, now I'm gonna cop it!' No doubt a few Consolidated Press employees might recall similar looks from the boss because of some stuff-up or other. Kerry chased me around the ring for a little while, a bit like a bull after one of those rodeo clowns, much to the amusement of all those watching. Mercifully I was rescued from the ring before suffering too much of a beating.

Geelong Grammar, like a lot of boarding schools, has gained a reputation as some kind of hotbed of homosexuality. My experience was different; I only knew of a couple of isolated incidents I was, however, always wary of other boys, and teachers for that matter too, alone especially in compromising places like changing rooms or in the dormitories. It didn't matter who it was either.

I remember one occasion when Kerry's older brother, Clyde, saw me one day in the dormitory as I was getting changed. Clyde Packer was enormously fat and a flamboyant type. I had just had a shower and was putting on my underpants. He said in his booming voice, 'My, you're a handsome boy.' You've never seen someone get his underpants back on as quickly as I did!

The most significant thing that happened to me at Geelong Grammar — you could even say it was life-changing — was that I discovered horse racing. Or rather, gambling on horse racing. I used to sit listening to the races on a crystal set with two of my classmates, Bill McKinnon and Bill Guest, and we would bet on the races using imaginary stakes. We gave ourselves £200 each in imaginary money, and by the end of the first term I was a few thousand quid in front. The two Bills, however, had gone backwards and I was making them advances.

I didn't really have any betting system, I just trusted my instincts. I would mentally record that certain trainers seemed to perform well at certain tracks, or were better at getting their horses ready first up. All this information was stored in my memory — I was never organised or meticulous enough to write it down for reference purposes.

That Easter break when I returned home to Hobart I told my mother about the horse racing and said, 'Mum, look, I think I can make some money out of this.' And for a short while we did.

* * *

After the double blow of a marriage breakup followed by the loss of a young son, my mother was to be dealt a third and final blow. On my regular returns home from boarding school I had noticed some alarming signs that all was not quite right with her. Sometimes she would be walking up the stairs and then would suddenly tumble and fall over. Quite often she would say to me, 'Richard, just let me lean on you,' and I would have to support her. It was as though she was drunk, except she wasn't a drinker.

She used to laugh about it as though it was all kind of comic. But the episodes became both worse and more frequent. My half-sister, Sally, had moved back to Craigow. Eventually, after a few visits to the doctor and various tests, they found out what was wrong with her. She had multiple sclerosis.

I've since read that a suspected cause of MS is lack of sunlight, so all those years cooped up in the sitting room playing Patience could have contributed to her illness. In those days treatments were neither as sophisticated nor as effective as today. As the disease took hold of her, she went down and down, but it took about fifteen years before she finally died. During this time Mum never lost her sense of humour.

My mother and I had become betting partners, and I guess the gambling for her was a bit of an amusement. Like Patience I imagine it momentarily took her mind off her troubles. At the start, we were quite successful at it, and after the first few weeks we were up about £45 –real money this time, not the imaginary stakes I'd been playing with at boarding school.

In those days, there were no TABs — you either bet at the track or with the local SP bookie, though they were illegal and included some pretty dodgy characters. We used one by the name of Alan Watt, who had been a bookie to my mother's father and worked out of a big betting hall in downtown Hobart.

Increasingly concerned about her illness, my mother travelled to Vienna to see a world-renowned specialist in multiple sclerosis, Dr Walter Stiazni, in the hope that he could provide a cure. While she was gone, I kept up the gambling. Unfortunately, when she returned from Europe she discovered that her fifteen-year old son had managed to get the family in debt with Alan Watt to the tune of about £1,400!

I guess if she had wanted to, my mother could have got out of paying Watt; after all taking the bets from a minor was hardly legal. But she paid him anyway, writing him out a cheque. However, that was Mum's cue to retire from the betting business. I, unfortunately, didn't learn the same lesson. For better or for worse, betting on horse-racing would continue to play a major role in my life.

CHAPTER 3

Geelong Grammar and I eventually parted ways, after I told my mother I wasn't going to put up with sadistic prefects belting me on the arse any longer. Instead I finished my education at Taylors College in the Melbourne CBD. In my opinion, it was a much more enlightened place of learning, with more of an emphasis on developing research skills rather than the rote learning methods favoured at Geelong. Plus, you didn't have the suffocating boarding school regime of always having to be at a certain place at a certain time.

After matriculating from Taylors College, I still had no firm idea of what I would do with my life. I did confidently declare to my father, when he was making one of his rare family visits, that I would be a millionaire by the age of forty. Dad, not normally a man easy to amuse, certainly got a big laugh out of that.

Initially I spent some time managing, or rather, mismanaging the family farm at Craigow. The problem was that for so much of my adolescence I had been cooped up at boarding school, and I was now enjoying a wonderful sense of freedom. This freedom, however, didn't combine well with the rigid routines of farm management. Often at seven o'clock in the morning, when the working day was just beginning, I'd just be getting home after a night on the town. Still dressed in my dinner suit I'd start the men, giving them their instructions on what to do for the day. It's not hard to imagine what they must have thought of this eighteen-year-old rich kid in evening wear. I think it was clear to everyone, not least myself, that I had no feel for the work.

I have to admit that the Managing Director of Rick Hore-Lacy Ltd in those days was a part of the anatomy just above the thighs and below the navel. Although opportunities to please the Managing Director did arrive, they weren't as often as I, or the Managing Director, would have liked. At that time, the contraceptive pill was not yet readily available, so most girls had a very real fear of pregnancy. Abortions were illegal, and in Hobart there were no doctors prepared to perform them, at least that I knew of. In the event of an accidental pregnancy, the girl would have to concoct some story to tell her parents of why she suddenly needed to travel to Melbourne. And with the cost of the abortion — £200 was the going rate — plus plane tickets, a single night of pleasure could turn out to be dismayingly expensive.

Meanwhile, my mother was pushing me to study Law at University rather than waste my time trying to run a farm. She'd say, 'Oh, your grandfather was a lawyer and your great-grandfather was a lawyer.' So, to please my mother, I applied for a place at Melbourne University and was accepted.

At university, I continued to enjoy my freedom to the full — like a newly released prisoner who is hell-bent on making up for all the good times he had missed out on while inside. I hardly ever attended lectures. Instead, my morning routine was to sit in the University cafe, drinking coffee, reading the form guide and doing a bit of bird-watching. Afternoons would be spent down at the pub, the Mayfair Hotel being my regular. Or I'd pop down to the local newsagent's, run by a punting-mad bloke named Jack, and listen to the races on his portable radio. In the evenings, it was off to a party which often stretched into the early hours of the morning. In the time-honoured university student tradition, my friends and I would sit around drinking red wine, discussing the world's problems and, usually by around 3 am, solving them. All in all, I thought it was a great life.

The first place I stayed was at a boarding house in Carlton, not ten minutes' walk from the university campus. I had to lock my room at night, not so much to keep out thieves but to protect me from the randy homosexual landlord. I didn't stay around there for long, but moved to another boarding house in the eastern suburb of Kew. There I had a little bungalow to myself alongside the main house. Most of the lodgers were migrants, including one English family with a rather attractive daughter, a fair-haired girl named Caroline. We both took a liking to each other which led to some sleepovers in my bungalow. The sleepovers came to an abrupt halt when Caroline's mother found out what we were getting up to. She screamed her head off — firstly, 'Richard, how could you?' And eventually sneering 'It's nice, isn't it?' She immediately left the boarding house and took Caroline with her — I never saw either of them again.

Despite my lack of interest in studying I had come up with a method of getting through my course. Law undergraduates were required to complete around six subjects a year, but in those days, unlike today, if you didn't sit the final exam you didn't fail the subject. So, every year, about six weeks before exams, I would decide to have a crack at two or three subjects, and the others I would just ignore. This method of mine was semi-successful, in that despite being one of the least conscientious students in the hallowed history of the Melbourne University School of Law, I only ever failed one subject. (That was a third-year subject called Equity, a fiendishly difficult unit that covered trusts and their labyrinth of contingencies).

The downside of my method was that in only passing 80% or two or three units a year, after ten years I still hadn't managed to complete my degree, which may have been some kind of record at the time. I had become the professional undergraduate, a breed of student who can still occasionally be found on university campuses around Australia today.

During the university breaks I would return to Tasmania. On one of those visits back home I went to a local church dance at St Joseph's Parish Hall. It was there that I saw a young woman dancing, always with a radiant smile on her face. I thought to myself, 'Gee, what a pretty girl.'

Apparently, a few others thought the same, because when I tried to get a dance with her I discovered her dance card was already filled. The pretty young woman's name was Maria Lauber. She made a real impression on me that night, though her memory of the evening is somewhat different. (She has no recollection of meeting me at all.)

I didn't see Maria again until a few months later, this time at a Young Liberals function of all places. I wasn't particularly interested in politics, but one of my best friends, who wasn't just interested but obsessed with politics, dragged me along. Michael Hodgman and I had been friends since childhood — his father, Bill, was one of my mother's many lovers.

Michael was to do with his life what I could have and probably should have done, if I hadn't been so intent on partying all the time. He became a lawyer, used that as a launching pad to a political career, ascending all the way to a position as Minister in the Fraser Government in the early 80's. His loud abrasive style earned him the nickname from the Labor Party and the Canberra Press Gallery of 'the Mouth from the South.' It was a more than apt title, for boy he could talk! As long as I'd known him Michael Hodgman was never short of a word.

Sadly, Michael passed away only a few years ago. Even when we were young I used to nag him about his smoking. The habit caught up with him eventually, and he spent his last few years suffering from emphysema, the illness that eventually killed him.

Maria was at that same Young Liberals function, pretty much by accident. Her girlfriend took her along. Such is the way fate contrives to bring things and people together. This time I managed to get an opportunity to talk to her. We hit it off, and a short time later we were dating.

I spent six fruitless months trying to convince her to consummate the relationship in the bedroom, but she put up a strong resistance. Eventually she relented, with the words, 'Ricky, if you ever let me down, I'll never forgive you.' Fortunately, she turned out to have a forgiving nature for, I'm not proud to say, I was to let her down again and again.

Maria's family background was a real melting pot of nationalities. Maria was born in the Ukraine. Her father was German and her mother was Russian. One of her grandparents was from England, and there's also some Polish blood in the mix. Maria and her family moved to Germany after the Second World War, and then settled in Australia in 1950.

Her parents were very much conservative Old-World types. When they found out that Maria and I were sleeping together — her mother discovering some tell-tale evidence on Maria's underwear — they were absolutely furious. They told Maria she was no longer welcome in their house and threw her out, so she had little choice but to move in with me.

Those early years together were difficult — I brought her a lot of grief in that time. After years of being trapped in the monastic existence of a boys' boarding school I was still busy sowing as many wild oats as I could. It was a real dilemma for me: I wanted to do the right thing and take Maria in and look after her, but at the same time I was clearly unready for a monogamous relationship. Instead we came to an uneasy arrangement, but the conflict was always bubbling under the surface, threatening to erupt.

I caused Maria grief not just with my roving eye but also financially. When I went back to university she came up to a Melbourne with me where she found a job as a legal secretary earning a modest salary with William Street law firm. My mother was sending me an allowance, £100 every three months, which I would promptly spend in the first week on partying and paying off betting debts. Once that ran out, Maria would have to bail me out until my next allowance arrived, which I would again waste in record time. For most of my university days we were church-mouse poor; all of it my doing.

Our impoverished circumstances did bring one unexpected benefit. Having no money forced me to develop some entrepreneurial skills to help us get by.

Melbourne University's student newspaper, *Figaro*, had a section advertising jobs. I saw a summer job for delivering Christmas trees and decided to give it a go. At first Maria and I would lug these Christmas trees around to various inner-city factories, hoping to sell them to the workers there. Initially we barely made a single sale, and neither of us was particularly enjoying dragging heavy trees around in the December heat for no reward.

'I'll never make any money.' I thought, 'taking these from factory to factory and selling them one at a time.' Then I got the idea that we might have more success if I added value to the product. I bought several boxes of cheap Christmas tree decorations at Coles, dressed up a tree and took it to one of the factories. There I conducted my first ever business negotiation, with the factory canteen manager.

'You know, you could really give this place a festive feel if we put this tree here near the counter.' I suggested. 'Yeah, it would look nice,' she agreed.

'I'd like to put a sign beside it, just letting people know they are for sale.'

'Well, I don't know if we can advertise –'

'How about.' I interrupted, 'If you take the orders I'll give you a free tree for every ten you sell? You just collect the money, and I'll come back and deliver the trees on pay day.' And so the deal was done.

I did the same at several other factories around the place, and it worked sensationally. Business just took off. I was selling hundreds of trees and could barely keep up with the orders. So well was our enterprise doing that I ended up buying an old Fargo truck and hiring a handful of fellow uni students to help me with the deliveries.

The next Christmas we did the same thing, this time with artificial Christmas trees, and business continued to boom. We'd buy the trees direct from the factory, J D Wire Products in Collingwood, and we had to rent premises to store them all. At this point, I'd like to say that the profits from the Christmas tree business were all sensibly invested in shares, bonds, a property portfolio. And that thanks to the joys of compounding returns, those reinvested profits have made me and my family extremely wealthy. I'd like to say that...however what I actually did was punt most of the money away. The remainder was spent on wine and women.

In 1963, after four years of living together, Maria and I got married. Perhaps we both hoped that the marriage ties would be a sufficient restraint and I would settle down. It didn't actually work out that way, but one benefit marriage did bring was to reconcile us with Maria's family. Her father turned out to be the forgiving type; he was a really nice bloke who worked as a typewriter mechanic. When we got married he helped out by paying off about £200 of my betting debts. Not your average wedding present, but for me much more useful than a toaster or a set of bath towels.

I continued to have little to do with my own father, who had moved to Victoria sometime after the marriage break-up. He had opened up a couple of real estate agencies, one at Moe in Victoria's Gippsland region, another one in Croydon — now an established suburb in Melbourne's outer east but then a semi-rural area. My father had undergone a kind of transformation, at least in name. He was no longer the rather posh sounding Basil Hore-Lacy, but now called himself Bill Lacy — much simpler and more egalitarian. He reckoned that his new name would go over better with his real estate clients, mostly young working-class families pursuing the Australian home ownership dream.

But Dad was not in the best of health. In 1963, he was diagnosed with prostate cancer, and had to undergo surgery to have the prostate removed. A few days later he was out of hospital and back at his home to recuperate.

It was only shortly after he returned home that I got a visit from my brother Dyson. I was surprised to say the least, as the two of us barely spoke to each other — we certainly weren't in the practice of making social calls. This visit, however, was not a social one, but to deliver bad news — my father was dead. There must have been post-surgery complications. A few days after he had got out of hospital he had gone to the bathroom, and that's where they eventually found his body. The story goes that father was constipated and was struggling to shit when he had a heart attack and died on the lavatory. How things have changed in one generation. In those days, they knew nothing about the benefits of daily exercise, not eating fatty foods, eating plenty of green vegetables and consequently the average death rate for a male to mid-sixties to early eighties!

Nine years after commencing university I had completed

seventeen of the twenty-one subjects required for a Law degree. However, by this time I had realised that I had absolutely no interest in being a lawyer. When I tried to picture a future law career I could only imagine days, weeks, years of unremitting tedium. Although I was still without any clear idea of what kind of career I did want, I was determined to have a job that I loved, not one that bored me tearless. So many other people seemed to be in jobs that were a grind, a means to put bread on the table and nothing else. The walking dead I thought of them — and I didn't want to turn out like them.

I dropped out of Melbourne University with just four subjects to go. However, Mum encouraged me to complete at least some kind of qualification so that the past nine years weren't a complete waste. She was of course disappointed that I wouldn't fulfil her dream of my becoming a lawyer. Fortunately, a lot of the pressure to be successful was taken off me by my brother, Dyson. In stark contrast to me, he had sailed through law school and had become a successful barrister.

To please my mother I returned to Hobart, took a few Arts subjects at the University of Tasmania and finally graduated with a Bachelor of Arts degree. I still had my millionaire ambitions, fuelled by the success of the Christmas tree enterprise, so I thought maybe I should get into business. Besides I couldn't see a way of making a quid out of my Arts Major, Philosophy and Political Science. There never seemed to be any jobs for philosophers or political scientists in the Situations Vacant columns of the newspaper.

I'm not sure what led me to office stationery. I was looking for something that would be in sufficient demand, that could be purchased cheaply wholesale and then on-sold with a healthy price mark-up. Not to mention something that was a little less seasonal and, hopefully, a bit easier to lug around, than Christmas trees. With this in mind I flew to the centres of cheap goods at the time, Japan and Hong Kong, touring the factories looking for suitable products.

I had identified several office products, mostly knick-knacks and novelty items, and had an address book full of potential suppliers and customers from my Christmas tree selling days. I was all set to embark on my career as international trader, but was faced with a hurdle familiar to just about every small business owner. What was I going to do for finance? I needed some start-up capital.

After more than forty years of running businesses, if there's one lesson I've learned it is this: all banks are bastards. I was to get my first lesson in this universal truth when I tried to set up the importing business.

I had a business plan, had done all the sums and costed it to show that the business would be viable. I had letters of credit from suppliers, signed orders from customers, the legal, insurance and customs boxes were all ticked. So, I was pretty confident of getting funding from the banks. However, all the banks were concerned about was what kind of security I could put up. 'Where's your bricks and mortar?' they kept asking me. Each visit to a new bank brought the same tiresome refrain, 'Bricks and mortar, bricks and mortar.'

Well, I didn't have any bricks and I didn't have any mortar, so it looked as if my bright business idea would be still-born. I called my mother for help.

'I haven't got any money, darling, but ask Frank, Frank Packer. He'll help you.' was my mother's advice.

Sir Frank Packer has earned a fearsome reputation from those who had dealings with him. He was known to be a something of a tyrant who didn't suffer fools gladly. He was also notorious for being careful — some might even say tight — with his money.

Nevertheless, I plucked up the courage to go see him. Maria and I flew up to Sydney, dressed in our Sunday best to make the right impression.

Maria even dyed her hair blond for the occasion. The Packers lived at 'Cairnton.' the mansion Frank owned in the exclusive harbour-side suburb of Bellevue Hill. We arrived on Frank Packer's doorstep on a Saturday morning, and I remember standing outside the gates of 'Cairnton.' peering into the massive grounds, its tennis court and beautifully designed and immaculately kept English gardens, and thinking to myself, 'What the hell am I doing here?' But then I reasoned with myself, he can only say no, and so I rang the bell and waited.

I expected a guard or servant to come to the gate, and got a bit of a surprise when it was Sir Frank himself who strode into the view. Like most of the Packer males he was a large man, and there was something very imposing and formidable in his posture and the way his eyes fixed on you.

I had my opening line. 'Hi, Mr Packer. I'm Rick Hore-Lacy.'

'So what?' he bellowed at me. That wasn't quite in the script I had rehearsed in my head, but I ploughed on anyway, a nervous actor perspiring in the spotlights. 'I'm Barbara Bond's son.'

'Oh,' he replied, thought about it for a couple of seconds. 'Well, I guess you better come in.'

So Maria and I were admitted to the Packer mansion, and there I gave my presentation. I had a briefcase full of signed orders and other paperwork, which he briefly flicked through. I could see he was inclined to help out because I was family, but he was also too astute a businessman to simply hand over money.

'Come to my office on Monday,' he said gruffly 'and bring all the paperwork with you.' And with that I was dismissed. As we walked away, he laughed to himself 'Bonnie and Clyde.'

So on Monday I fronted at the Consolidated Press headquarters in Castlereagh Street in the city. In his office, he made a phone call, and a few moments later two of the Consolidated Press financial advisors came in — one of them could well have been Jim Flahdon, a senior Packer financial exec. Packer gave his sidekicks my paperwork, 'Take this away and see if he can make a profit.'

An hour or two later I was back in Sir Frank's office to hear the verdict. The figures suggested the business had legs, which I, of course, already knew. Sir Frank Packer agreed to go guarantor for me, and put me on to a confirming house called S H Lock and Co. The arrangement was that I would pay the suppliers through the confirming house ninety days after the goods were delivered. If for whatever reason I didn't pay, Frank would put up the money.

The business justified the faith Frank Packer had shown in it. It quickly became a nice money-spinner, and we always paid on the dot.

One of the Hong Kong factories I had gone to was run by a Chinese bloke called Louie. We had hit it off and I sensed he was someone I could trust. Louis thus became my main supplier.

Louie once boasted to me that he had slept with over three thousand women in his eventful life. Louie passed away several years ago; I'm not sure of the cause of death — possibly heart failure! It was Louie who took me on my first, and only, visit to a brothel. It was an unusual way to consolidate our business relationship, but very typically Louie. We had to climb several flights of stairs of this establishment, at the top of which was a crowded waiting room. There seemed to be an endless procession of women in black uniforms who would appear from one room, a key in one hand, collect a customer and disappear with into another room down the corridor. Another woman, the traffic controller, kept the production line moving, periodically yelling out 'Next!'

We had barely arrived at the waiting room when I got cold feet. 'Look, I'm sorry but I just can't go through with this.' I told Louie.

And so we left, much to Louie's annoyance. When it comes to sex I've always preferred enthusiastic amateurs to the dispassionate professional.

Our business 'headquarters,' were a small apartment that Maria and I were renting in the inner-northern Melbourne suburb of Parkville. The business soon outgrew the apartment, taking over just about all available living space. Rather than continue to trip over the mountains of boxes everywhere, we took out a second lease on a neighbouring flat, and that became our warehouse.

I named the business Goodcheer Industries. It was a bit cheeky because our main competitor was a firm called Goodwill Industries. I imagine they were none too pleased about the name similarity. We sold a motley range of office stationery. For our upmarket clients we had some fancy, embellished products, while novelty pens with a photo of a nude lady on it who undressed as you wrote were a big hit with the scrap metal merchants, auto parts suppliers and so forth. However, the real big sellers were the diaries. Clients would buy these up in bulk towards the end of the year, and we would often be selling hundreds of the product with the same order.

I need to be a little careful here, as I'm not sure if there's some kind of statute of limitations that protects me from past business misdemeanours. I'll just say that there was a particular brand of diary with a name that sounded like Dilly Dally Diary. The diary had one page per day, and on the other side a raunchy girlie cartoon, usually involving a buxom blonde. I started a range of window diaries, using modified versions of the Dilly Dally cartoons. To this end I employed a commercial artist, an Arab called Nubah. He was a funny bloke with a great sense of humour, and he could draw a cartoon incredibly quickly and the dirtier the better, but also an absolute whiz with the pen as quick as anything. I'd change all the cartoon punchlines, just a word or two, while Nubah's job was to alter all the illustrations. Then we'd sell the diaries under our own brand name. With 87.5 percent of a Law degree behind me, I confidently adjudicated that the alterations were enough for us to avoid any copyright infringement. With hindsight, it was probably just as well we never had to test out my legal judgement in the courtrooms!

The business was growing to the point where we went national, with salesmen in Sydney, Adelaide and Perth. Sir Frank continued to go guarantor for us — it was a ritual that I would embark on every year, going up to his Sydney office, opening our books to him, and then he would back us for another year. However, in 1974, Frank Packer passed away after a succession of illnesses that had left him increasingly weakened and frail. The next time I went to 'Cairnton.' my old sparring partner, Cousin Kerry, was running the show. He was to prove to be less generous than his father.

'What are you doing here, you little bastard?' he said to me in his typically direct manner. 'You only ever fucking-well come up here when you want something.' And I thought, well, there's a certain amount of truth in that. That was the last time I went cap in hand to the Packers. Fortunately, the business was going well enough that the banks were happy to loan us money when we required it.

Around this time too, after years of putting it off, Maria and I had started a family. Our first child, a son Ricky, was born in 1971. It was like a baton change between the generations because, not long after Ricky was born, Mum passed away at the age of sixty-seven. She had hung on for around twenty years with multiple sclerosis, a long time for someone with the illness, but eventually, inevitably, the battle was lost. She spent the last months of her life bed-ridden, no longer able to walk, the Catholic nuns looking after her at Calvary Hospital in Hobart. Those nuns did a marvellous job, even though our family was nominally Church of England. My mother had been deserted by all her old friends, and often remarked that the nuns were a lot more caring towards her than anyone else.

It was a painful time for me, observing her body gradually packing it in. She began to lose control of her bodily functions, and they had to tie her forehead to the bedstead to stop her slumping forward. It seemed an undignified end for someone who in her youth was the belle of the town. With her wealth, beauty and winning personality, she must have thought in those halcyon days that she had the world at her feet. Her life certainly had its ups and downs, more downs than ups in the final analysis, but as least she lived life to the fullest — and I loved her.

CHAPTER 4

I had been betting on horses since I was at school and through my university days, and more often than not I would come out on the losing end. I then found another guaranteed way to lose money at the track — racehorse ownership.

The first horse I bought was called Miss Testatrix who had been purchased as a yearling by a trainer, Ron Maund. Ron was then in the early stages of what was to become a successful training career. At that time, he had a major client, the Grant-Hay family who were originally from Tasmania. My parents knew them pretty well, and so I decided to use Ron as well.

Miss Testatrix raced a couple of times, her best finish was a fourth. She then developed problems with her knees, broke down and wasn't raced again. We tried to breed a couple of foals out of her, but none of them amounted to anything. And that was my introduction to the joys of horse ownership. Nevertheless, the distinct lack of success didn't matter, the bug had bitten.

I purchased a few more horses, and even got my own private trainer. Ron Crawford was a retired jockey who was looking for a new career. I set Ron up on a property out at Pakenham on the eastern fringes of Melbourne, paid him a weekly wage and let him live on the premises. Ron was one of racing's Mr Nice Guys, with an easy-going nature and always with a smile on his face. He needed that friendly relaxed temperament, because I was the type of owner that most trainers dread — the Interferer. I'd be down at the stables almost every day, pestering Ron with questions, giving him unasked for advice. Ron was too nice a bloke to say anything to me, but I'm sure he didn't appreciate the interference.

Prize money in those days was nowhere near the generous amount that racing clubs provide now, so unless an owner had an out-and-out champion it was difficult to make money from prize money alone. The real money came from betting on your horses. Betting plunges, where an unfancied runner is backed from long odds in to favouritism and large amounts of money are taken out of the ring, were almost a daily occurrence. In those days, on some provincial track somewhere in Australia, some well-informed punter was parting hapless bookies from large sums of money.

I was fortunate to be the architect of a successful betting plunge or two. One of our earliest ones was with a horse called Sweetbread at the provincial Victorian track of Hamilton. It was Hamilton Cup day, and Sweetbread was ridden by Garry Clarke, older brother of the top jockey Michael Clarke. Though not in Michael's class, Garry was a very good jockey who, I think, had his career ended prematurely because of injuries. Sweetbread started at long odds, and duly won by six lengths. The day has been recorded for posterity in a photo I have of a beaming Ron Crawford, thick wads of twenty-dollar notes sticking out of his pockets.

I have learnt the hard way that gambling is like a disease. For those caught in its grip it can bring untold misery and hardship. But all serious punters also experience moments of indescribable euphoria. The rush of excitement that courses through you when you see your pick storming home is like a shot of pure adrenalin. My most euphoric moment as a punter was in October 1974, Cox Plate Day. It was a day that was to alter forever the course of my life.

I had gone down to a country race meeting at Trafalgar in Victoria's Gippsland. Before the races started I popped into the

TAB in town, deciding to place a few bets on the quadrella for the Melbourne meeting. A quadrella involves picking each winner of four selected races, usually the last four races on the card. I had studied the form and identified a few stand-out selections, and must have felt reasonably confident because I spent $300 — a hundred on three separate quadrellas.

Isn't Fate an odd thing sometimes? As I was walking out of the TAB I glanced down at the tickets and noticed that two of them were exactly the same — I had filled one in incorrectly. So I went back to the cashier and changed one of the tickets, selecting a couple of different runners. If I hadn't made that quick double-check… well, my life could easily have taken an entirely different course.

I can still remember the four winning horses of that quadrella. Moonee Valley was an absolute bog track that day. Pure Luck won the sprint, and I had Battle Heights, a champion horse, in the Cox Plate. When they rounded the bend, he was last in the field, and even with 400 metres to go they were still calling him last and I was mentally tearing up my betting ticket. Then he stormed home on the outside to win at odds of 7-1 in one of the most famous Cox Plate finishes ever. The third leg of the quadrella was the Mooney Valley Cup, won by a horse called Lord Metric. By that stage one of my tickets was still alive — it just needed Romantic Sun to win. He was a 10-1 chance in the last race and trained by Colin Hayes. He led all the way and won by a neck!

In those days, of course, there were no big screen televisions at the track; instead the races were broadcast over a crackly old PA system. As they came down the short Moonee Valley straight, my palms were wet, butterflies inside my stomach, I may have even stopped breathing for a few seconds. And Romantic Sun — how I loved that horse at that particular moment — flashed home to win.

Then there was the wait. Payouts weren't officially declared until half an hour after the last race. By then I was in the car heading back to the Pakenham stables. It was a frustrating trip, constantly twiddling the dial of the car radio, trying to find out how much the quadrella had paid. Being out in the country it was next to impossible to get any reception at all –just static occasionally interrupted by a local radio station playing easy-listening classics.

Before I left Trafalgar I had phoned through to the stables to tell them the news of my win. When I got to Pakenham, the young lad who worked at the stables came rushing out to greet me. This kid had a bad stutter, which got worse whenever he was excited. 'It paid f-f-f-f….' he shouted at me.

'What was that again? How much?'

'F-f-f-f…'

'Just take a deep breath and relax.' I told him, trying to calm him down.

'F-f-f-four…'

But by this time, I had gripped him by the shoulders, prepared to shake the answer out of him. 'Just tell us how bloody much!

Fourteen hundred and forty-four dollars seventy cents for 1 unit was what he was trying to say. I had a hundred units on it, which meant my collect was $144,470. To give you some idea of how much money that was in those days, the average suburban home in Melbourne was about $25,000. You could buy a house in Toorak for $70,000! There was approximately half a million dollars in the quadrella pool and I had a ticket which entitled me to one third of it!

The TAB system operated differently back then, in that you had to go to the place where you had placed your bet to collect your winnings. So I drove back out to Trafalgar — I had to wait until the Monday — and the woman at the TAB was very polite and courteous. 'Would you like it by cash or cheque?'

I said, 'Thanks darling, but I doubt there'd be that much cash in all of Gippsland.'

'No, that's alright,' the ever-helpful cashier replied. 'We can get a truck down here if you'd like.'

Although the thought of a truck load of cash — all of it mine — was a tantalising one, I said thanks all the same, but I'd just take the cheque.

I was now wealthier than I'd ever been, and the first thing I spent my riches on was a stiff drink. I drove back to Melbourne and headed straight for the Continental Hotel on the corner of Russell and Lonsdale Streets in the city, a regular drinking place of mine and the publican there, Tommy Gabriel would often cash cheques for me; ten dollars, sometimes twenty dollars, when I wanted to have a beer. So I sidled up to the bar, handed over my winnings cheque, and very casually asked, 'Cash this for me, Tommy, will you?'

'Sure, Rick.' Tommy took the cheque, put it on the top of the till, glanced at it. He did a double-take, exactly like they do in the movies, lifted the cheque to get a closer look. I'll never forget the expression on his face before he threw the cheque back at me.

Needless to say, I ended up getting quite pissed that evening. I also got the fright of my life towards the end of the night. Some smart-arse had pick-pocketed my pants where I'd put away the cheque, then asked me, 'C'mon on Rick, show us the cheque, let us have a look at it.'

He strung me along for a while as I grew increasingly panic-stricken, frantically checking all my pockets, the floor around me, retracing my steps. I was too drunk to notice everyone else having a good laugh at my expense.

* * *

Racing had given me this massive windfall, and I decided to plough some of it straight back into racing. I went across to New Zealand, to the yearling sales there. New Zealand has long had a reputation for breeding champion thoroughbreds — the temperate climate and reliable rainfall produce lush green pastures that horses just seem to thrive on. I also reasoned that because it was a little out of the way, I'd be more likely to unearth some bargains. (Nowadays it's a completely different story — New Zealand horses are amongst the most over-priced in racing.)

Everybody in the racing game has the same conceit...or should that be delusion? We all think that we can pick a good yearling when we see one. I was no different, despite being involved in the industry for just a couple of years. However, it was probably good luck more than good judgement that any of the horses I bought on my first buying trip turned out to be any good. Anyway, I spent about $45,000 on eleven yearlings — I just picked nice strapping types that looked good to me — and returned to Australia.

Ron Crawford was still my private trainer, and I was still pestering him every day with questions and unwanted advice. I'd also bought a couple of books on the subject of horse-training, 'Feeding to Win' and 'Conditioning to Win' were my two bibles, and was starting to believe that I was at least a little knowledgeable on the subject. Often, I found myself thinking, 'Gee, I wouldn't mind doing this for a living.'

The fact is that after several years of building up a nice little import business, I was growing restless. Although financially rewarding, frankly, I found running the business a bit tedious and repetitive. Just as I had baulked at the idea of spending what I thought would be a less than exciting existence as a lawyer, I now realised that I wanted more out of life than importing thousands of diaries and ball point pens for the rest of my working days.

So I made the decision to strike out on my own, applied for and was granted an owner-trainer's permit. I had my eleven yearlings, now maturing into 3-year-old colts and fillies, plus some older horses. These I either owned outright or in partnership with a mate of mine, Gary Needham, with whom I'd studied Law at university.

I sold the importing business to my brother-in-law, Bill — my wife Maria's brother — for about $100,000. I'd already written most of the orders for the year, a lot more than $100,000, so the profit was already there and it wouldn't take him long to get his investment back. So it was a great deal for Bill; I just wanted to be rid of the business. Bill still runs the business today and has done very well out of it; it has made him a million or three. Even after a messy and expensive divorce where his ex-wife cleaned him out for half his assets, he's still doing nicely.

I've made more than my fair share of poor money decisions over the years; they usually involved spending money that should have been invested. This time, however, after selling the business to Bill, I thought I was doing the smart thing by investing in real estate. I bought an 800-acre property out at New Gisborne which is about 40 kilometres north-west of Melbourne, using the $100,000 from the business sale and $300,000 in borrowed money. 'Elderslie' was a historic property that had been in the one family, the Hamilton family, for almost 150 years. The property had a beautiful old colonial-style house on it, a National Trust sandstone mansion with parapet gables and beautiful French doors opening on to the verandah, all surrounded by paddocks as far as you could see.

My investment plan was beautiful in its simplicity. I intended to subdivide half the property into 40-acre blocks. I had worked out that I could sell them for about $1,000 an acre, or $40,000 per block. I'd sell ten of them, recoup my costs, and still have 400 acres and the house — for nothing! It was a property investment master stroke — Donald Trump would have been proud of that one. Or would have been, except that the Shire of Gisborne suddenly changed their zoning laws, decreeing that there would be no more subdivisions in Gisborne pending the release of a new town plan.

Suddenly, instead of an investment goldmine, I had a huge block of land that I couldn't do anything with, and a $300,000 mortgage — a massive amount of money at the time. The wheels of bureaucracy down at Gisborne Town Hall slowly creaked forward and eventually, three and a half years later, they allowed me to sell a single 40-acre block. That's all I got out of it. By that time, the original owner had taken back 500 of the 800 acres when I couldn't make a payment.

As a footnote to my property investment venture, the 500 acres were later sold to a company called Associated Securities. Then shortly afterwards — you guessed it — the area was re-zoned, Associated Securities more or less did what I had wanted to do, and made a bucket-load of money out of the deal. And a great time was had by all... except, of course, me.

* * *

One of the horses I had bought in New Zealand was sired by Even Stevens and we called him Toss. No one would remember that horse now, but he will forever hold a special place in my heart. I had given him a couple of closed trials as an unraced two-year old and he was very impressive. He looked like a potential city winner, and so it occurred to me that, if I could find a suitable race for him this could be the best bet of all time. I nominated him for a Maiden Handicap — that is a race for horses who had yet to win a race — at a mid-week meeting at the country track of Kilmore.

Toss's racing debut couldn't have had a more inauspicious setting. It was a cold, wet and windy day — late September- but it might as well have been the middle of winter. Despite being a small mid-week country meeting, in those days there was always a vibrant betting ring with about forty bookmakers operating at the track.

The bookies operating at Kilmore that day knew nothing about Toss — some untried colt out of a lesser-known sire and trained by someone who had never trained a winner. The horse consequently opened at long odds. Now if I had fronted a bookie and plopped down $1,000 on Toss at long odds, two things would have happened. The bookie, seeing this large amount of money for a horse he knew nothing about, would refuse to take the bet. And the other bookies, sensing a plunge, would have immediately and dramatically shortened their odds. So I needed to be a bit more strategic.

To this end I had enlisted a few of my university mates to travel up to Kilmore with me. My mates and I started to lay small bets, twenty dollars here, fifty there. The best odds we got were 33 to 1, a few bets were laid at 20 to 1. Eventually, with the money continuing to come in, the bookies realised something was up. In the end we backed Toss in from 33s to 7 to 2.

Toss, with Garry Clarke again on board, didn't just win…he bolted in; I think the official winning margin was ten lengths. I had trained my first ever winner. That alone was enough to make me ecstatic, but I had also won a small fortune off the bookies. It was estimated that over $40,000 was taken out of the ring that day.

No doubt there was a bit of a strut in my walk as I led Toss back to the winner's circle. I was questioned about the betting plunge, to which, of course, I professed ignorance might have then loudly regaled all and sundry with tales of my training exploits. There were a couple of remarks behind my back, along the lines of 'smug bastard.' One fellow trainer was reported as saying, 'Smartarse. He won't last long.'

We organised a lot of successful betting plunges in those days — that's pretty much how I made my living because prize-money alone certainly wasn't going to support me. These days, in contrast, it's next to impossible to orchestrate a major betting plunge, and at a country meeting there would be absolutely no chance. Today there's just half a dozen punters in the rings on the country tracks, the handful of bookies there aren't laying anything, you can't get set for five bob. What betting that is done is done by phone.

Raise The Kitty was the subject of another betting plunge I remember, when we backed him from long odds into favouritism in a Maiden at Bendigo. The horse ended up winning by 12 lengths, ridden by Brent Thompson. Brent was just starting out in Australia; he'd come over from New Zealand where he was the then wonder boy of racing. He had the nickname Babe because he was winning New Zealand jockey premierships when he was no more than a kid. I remember he always had the most impeccable manners, and spoke as if he had been educated at the best public schools in Britain. After the big win on Raise The Kitty, Brent actually came up to me and apologised after the race.

'I'm sorry, Mr Hore-Lacy. I didn't realise I was so far in front.'

I guess he knew there would be no more betting plunges on Raise The Kitty after that massive win.

Bookies, once bitten, tend to learn their lesson quickly. Word got around that this Hore-Lacy was up to having a huge gamble on his horses and the gamble more often than not came off. So it became increasingly difficult to get set at the track. As soon as there was even a trickle of money for one of my horses, the bookies would immediately over-react and shorten the price off the map.

I was also betting with the SP bookies. Harold Price was one of the biggest SP bookmakers in Melbourne, and I used to place a lot of bets with him. At first, I was winning some big money on my horses, but Harold — a wily old fox — soon came up with a method to beat me. He had an assistant, a young Greek bloke; many years later I met this Greek and he spilled the beans about how Harold got the better of me.

Let's say I had a horse I fancied running at Ballarat. After I laid a bet with Harold he would phone his man at the track (there was a public phone box outside the track at Ballarat it was before the days of mobile phones), the Greek lad, and say, 'Hore-Lacy's just had a thousand each way on so-and-so. Go into the ring and knock the price off.'

Betting with the SPs meant that although my horse might be at 10 to 1 when I placed my bet, I was on at the starting price. So Harold's assistant would go into the ring, start making bets, and knock the price down to 3 to 1. Then, if the horse won, Harold would pay me out at 3 to 1. (Harold, meanwhile, would have got 10 to 1 for it in the ring). As I said, he was as cunning as they come, as I guess he needed to be if he wanted to remain the most successful SP bookie in Melbourne.

I was quickly learning that punting was a mug's game, and it was increasingly difficult to get a good price on my horses. As the prize-money barely covered expenses, I was confronted with a choice: either give up training altogether, or become a public trainer and get others to pay my training bills. So I applied for my trainer's licence. And I guess I've been broke ever since!

* * *

My old university mate and partner in horse ownership, Gary Needham, had moved to Bendigo to start a law practice there. He continued his involvement with horse-racing, and became Chairman with the Jockey Club there.

One day I got a call from Gary. 'Rick, these new stables are about to become available at Bendigo. You should consider leasing them.'

The Bendigo Racing Club was in the process of adding a brand new thirty-stall stable at the racetrack. I went out to have a look; the facilities were good, and it would be much more convenient to have my horses stabled at a racetrack rather than at my New Gisborne property. I had laid out a small training track at the Gisborne place, adequate for cantering the horses, but using the Bendigo facilities for track work would be a huge improvement. So I signed the lease. It ended up being one of the biggest mistakes of my life.

A few of the local trainers at Bendigo also had their eyes on the new stables. Some might have even felt that, as local established trainers, by rights they should have been first in line. So when this inexperienced upstart jumped the queue, a few feathers were ruffled. Not that I was aware of it immediately. In the early days, I went about my business blissfully ignorant of the resentment that was building up towards me.

I didn't have much to do with the other trainers. Maria and I and our three children — Ricky and our two daughters, Kate born in 1973 and Emma in 1978 — were living just a few miles out of Bendigo at a small town named Junortoun, so we were a bit isolated. And I really didn't have a lot in common with the other trainers. We all trained horses of course, but that's where the similarities ended. We had completely different upbringings, different educations, different outside interests. So I pretty much kept to myself, no doubt reinforcing their perceptions that I was some snobbish silvertail.

I am certain that there was some professional jealousy towards me as well. I was having a decent amount of success with the yearlings I had bought in New Zealand, as well as several tried horses purchased over there. The other Bendigo trainers resented the fact that over the course of two years, I trained more city winners than the rest of them put together.

My training methods were pretty simple, and I'm not ashamed to admit that anabolic steroids were a big factor behind my early success. I found that I could buy horses in New Zealand who were just short of being open class handicappers, and by giving them anabolic steroids and proper feeding, they could be improved substantially. They'd eat better, they'd build up muscle and the geldings would develop the confidence of a stallion. They'd then go out and win open handicaps here in Australia by many lengths.

It was all perfectly legal at the time. Many of the top trainers were also using anabolic steroids, but hardly any of the smaller trainers. I was enjoying a good run of wins, and a few of the other Bendigo trainers resented me for it. I was some upstart from out of town with virtually no racing background, who had seconded the best stables for himself, and whose success, in the other trainers' eyes, was no more than an extended fluke.

A lot of my early training success was with jumpers, and again anabolic steroids were a key ingredient. Most of the jumpers in those days were, to put it harshly, failed flat track horses. If there were a prototype for a successful jumps racer, it would be a one-paced plodder who had shown some staying ability. That was the conventional thinking.

Not having a horse training background meant that I was more open to unconventional ideas. My view has always been that just because something has always been done the same way for a hundred years, doesn't mean we have to keep doing it.

What I discovered with jumps racers was an opportunity that no one else appeared to have stumbled upon. New Zealand has always produced great stayers — you'd only have to look at the history of Melbourne Cup winners to confirm that I was certain that if I bought Class 2 handicappers in New Zealand — that is, horses that weren't top grade handicappers but at the next level — then taught them to jump and beefed them up with anabolic steroids, they would do well in Australia. That was the theory, and that's exactly how the theory panned out in practice.

One of the yearlings I bought on my first trip to New Zealand was such a horse. We named him Lord Rocky Red. It turned out he was a natural jumper, and when we raced him in the steeplechases he would blitz the field. I took him to South Australia for one of the major steeplechase events, the Great Eastern Steeplechase, which is held every Easter weekend at Oakbank.

The Great Eastern is a punishing test for any horse. It's run over 4950 metres which makes it the second longest horse race in Australia. That year, 1980, Lord Rocky Red was up against a true steeplechase champion, Chocolate Royal, who had just completed a hat trick of wins in the other major South Australian steeplechase, the Von Doussa. But the younger and lighter-weighted Lord Rocky Red, helped by an outstanding ride from Bobby Challis, prevailed to win by seven lengths. Lord Rocky Red's Great Eastern Steeplechase victory was my first major race win. It was like a vote of confidence: that my training methods were sound and that I was no longer a hobby trainer — I was the real deal.

The next major steeplechase event on the racing calendar was the Grand Annual Steeplechase, held around the first week of May each year in the Victorian coastal town of Warrnambool. It's part of the Warrnambool Racing Carnival, arguably Australia's major country race carnival. The four-day meeting regularly attracts thousands of visitors to the picturesque track. There's always a great atmosphere there — it has a friendly down-to-earth feel of a picnic race meet, but at the same time there is the sense of occasion and excitement of a major event. The crowds, too, are enthusiastic and knowledgeable about racing.

In the Grand Annual, horses race over 5500 metres and 33 jumps. The fences include three treacherous 'doubles.' that is a set of two fences placed only metres apart that leave no margin for error. The handicapper gave Lord Rocky Red 67 kilograms after his win in the Great Eastern. It was a massive impost; I think the highest weight given to a horse since the sixties. Despite the weight, the punters sent Lord Rocky Red out a short-priced favourite, ahead of the previous year's winner, Thackeray. Lord Rocky Red had immense heart and courage, but he was a sometimes-erratic jumper. I think the Grand Annual course was just a bit too demanding for him, and crashing into the fence at the half-way mark certainly didn't help his cause. He finished out of a place in a tight finish, with Thackeray winning for the second year in succession.

The next year, 1981, I happened to have another star jumper on my hands, called Kaimoto. The premier Steeplechase event in Australia at that time was the Grand National Steeplechase, run every July at Flemington, and I set Kaimoto for that race. He was unbeaten in his early season races leading up to the Warrnambool Carnival in May. However, I dropped a bit of a bombshell by telling the press that I was considering giving the Grand Annual at Warrnambool a miss because the prize money wasn't attractive enough. Of course, I always intended running him in the Grand Annual, but I did want to make a point — that the $18,000 prize money was on the light side, especially considering the prestige of the race.

It would have been more profitable sending my jumpers to New Zealand and racing them there where richer stakes were on offer. My candour, however, no doubt did little to endear me to the Victorian racing authorities.

There was a bit of musical chairs amongst the top jumps jockeys in the lead up to the Grand Annual. Bobby Challis had been a regular jumps rider for me, including on Lord Rocky Red, but I had let him go. Instead he had picked up the ride on the reigning Grand Annual champ, Thackeray, who was looking to go three-in-a-row. Previously Thackeray had been ridden by David 'Butch' Londregan, but Londregan had been disqualified for four years as a result of a ride in Tasmania that the stewards didn't approve of. It was an extremely harsh penalty and Butch fought the decision, even taking it to the Supreme Court. It cost him a small fortune to clear his name, but the Supreme Court quashed the suspension just weeks before the running of the Grand Annual. But by this time the connections of Thackeray had already committed the ride to Bobby Challis.

Kaimoto's regular rider was a jockey called Paul Hely, who had done everything that could have been asked of him in the lead-up races. Unfortunately for Hely, he injured himself in a track fall just days before the Grand Annual. I needed to find a replacement in a hurry, and called up Butch Londregan. He was only too happy to take the ride.

Kaimoto went into the race slight favourite, though there was no doubt who the crowd favourite was. Everyone wanted to see Thackeray win the race for a record third successive time. Kaimoto started off well, and Londregan took the initiative half-way through the race by taking the lead. So far so good. The course is gruelling — it's so large that two race-callers are required to cover it. The horses complete the circuit twice, but there's one part of the course (Butch Londregan nicknamed it Devil's Bend) that plays tricks on some of the smarter horses. The first time they navigate the bend the horses turn left, but the second time around they have to turn right.

As they came to Devil's Bend the second time, 1200 metres from the finish line, Kaimoto had galloped away from the pack and was leading by 20 lengths. He just needed to stay on his feet and the Grand Annual was his and mine. But at the bend, Kaimoto thought he knew what he was doing and turned left again — the wrong way and in the opposite direction of the finish line. Londregan had to yank the horse back in the right direction, but in doing so pulled the bit through the horse's mouth. Ring bits had not yet appeared.[1] This meant he was steering with the reins in the horse's mouth for the last half mile of the race, which couldn't have been comfortable for Kaimoto — we have a photo! Kiamoto lost at least 200 metres.

Londregan told me after the race that at the point he thought that he had blown it and the race was lost. The horse in second place had made up ground in the mix-up at the bend and raced past Kaimoto. But Kaimoto was a tough athlete; he quickly hit his stride again — reins in mouth and all — and gathered the leader in, then regained the lead. At that moment Thackeray made his move. Thackeray had had no luck up to then; a horse had fallen just in front of him early on, hampering his progress. Then another, riderless, horse got in his way and held him back for a time. But once he got a free run he rapidly began to make his way through the field. I could see him looming, and at the turn he was just three lengths behind Kaimoto. It seemed inevitable that Thackeray — famous for his blistering finishing bursts — would storm home to win.

But Kaimoto was equal to the challenge. He found his second wind and Thackeray could take no further ground off him, Kaimoto going on to win by three lengths. Three lengths sounds a comfortable distance, but when they've just run 5500 metres it's little more than a hair's breadth. Even today, jumps aficionados

---

1 Ring bits. Whereby a ring was attached to the bit were introduced at this time. This prevented the bit being dragged through a horse's mouth as was the case with Kiamoto.

regard Kaimoto's victory one of the most memorable Grand Annuals ever.

Kaimoto then did the job again two months later in the Grand National Steeplechase at Flemington. This gave him, and me, the double of the two major steeplechase events in Victoria. At that time Kaimoto was just the third horse in over one hundred years to complete the cherished double.

* * *

Another problem I encountered at Bendigo was that, in spite of the success I was having, it was difficult for me to attract owners. Most owners are based in the city, and were reluctant to entrust their horses to a trainer out at Bendigo. I guess all owners have the same aspiration for their horses, of winning metropolitan races and ultimately a group success or two. No owner dreams of having a horse that runs around in country handicaps with the occasional city raid. Where's the glamour in that, although for most owners it is the more realistic scenario. Anyway, the wash up was that, after making the decision to train for others, I found that apart from Gary Needham and one or two other locals, I had no clients.

If that wasn't bad enough, a spate of positive drug tests found me continually in trouble with the stewards. Performance-enhancing substances are a bit of a grey area. A substance only becomes banned once the authorities develop a test to detect it — they can't ban something if they've got no way of knowing if it's been used or not. And trainers are always looking for something they can use to improve a horse's performance and which can't be traced.

Solu-Delta-Cortef was one of those drugs that couldn't be traced. It was an anabolic steroid being used by most trainers at the time, including myself, that put more oxygen into the blood. In 1980, however, a test was developed that could now detect Solu-Delta-Cortef. Usually, when a new drug detection method was introduced, the authorities would notify all trainers that they would now be testing for the drug; in many cases a few months' grace period was given. If the authorities warned us that Solu-Delta-Cortef would now be tested for, well I never got the memo.

Obviously, if they start testing for a drug that the majority of trainers are using, then a lot of people are going to get caught. And if they then suspended all the guilty parties, it would decimate the industry. All those trainers out of action would make a farce of race meetings — there'd only be a handful of horses running around. The few 'clean' trainers would be inundated with more horses than they could handle while the banned trainers sat out their suspensions.

What the authorities needed was a fall guy, someone to serve as a warning to all the others. It turned out that I was the fall guy. The authorities developed the test, and the racing world was surprised to discover that only one person in the whole of racing was using Solu-Delta-Cortef — Rick Hore-Lacy! The stewards sprang me after a Raise The Kitty victory, testing him and finding the drug in his system. I remember the saga dragged on for almost a year — they had to send samples overseas for further testing and it took an eternity to get the results back.

They suspended me for twelve months, which I appealed, managing to get it reduced by three months. Still, nine months out of racing was very harsh. A suspension is a heavy punishment for a trainer to endure, because it meant that for nine months I was without a livelihood and regular income, and several of my owners took their horses away, permanently, to give to someone else to train.

That unfortunately was not to be the end of my run-ins with

the stewards over banned substances. On one occasion, I took a horse called Storming Diamonds to Adelaide, and there I stalled the horse at the property of Byron Kozamanis, a trainer who was based in South Australia at the time. Storming Diamonds won his race by a several lengths, but I got a phone call from the stewards a few days later.

'Your horse has tested positive to Circulon.'

'What?!' Storming Diamonds had never been given Circulon, a treatment for horses with bad feet, in his life.

'Did you clean his feeder bin out?' Circulon was administered with a horse's feed, and even if the slightest residue gets into a horse's system it will show up positive in a drug test.

'Yeah, the feeder was clean.' I mean, I didn't know for sure, there might have been a few crumbs on the sides of the bin.

'You should've washed them out, you didn't clean it out properly.'

'I couldn't. It was a fixed feeder. It was screwed to the wall.'

An inquiry was held into the incident a week or two later, and from that it emerged that Kozamanis had had a horse in there that was on Circulon just before my horse was there. The stewards concluded, 'Just the same, you didn't clean the feeder out properly so you're liable.'

They fined me $5,000 and took the race off me, which was worth a bit of money. At least this time they didn't suspend me, because they realised that I hadn't doped my horse.

My final run-in with the stewards over banned substances took place in 1983. My stable foreman at Bendigo was a bloke who we shall call Sam, originally from Yugoslavia. Obviously, a lot of migrants from that troubled land with its centuries of bitter internal warring have become hard-working, law-abiding citizens in their adopted country. And a few of them were outright crooks. My father worked for a few years on the Snowy

Mountains Hydro-electric Scheme, and he always maintained that the Yugoslavians there were all madmen.

I can remember we were preparing for a race meeting. I had a horse called Diwali, who was my champion jumper at the time, and who I had bought in New Zealand for about $20,000. I had great expectations for Diwali, who I considered the equal to Kaimoto and Lord Rocky Red. In the 1982-83 season Diwali was just about unstoppable, winning everything he raced in.

As we were loading Diwali into the float, Sam was chatting away to the horse.

'You feel good today, boy. You gonna run good today. Yes boy, you gonna win today.'

He was almost gleeful in his excitement. Was this some kind of motivational tactic, that a pep talk would give the horse some added confidence? I know that many horses are very intelligent — smarter than some humans I've known — but this was very strange.

Diwali went out and won his race, by six lengths. Perhaps, I thought, there's something in Sam's version of horse-whispering after all. However, a week later, we were about to run Diwali in another steeplechase. When we arrived at the track a couple of vets went over to Diwali, started to take blood from him.

'What's this all about?' I asked, a little surprised.

'The stewards want to see you,' was all they said.

Well, it turned out that after his race the week before, Diwali had returned a positive swab for the banned substance BTZ, commonly known as Bute. In fact, there was so much Bute in his system that the measuring needle on the machine had gone off the graph paper.

'It's just not possible,' I pleaded with them. 'He hasn't had any Bute at all, not at all.' I was almost in tears, because the stewards then disqualified Diwali from running that day. It was an important lead-up race to the Grand National Steeplechase — the premier steeplechase event in Australia — which I had set Diwali for.

I was stunned by the news of the positive swab. Bute is a drug that acts as a painkiller; it allows a horse to run better because it is able to ignore all the normal aches and pains, the wear and tear that a lot of horses feel, especially when they are in the middle of a campaign. The drug is legal in some parts of the racing world, but in Australia it was a banned substance, and to be caught administering a banned substance was a serious offence. I pleaded my innocence, my ignorance, in fact, as I genuinely had no idea how the drug got into Diwali's system. Though when I thought back on Sam's pre-race behaviour I had my suspicions.

I think the stewards believed I had nothing to do with the doping. Nevertheless, I was taken to task for not having sufficient security at my stables. As it was a new facility there were no fences to keep people from wandering in or out. I was also told I should have guard dogs on the premises. I didn't bother pointing out to the stewards that all the security in the world wasn't going to help if it's an inside job.

Needless to say, I fired Sam after that incident. Not that there was much work for him anyway because the stewards suspended me for three months as well as hitting me with a fine.

At least the suspension didn't commence until after the Grand National Steeplechase. Diwali was able to take his place in the field, and was now completely Bute-free. He won the Grand National too... by a furlong! The second placed horse wasn't even in the photo of the finish, it was just completing the last hurdle when Diwali went past the winning post. Sam should have had more faith in the horse, and saved us both a lot of problems.

The biggest doping scandal that I was involved in was to happen about a year or so later.

Perhaps I've always been a bit too outspoken, and on occasion may have rubbed a few people the wrong way. It has been suggested to me that a couple of fellow Bendigo trainers were bad-mouthing me to the racing authorities. However, I was genuinely unaware of any bad blood between myself and the stewards, racing clubs or any other racing authority. So I was completely baffled — and remain so to this day — as to why I might have been singled out.

I served my suspension, but the succession of positive drug tests was making me edgy. I was at the stage where I dreaded every phone call after a race. If I saw a steward walking towards me at the track, my heart would immediately quicken, I'd feel my legs go weak. And because I was aware of the resentment towards me from the other trainers, I was vigilant to the point of paranoia, concerned that someone might try to slip a powder to one of my horses. However, it wasn't another doping scandal that was to push me over the edge. Something much worse was about to happen that would force me out of Bendigo once and for all.

CHAPTER 5

If copping a three-month suspension for something I didn't do wasn't bad enough, more salt was rubbed in the wounds when I then lost Diwali to another trainer. Because I couldn't train, the owners transferred him to Eddie Laing who was based in Cranbourne. It was obviously disappointing to lose a champion like Diwali; however, the swings and roundabouts of racing were about to once more take me on a ride. Not long after losing Diwali to one trainer, I, in turn, was to get a good one from another. In early 1984, I was approached by a woman named Emmaline Smith. She was from Melbourne and she owned a couple of horses. She and her husband were both a little on the eccentric side — Emmaline always reminded me a bit of Blanche DuBois in the film *Streetcar Named Desire*.

Emmaline Smith approached me one day and said, 'I'd like you to train Star Pyramul for me.

Star Pyramul was a two-year-old colt who at that time was in the hands of a local Bendigo trainer named Jack Hearps. Hearps had originally been a farrier by trade and had graduated into horse training. Jack Hearps is long dead, but some of his sons are still training. I was no mate of Hearps, a big oafish man — and I'm sure he didn't think much of me either. Nevertheless, I had no desire to take one of his horses away from him, especially having recently lost Diwali the same way.

'I'm sorry, but I'm not interested.' I told Mrs Smith. 'I'm already in the bad books with the local trainers. This will just make me an even bigger enemy.'

'If you don't take him, I'm only going to give him to someone else. I just don't want Jack Hearps training him anymore.'

For this reason, I, reluctantly, agreed to take Star Pyramul. The horse had shown plenty of early ability, even winning a Blue Diamond Prelude. He should have raced in the Blue Diamond, but apparently Hearps forgot to submit the paperwork, which might have been why Emmaline Smith was searching for a new trainer. Hearps never confronted me over my taking the horse off him, but I'm sure he wouldn't have been too pleased about it. For a battling trainer like him, it would have been an especially bitter experience to lose possibly the best horse he'd ever had.

After the various doping incidents that had befallen me in 1983, I was in no doubt that someone had been slipping my horses a powder. Security at the Bendigo stables had been improved; however, as I repeatedly told the stewards, if it's an inside job the best security system in the world isn't going to prevent something from happening.

On the evening of March 10, 1984, my wife Maria and I were at a function in Melbourne, in the city. It was a Saturday night, and we were sitting down for dinner when I was called to the phone. The call was from Bendigo.

'The horses have got out.' a distraught stable hand told me over the phone. 'They're running loose on the highway.'

'Which horses?'

'All of them!'

I had eleven horses stabled there at the time. Each of them was quartered in its separate stall, each stall secured by a steel chain. I was stunned.

'How could every one of them have got out?'

Maria and I got straight in the car and raced back to Bendigo. A sick feeling was welling in my stomach — someone had deliberately let the horses out. My suspicions only grew stronger when I arrived. The chains to the stall doors had been slipped off. The horses could have then gone one of two ways. They could have turned left and gone towards the training track — a familiar enough trip for the horses. Or they could have gone right, up a narrow road that led to the Midland Highway about a kilometre away. All the horses, every single one of them, had turned right and out on to the highway. Or more accurately. 'some people' — as it would have been impossible for someone acting alone to have done it.

'They've been herded on to the road,' I told no one in particular. 'Someone has driven them out on to the highway.'

Two of my horses were killed that night, hit by cars or trucks. All the horses came storming on to the highway in a pack. 'It was like the Charge of the Light Brigade.' one witness described it. 'It was chaos, you could see the sparks coming off their hooves as they charged up the road.'

One elderly driver had his car completely written off and he himself was lucky to be alive. The poor bloke was driving along at 100 kilometres an hour on a fairly dark stretch of the highway, and a horse suddenly loomed up in the arc of his headlights. The horse, a two-year-old colt called Stillarto, was badly messed up by the collision — one of the policemen on the scene had to shoot him to put him out of his misery. The other horse that failed to survive, Waideene, was one of my jumpers and the winner of nine races. He had to be put down a couple of hours later because of his injuries.

I'll never forget the sight of the dead horses lying in pools of blood. It felt like all my dreams of being a successful trainer now lay in ruins around me. We then spent hours trying to round up the other horses; some of them had bolted for miles. Others had been hit and were nursing cuts and gashes. The local vet and I were up until half past one that morning stitching up horses. All were severely distressed by the event.

The police, including the police racing squad, conducted an investigation. I had no doubt who were the people behind it. Unfortunately, I had no proof and the police weren't able to find any either. As a result, no one was ever charged over it — the culprits got away scot-free. I have no doubt that it was a local trainer and a couple of his sons but I can't prove it and can't publish it.

That same day that I lost the two horses, victims of sabotage, the Colin Hayes-trained two-year-old Frame raced in the Sires Produce Stakes at Flemington. Beautifully bred, he had been Hayes' most expensive yearling purchase up until then, bought for over $400,000. He was in dazzling form in his first couple of starts, and Hayes declared that he was the best horse he had trained since the ill-fated Dulcify. He was sent out as odds-on favourite for the Sires Produce, finished last, then dropped dead two hundred metres past the post. An autopsy was unable to determine the course of death. A mournful Hayes remarked that racing is a sport that produces the ultimate highs and lows, and this was one of those lows. I knew exactly what he was talking about.

The next day I discussed our future with Maria. Neither of us had any hesitation in deciding what to do next — get out of Bendigo as soon as possible. I fronted the Bendigo Racing Club, and told them that I wanted to terminate my lease, effective immediately. A week later we had vacated the stables and were out of there. Only one fellow trainer named Alan Browell, who I got along with well, could spare a word of commiseration for me before I left.

I was so disillusioned with the events in Bendigo that I seriously considered giving the training business away. However, I didn't want to give the people who turned my horses out on the road the satisfaction of being responsible for my quitting. Besides, I loved training too much to just throw in the towel. And so, I vowed to make a new start.

It seems to have been my lot to be constantly on the move, shifting from one place to another. Maria has calculated that we have lived in twenty-three houses in fifty-three years of marriage. It must have been unsettling for the children in particular –especially once they reached school age, and each move meant they had to find new friends.

I moved the family back to Gisborne where we rented a place. I had submitted an application for a city trainer's licence, and was still awaiting the outcome. In the meantime, somewhere needed to be found to stable the horses.

David Hains, a Melbourne merchant banker and frequent listee in the BRW Rich List, is also a highly respected thoroughbred breeder. He's probably best known as the owner and breeder of Kingston Town, the racing superstar of the early eighties and one of the two best horses I ever had the privilege to watch race. (Tulloch is the other one).

Hains owned the Kingston Stud on the Mornington Peninsula which also operated as a training complex. I had a passing acquaintance with him from my attendance at yearling sales, and after I left Bendigo I gave him a call to inquire about stable availability.

'Sure, you can rent the stables.' Hains told me. 'I'm not currently using them.'

Hains' property was on the Mornington Peninsula on the south-eastern outskirts of Melbourne, that is, on the other side of town from Gisborne. It would take me an hour to drive there, and I made that trip almost every day for the next several months. It was a real grind but I was determined to persevere and get my training career back on track.

Horse-racing really is a roller-coaster ride for everyone involved — trainers, owners, jockeys, punters. One moment you are at the top of your game and everything you touch turns to gold, then suddenly the rug is pulled out from under your feet and you're left sitting on your backside feeling sorry for yourself. Events at Bendigo had brought me down, but my fortunes were about to take an immediate turn for the better. Fittingly it was in partnership with someone else who, like me, had been given a fair battering by racing over the years and was also on the point of throwing in the towel.

Alec Dodson was a self-made millionaire; born in England he came out to Australia as a young man in 1927, with the proverbial £5 note in his pocket. He had chosen Australia because he thought the climate would be better for a chronic respiratory complaint he suffered from. Rather than travel half-way around the world, a simpler solution for his health problem might have been to give up his three pack-a-day smoking habit. Australia never cured the respiratory complaint, but it did help make him a wealthy man.

Alec had a bit of a mining background, having worked as a clerk for a mining company in London. He knew that the Australian outback was a vast treasure trove of hidden minerals, but his plans to launch a prospecting mission had to be delayed because of the Great Depression. Then in the early 1930s he and a business partner headed into the desert to do some gold prospecting.

They took a truckload of supplies with them; like good adventurers they had a Plan B, which was to set up a general store if their prospecting didn't work out. However, like not-so-good adventurers, they got lost in the desert, and never got the opportunity to enact either Plan A or B. They had ventured into the Simpson Desert, where they would have certainly died if it hadn't been for the help of a tribe of aborigines. Those aborigines took pity on the hapless two white fellas wandering around in the blazing sun, and led them out of the desert and back to a settlement. Alec said that he went into the desert weighing thirteen stone, and six stone when he eventually wandered out again. They had also lost or traded away all their supplies, so the whole ill-fated expedition was a disaster.

Alec could have quit then, but he remained determined to make his fortune. His next port of call was Papua New Guinea, again in search of gold. Somehow, he ended up in the Portuguese colony of Timor, this time an oil explorer. Here he found success, becoming a key player in establishing off-shore oil rigs in the Timor Strait. He became the inaugural Managing Director of the Timor Oil company, and later also set up the Moonee Oil Company, building the first off-shore rig in Queensland.

Meanwhile, he began dabbling in property development, buying up a lot of land around Doncaster, now an established suburb of Melbourne but then a semi-rural area. Alec was by this time a wealthy man, but really hit pay dirt in 1956 with the Suez Crisis. Egypt declared it would nationalise the Suez Canal, the British, French and Israelis responded by attacking Egypt, oil prices soared and Alec's oil companies profited.

Alec had bought his first race horse in 1950 and then for thirty-three years raced and bred horses with at best mediocre success. The good fortune that had shone on him in his oil and property ventures seemed to strangely turn off whenever he turned his attention to horses. When I met him, he was on the verge of getting out of horse-racing after three decades of frustration. He was seventy-six years old at the time, and not in the best of health. Although he had given up the cigarettes ten years earlier, the damage had been done and his chronic respiratory complaint had deteriorated into emphysema. Perhaps I was the last throw of the dice for him.

It's interesting that despite the enormous influence he was to have on my life, I'm not entirely sure when it was we first met. I do remember a plane flight sometime in 1983; he happened to be sitting next to me on the plane and we got to chatting about horses. And out of that chance meeting, I later got a call from him asking if I'd be interested in taking on one of his horses, a filly called Adios Belle.

'Look, I'll give it to you to train,' Alec suggested. 'See how you go with it.'

I agreed, and not long after the horse won a race at Moonee Valley. Alec was pleased no end.

Although I was then primarily known for my success with jumps racers, Alec had a lot of faith in me and my training methods. He basically opened his wallet to me, and gave me the go-ahead to purchase some yearlings for him. This I did, at the Victorian Sales, of which at least one, Lost Art, developed into a handy galloper.

Before meeting Alec Dodson, I had just completed my three-month suspension because of the Diwali doping incident. With nothing else to do, I turned the suspension into an enforced vacation, travelling to England, the United States and New Zealand. The vacation was very much a busman's holiday, as I toured various racetracks, stud farms and training complexes. One of the highlights was in England where I was invited to the training operations of John Dunlop at Arundel in Sussex. Dunlop was a very pukka English gentleman whose major client was the founder of the Massey-Ferguson tractor fortune.

While in New Zealand I bought some more horses. One of them, a tried galloper, was the result of a tip I had received. The horse had had five starts, won a couple of them, and had shown plenty of ability, but the owners were keen to sell. The horse was called Foxseal. I got hold of a video of Foxseal racing and was immediately impressed. He was a big athletic type with a powerful burst of acceleration — both his wins had been last-to-first finishes.

Foxseal was bred at the Kiteroa Stud in Waikato. The sire was Imperial Seal and the broodmare Foxton, who was, to put it mildly, a reluctant mother. Foxseal had been her first foal, at the ripe old age of 16, that is, an age when she should have been retiring from broodmare duties.

I ended up paying $100,000 for Foxseal, much more than I'd ever spent on a horse before. New Zealanders are some of the shrewdest negotiators I've encountered, and always knew how to drive a hard bargain. You had to get up early to outwit a Kiwi horseman at the negotiating table — perhaps the two-hour time-zone difference had something to do with it!

Despite the hefty price tag, I had an intuition that Foxseal would repay the initial investment. Besides, I had a buyer for him in Melbourne already lined up. Or at least so I thought.

Cliff Pannam QC, a celebrated barrister in the Melbourne legal scene, often represented people in the racing industry. I had consulted him a couple of times on legal matters relating to my import business and we had struck up a friendship. He also represented me during my appeal against the Diwali suspension. Cliff had established a flourishing practice over the years, and had become quite wealthy as a result. Like many rich people, Cliff had decided that racehorse ownership might be an enjoyable way to fritter away some of that wealth. I saw Foxseal as a potential big race winner, and thought he would bring some success and a lot of enjoyment to Cliff as an owner.

Cliff agreed to buy Foxseal and once I returned to Melbourne I sent him a bill for $105,000. The additional $5,000 was basically to cover my expenses; I had flown to New Zealand and spent a week there, which certainly didn't come free. Then I got a call from Cliff.

'It just occurs to me, Rick, that you'd be making a thumping great profit on this transaction.'

'Well, I'm not sure about a thumping great profit.' I replied, 'but as a matter of fact, I'm making $5,000 on it... to cover my expenses.'

Cliff seemed a bit put out by this, and a few days later I got an emotional letter from him, the gist of which was: 'How could you do this, Rick? I thought that we were friends,' which I thought was a bit rich. It hadn't been that long ago that he had charged me $2,600 for a day in court. Customs had caught me undervaluing office diaries so that I would pay less import duty back in the days when I had the import business. Even Cliff Pannam's renowned advocacy skills were not enough to get me off and the Court fined me $44,000. However, I never used Cliff's legal bill as a test of our friendship!

So Cliff, his feelings hurt, didn't take the horse, and all of a sudden I was left in possession of a $100,000 horse and no owner. After I met Alec Dodson, I told him the story. Alec was always straight as a barrel in his dealings with me. He simply said, 'That's alright, I'll take the horse.'

He then added, 'You know, Rick, you should've charged Pannam ten percent, that's the normal agency fee. Five percent wasn't enough.'

True to his word, Alec paid me $110,000 and Foxseal was now his, in partnership with his wife, Ethel. Actually, despite his unhesitating offer to buy Foxseal, Alec had never paid so much for a horse before either. So we were both more than a little nervous when it came time for Foxseal to have his first Australian run.

The first few starts here, Foxseal was a disaster. He showed absolutely nothing at all. One run in a handicap at Caulfield, he flopped so badly that I thought, 'Oh hell, the Kiwis have got me again. It was a deflating experience; I had just had the good fortune to come across a wealthy, generous owner prepared to place his faith in me, and I had sold him a dud.

Two things swayed me to give Foxseal another chance. We had at least discovered why the New Zealanders had been sellers in the first place. Foxseal had a curious anatomical problem; when he was running at full speed his back passage would open, air would be sucked in and fill up his belly. The result was that if he was forced to run at full stretch for anything longer than a few hundred metres he would become so bloated that he would start to pull up out of discomfort. Going back to his past racing history I saw that he only raced well when he was ridden stone cold, that is, off the pace and at the back of the field. He then could be unleashed in the final few hundred yards. This style of riding him only worked, however when there was a strong pace on throughout. If there was no pace on, and all the horses started sprinting at the end, he'd be too far back to make up the ground.

The second thing I wanted to test with Foxseal was whether he could run over further distance. Up to this point he had only been raced over the sprints. Much to my and Alec's relief, once we put him in some longer races and allowed him to be ridden cold, he began to win. It was about this time that I started to think we might have a good one on our hands.

* * *

My application for a city trainer's licence was approved around April 1984. I had my eye on a property next to Epsom, virtually across the road from the track entrance. Epsom, in the south-eastern suburb of Mordialloc, was at that time the second biggest training complex in Victoria. The site I had in mind was a former factory up for sale, and I thought it would be an ideal spot for stables. The towering red brick walls that surrounded the factory like a prison wall also had a certain appeal, given what had happened to me in Bendigo.

I estimated the cost of purchasing the factory and converting it to stables to be around $400,000. It was a prohibitive price for a broke trainer, except once again Alec came to my rescue. He thought it was a great idea and paid for everything!

Once we finished the conversion I had some of the best training facilities in the state. From memory, I had forty-four boxes there, we had enviable staff amenities, and a modern feed room. This was in the days before packaged horse feed (the feeding process is one of the most important components of horse-training). The stable even had its own laundromat in the interests of cleanliness and hygiene. The finishing touch to the new stables was the installation of an absolutely ferocious Alsatian guard dog named Kaiser — just in case anyone got the notion to launch another vendetta against me.

The move to Epsom began to bear fruit almost immediately. In the first month of the 84-85 season, in August, I trained my first city treble.

It may have been only a mid-week meeting at Sandown, but I was particularly proud of the achievement as I had managed to defy conventional thinking. All three winners that day were backing up from runs a few days earlier. Many people at the time believed that I asked too much of my horses, that they would not be able to recover in such a short space of time, particularly as Melbourne had had constant rainfall over that period making the conditions even more trying for the horses. However, I was confident in the fitness and conditioning of my three runners and all of them were eating well in the lead-up to the races. A simple rule of thumb I often used is: if the horse is licking out its feeding box, it's okay to run.

The track was rated Heavy that day at Sandown. In the first

race, I had a horse called Fast Food running. Fast Food, sired by Kirrama out of Microwave, was a six-year-old gelding that I had only recently purchased for $30,000. He had been racing up in New South Wales where he had won eight races, and was good enough to run fifth in the Group One Sydney Cup a few months earlier. He was a big, impressive looking horse, and when I trialled him over the jumps he took to it like a duck to water. I had just raced him over the flat in a middle-distance event on the Saturday, and was now backing him up in a hurdle event over 3100 metres. He was a class above the other runners, and just needed to jump cleanly, which he duly did, winning the race by twelve lengths.

Planinca, a four-year-old grey gelding by Caledonian Planet, was one of Alec Dodson's horses that he had now put in my care. Alec was almost ready to give up on Planinca, but I felt that if we chose the right races for him, that is, middle distance races in the winter months when the fields are relatively weak, we could get a few wins out of him. He was later to exceed even my expectations, but at that point I had no inkling of his real potential. The previous Saturday he had run a solid, though hardly eye-catching, seventh over 1600 metres. However, the Wednesday meeting was much more suitable: he loved the wet, and the track was a bog. He was now running over 2400 metres and it was a much weaker field. He went into the race favourite and won by one and a half lengths, with boom apprentice, Darren Gauci, on board. It was a grinding hard-fought win where Planinca had managed to wear down the leaders. It would turn out to be a typical performance from this honest, courageous horse.

My third winner was another jumper, Get The Rent. This time, however, I had switched him back to the flats for a 2400 metre handicap. Often horses that have been racing over the arduous jumps circuits relish the return to flat racing, and that was the case with Get The Rent who won by one and a half lengths. The nine-year-old was sold soon after that win, as I started to bring younger horses into my stable.

* * *

Encouraged by Foxseal's most recent performances over the longer distances — he won two races in ten days in July — we nominated him for the two premier Spring Carnival staying races, the Caulfield and Melbourne Cups. I thought he was a genuine chance in the Caulfield Cup over 2400 metres. The Melbourne Cup nomination, however, was just to be on the safe side. Imagine how upset I would have been if he had turned out to be a brilliant two-miler and I had neglected to nominate him for Australia's greatest race!

As part of Foxseal's spring preparation we took him up to Sydney to run in the Group One Metropolitan Handicap over 2400 metres. The Metropolitan is often chosen as a good lead-up race to the big Victorian Cups and usually attracts at least a couple of high class stayers. Jockey Bruce Compton followed my instructions to the tee in the Metropolitan, and Foxseal came from almost last to storm home. Unfortunately, he wasn't quite good enough to haul down the Jim Lee-trained Hayai who held on to win his second successive Metropolitan. Foxseal finished a length behind in third, which provided Alec Dodson with a handy slice of the $175,000 prize-money. Foxseal's run caught the eye of many punters, and his odds for the Melbourne Cup shortened from name-your-own-price to 25 to 1.

After the Metropolitan, we brought Foxseal back to Melbourne. However, it occurred to me that the $50,000 Canberra Cup to be run the following week over 2400 metres could be a good opportunity for him. So Foxseal was back on the float and up the

Hume Highway again the night before the race. Not all horses travel well, and this would be Foxseal's third long-distance road trip in just over a week. But he had one of those calm, placid natures and not much fazed him. We arrived in Canberra about 9:30 the morning of the race, gave Foxseal a lick of grass and the horse showed there was nothing wrong with his appetite — he was ready to go.

Bruce Compton was engaged again for the ride. Compton was a former New Zealand jockey who had crossed the Tasman a few years previously and became stable rider for one of the top Sydney trainers, Paul Sutherland. Foxseal went into the race favourite, and Compton again provided a faultless ride, timing Foxseal's run to perfection. He came powering home to win by a length. By this time, I was convinced he deserved to start in the Melbourne Cup.

The next race on Foxseal's schedule was the Caulfield Cup two weeks later. He finished eighth in that race, but came from last to be only two or three lengths behind the winner, Affinity. Punters again took note and his Melbourne Cup price shortened from 25s into 15-1.

He had one final run before the big race, in the Dalgety over 2500 metres the Saturday preceding the Cup, finishing a solid fifth.

There is nothing to compare to Melbourne on that first Tuesday of November — it really is one of the great sporting rituals in the world. This was the first time I had ever had a runner in the Cup, and I tried to treat it just like any other day in terms of going about normal duties around the stables and getting the horse ready. However, it was impossible not to get caught up in the excitement and tension of the occasion.

On Cup Eve the Call of the Card is held at the exclusive Victorian Club where bookmakers takes bets from the various racing identities, business leaders and celebrities in attendance, not to mention some big-time and often anonymous professional punters. The Call of the Card provides a good insight into who the experts fancy, just through sheer weight of money. Foxseal, a little to my surprise, attracted some big wagers. In fact, at 15 to 1 he was backed to win about $450,000. (Black Knight was the only other horse whose win would have been more costly for the bookies).

Much of the day itself was a blur to me. Then before I knew it, several races had been run and the Cup was the next race on the card. As the horses were led to the barriers I had time to reflect that just nine months ago some low-life had turned my horses out on the road and I was ready to give the game away. Yet here I was, saddling up a potential Melbourne Cup winner.

I had allowed myself to dream that Foxseal could win — after all, this glorified 3200 metre handicap has always been a bit of a lottery that only sometimes rewarded the best horses. Realistically, however, we needed everything to go our way plus a generous serving of luck.

A little more than three minutes after the barriers were thrown open, the race was all over for another year. There were hard luck stories, as there always have been, but Foxseal wasn't one of them, and I couldn't fault Bruce Compton's ride. Foxseal was ridden from well behind — Compton as always had to hold him back so that the horse's back passage didn't fill up with wind. When Compton let him go the leaders were too far away and too strong at the finish for Foxseal to overhaul them. But the horse was as game as ever, finishing fifth ahead of a lot of better credentialed horses.

The Cup winner for 1984 was Black Knight, ridden by Peter Cook and trained by George Hanlon. Although Bart Cummings is rightly known as the Cups King, Hanlon's achievements should also be recognised, considering he had only a fraction of the number of horses Bart had to work with. Black Knight was Hanlon's third Melbourne Cup winner, a terrific feat as plenty of good trainers have failed to win one. The horse was owned and bred by the business entrepreneur Robert Holmes à Court, who had invested a fortune building up his racing and breeding operations. So although the Melbourne Cup once in a while ends up in the hands of a battler, it never hurts to have a bit of money behind you if you want to take the Cup home.

Things have completely changed since then. The Melbourne Cup is no longer the almost exclusive domain for New Zealand bred horses. It has become a wonderful international race that attract some of the world's best horses, jockeys, owners and trainers.

* * *

Fast Food was a six-year-old gelding that I purchased in mid-1984 for $30,000. He had been racing up in New South Wales where he had won eight races, and was good enough to run fifth in the Group One Sydney Cup a few months earlier. He was a big, impressive looking horse, and when I trialled him over the jumps he took to it like a duck to water. We knew immediately he was going to be something special. He had such a great leap and a lovely smooth-running style — the phrase 'poetry in motion' might have been coined just for him when he was in full stride. He made his jumps debut in a mid-week steeple at Sandown and won by twelve lengths, simply confirming his exciting potential.

Fast Food was given a lengthy spell and brought back in preparation for the Grand National Steeplechase at Flemington in July the following year. We raced him in three hurdles events; he won two and was beaten a short half-head in the other. But it was over the tall timber of the steeplechases that he really shone. His first steeplechase race that 1984-85 season was the Von Doussa Steeplechase which he won by six lengths. I button-holed one racing journalist after that win, the Age's Mark Harding, and told him, 'Do yourself a favour, and back him in any jumps race he's entered in.'

When Harding gave me a slightly doubtful look. I added, 'I'm telling you, he will not be beaten in any steeplechase.'

We skipped the Warrnambool Carnival, sticking to city events. (In those days jumps races were held at three city tracks, Flemington, Moonee Valley and Sandown). His next race, a lead-up to the Australian Steeplechase, he won by seven lengths.

The Australian Steeplechase was held each June at Sandown over 3900 metres. Despite the grand name of the race, the prize-money was on the paltry side, at just $18,000. I was a bit outspoken about the small prize-money on offer, threatening on more than one occasion to take my jumpers across the Tasman to race. This was at a time when Australian racing was just entering an increasingly destructive period of price inflation. It coincided with a period of deregulation in the economy as a whole. Credit controls had been loosened up and some high flying business entrepreneurs were borrowing and spending money as if there were no tomorrow. Some of these entrepreneurs — Holmes à Court, Robert Sangster, and the Western Australian mining millionaire Laurie Connell — had become involved in horse-racing. They went to the yearling sales armed with big cheque books and got caught up in bidding wars that were pushing yearling prices to obscenely high levels. Yet at the same time, prize-money was failing to keep pace with the rising prices, particularly in jumps racing.

Fast Food went into the Australian Steeplechase as a short-priced favourite with Nick Harnett in the saddle. Harnett was a great rider but was forced to specialise in jumps racing because of a constant battle with his weight. I think his lightest riding weight was 63 kilograms, and he had to 'sweat' to make that. He rode winners in most of the top jumps races in Australia, and then went on to have a successful career training jumpers.

Fast Food and Harnett were never troubled in the Australian Steeplechase; they went on to win it by eight lengths. After the race, I declared that Fast Food was the best jumps racer I had trained, better than Kaimoto, better than Diwali. And at that time Fast Food really had captured the imagination of the racing public. The media attention, the cheers he got and crowds he attracted were equivalent to the star flat racers going around then like Red Anchor. Plenty of people who knew their jumps racing were comparing Fast Food to Crisp, the great Australian jumper who went to England and despite carrying a massive weight almost beat the mighty Red Rum in the Grand National. Alec Dodson and I both had great ambitions for Fast Food. Alec wanted to see Fast Food take on the great jumps events in Britain, while I was keen to see how he would go in the United States, in particular in America's most prestigious steeplechase, the Colonial Cup in Maryland.

Meanwhile, at the same meeting where Fast Food was basking in the limelight of his Australian Steeplechase win, his less celebrated stable-mate Planinca was lining up in the Australian Hurdle. Just two months earlier I had made the decision to try him over the jumps. Although not a natural jumper, Planinca did possess one outstanding attribute, and that was dogged determination. It was typical of the two horses' contrasting temperaments that after Fast Food blitzed the field in brilliant fashion in the steeplechase, Planinca was slugging it out in the hurdles. The race appeared to be lost, but somehow through sheer courage and stubborn force of will Planinca managed to get his head in front to win, Nick Harnett again getting the job done.

The Australian Steeplechase-Australian Hurdle was a rare and prestigious double for me, but eight days later an even bigger cup win was to be in my grasp.

CHAPTER 6

Foxseal's effort to run fifth in the 1984 Melbourne Cup was a creditable one, yet I was still not entirely convinced that he was a genuine two-miler. I had taken him to Perth the following month to run in the Perth Cup but he finished a disappointing eighth. In May 1985 he ran in the Adelaide Cup and again he failed to run a place, coming fourth.

Foxseal's old rider, Bruce Compton, contracted to the Paul Sutherland stable in Sydney, hadn't been available for the interstate rides so I had engaged Greg Hall instead. Greg was one of Melbourne's top jockeys but he was also a freelancer. In those days, most of the Victorian jockeys tended to stick to rides in their home state, but Greg was different. He loved riding in the big races and would make himself available for all the major racing carnivals no matter what city they were held in. For this reason, Greg never won a jockey's premiership, although he certainly had the talent to do so.

He was also, to be frank, his own worst enemy. He enjoyed the good life, and really enjoyed a drink — his battles with the bottle have been well-documented including in his own autobiography. There were times when he was required for early morning trackwork and he would have the shakes, still working off the effects of the previous night's drinking session. However, when race time came he was always the complete professional, and the two of us shared some great successes together. At one time, I even considered offering him the role of stable jockey, but Greg preferred his freelancing ways.

Greg had recently returned from a short but eventful spell riding in Hong Kong. As he tells it, he hadn't been prepared to follow the 'riding instructions' passed on to him by Hong Kong's notorious Triads, and as a result made a hurried exit in fear of his life. He had started riding Foxseal for me in the Autumn '85 carnival, including the Adelaide Cup failure. He, too, doubted that the horse was a genuine two-miler. In fact, Foxseal's best performance that campaign was over the mile, when he ran second in the Group One Doncaster Handicap (the year it was won by the 100-1 long-shot Row The Waves in one of the biggest boilovers in the race's history). Nevertheless, when I entered Foxseal in the Brisbane Cup, which back then was a 3200-metre race, Greg agreed to take the ride. The Brisbane Cup is run every June, one of the main events of the Brisbane Winter Carnival. It was then a Group One Event, but has since been reduced both in distance and status, to a Group Two, and had been won by some classy stayers over the years, Tulloch being the most famous.

One of the reasons why I was keen to run Foxseal was because despite the race's Group One status, it was a relatively weak field. I felt that I wouldn't get many better opportunities to snare a Group One race than this one. The bookies appeared to share jockeys' and trainers' doubts about Foxseal getting the distance, and sent him out at generous odds. And I'm sure that many of the bookies and punters felt that Foxseal had been up for too long. He had been racing since March, travelling from Melbourne to Sydney to Canberra to Melbourne to Canberra to Sydney to Adelaide to Brisbane — my motto might well have been, 'Have horse, will travel!'

I have been criticised for keeping my horses racing for too

long. Funnily enough, I've also been praised for my ability to get horses to show consistent form over a long campaign, which only goes to show that you can't please all the people all the time. The reason why my horses stay up for so long is because they do very little galloping between races. In fact I might have been the only trainer in Melbourne who didn't own a stopwatch! I also used swimming as part of the horses' conditioning regimen. Based at Epsom, the Mordialloc beach was just a kilometre or two away and we would load some of the horses on the float and take them down for a swim. The horses loved it, and more importantly, it kept them in tip-top condition.

The logic behind my training methods was only common sense — if a horse is at peak fitness, then I don't need to gallop it to get it fitter, in the same way that you can't get a glass of water fuller than full.

In the Brisbane Cup Greg Hall gave Foxseal the perfect ride. As usual he was ridden from the back, but Greg gradually worked his way through the field. Usually when the horses entered the straight Foxseal would be at the tail, fifteen or twenty lengths back, and have to storm home on the outside. This time, however, Greg had stuck to the inside rail and when one of the front-runners started to tire, Greg used Foxseal's big frame to advantage, muscling his way past. With a clear run home now, Foxseal just took off and hauled in the other leaders. It looked to be a cakewalk from that point but then the two miles began to really test him. Watching in the stands I could see him running out of steam. But Foxseal was as game and courageous as they come, and he managed to hold on to win.

Foxseal's Brisbane Cup victory was the biggest win of my eight-year training career. Just as rewarding, however, was that I had also finally broken Alec and Ethel Dodson's thirty-year major race drought. And with the $155,000 prize money, Alec had now well and truly recouped his $100,000 investment in the horse. I couldn't help wondering how Cliff Pannam now felt at having knocked back the chance to own Foxseal... so I made a point of asking him every time I saw him!

* * *

After Fast Food's slashing victory in the Australian Steeplechase in May 1985 I set him for the Grand National Steeplechase in July, the same event that I had won with Diwali two years earlier. Alec was very keen to then send Fast Food to England to run in the prestigious Cheltenham Gold Cup the following March. Alec still had family in England and would have loved to return to the country of his birth and lead a Gold Cup champion around the Cheltenham winner's circle. It would almost be a vindication of that momentous decision he had made fifty-five years earlier to start a new life in Australia, and the tangible proof of what a success he had made of his life.

Such was Fast Food's brilliance, neither Alec nor I had any doubts that he would be successful in England. My own plans, once he had conquered Britain, were to then send him on to America to contest the classic jump races there, including the Colonial Cup. Those were our dreams, however, racing was to throw up yet another cruel twist of fate.

In preparation for the Grand National at Flemington, Fast Food had been entered in the Roussel Steeplechase. A few days before that race I noticed some heat and swelling on Fast Food's off foreleg. The vet diagnosed it as an infection of some sort and we had to scratch him from the Roussel. I wasn't particularly concerned as he still had plenty of time to recover for the Grand National.

The infection refused to go away. In fact, it was worsening, to the point where Fast Food could barely walk. Bewildered by the infection's persistence, I took the horse to the Melbourne University Veterinary Clinic at Werribee in Melbourne's west where they conducted some tests. We didn't have to wait long for the test results. It was bad news.

Fast Food had been diagnosed with osteomyelitis which is a bone marrow infection. It's uncommon in horses, and in many of the rare cases the outcome is fatal. What had happened was the soil in our yards out the back of the stable had become toxic, and Fast Food picked up the infection. The infection had eaten into the sesamoid bone, and the only course of action now was to remove the sesamoid before the infection spread further. Obviously the Grand National was out of the question, in fact, Fast Food's life now lay in the balance. If the operation was unsuccessful and the infection wasn't stopped, the only merciful thing to do would be to put Fast Food down.

The vets operating on Fast Food, Drs Vic Spiers and Alistair MacLean, didn't sugar coat the facts. The operation was a dangerous one and the chances of a successful recovery were only about 10%. Still, it was a chance we had to take. The two vets did a wonderful job and through their surgical intervention halted the infection. But Fast Food was still not out of the woods. If an arthritic problem had developed in the fetlock joint he would be a virtual cripple for the rest of his life.

Over a three-month period, the horse was slowly nursed back to health. Fortunately, he gradually improved and was eventually able to move freely again — the doctors attributed his recovery to his placid nature. He was a horse that just seemed to take everything in his stride, even a brush with death and months of painful recuperation. Unfortunately, however, Fast Food — who for a brief period had lit up the Australian jumps scene — was to never race again.

Racing is never short of what-if scenarios, and Fast Food was one of them. What if he had stayed healthy, gone to England, gone to America? Might he have gone down in history as one of our greatest racing exports ever? It's all conjecture now, but a lot of good judges at the time felt he was more than capable of achieving greatness.

While Fast Food was dicing with death, Planinca took the opportunity to emerge from his stablemate's shadow. In my view, Planinca was the perfect winter horse. When the better horses were spelling, and the tracks became slower and heavier, Planinca really came into his own. The grey gelding was tough, full of courage, and he loved it when the ground was wet. That winter of '85 he was in domineering form, winning six out of seven races over both jumps and the flat. Even his only loss was an honourable one, beaten by a short half-head.

While Fast Food had been set for Flemington's Grand National Steeplechase, Planinca was prepared for the Grand National Hurdle at the same meeting. He was sent out equal favourite that day, Nick Harnett again on board. The two horses to beat were the other favourite, New Zealander, Gogol, and the previous year's winner, Zamenhof.

Considering the ill fate that had struck Fast Food, it seemed only just that Planinca would get the lucky breaks that day. First Zamenhof lost its rider at about the halfway mark. Then Gogol, just when he was looking to challenge, clipped a hurdle and fell. The rest of the field weren't up to the challenge and Planinca did what he did best — kept going, kept grinding, and eventually won by 4 lengths.

The greatest memory I have of that day was Alec and Ethel Dodsons' jubilation when Planinca crossed the finish line. I've never saw Alec happier and more excited than after Planinca's Grand National win.

'Rick, that's my greatest satisfaction in almost forty years of racehorse ownership.' he told me immediately after the race. Unlike Foxseal, which I had bought for him, Alec had bred Planinca himself — no doubt the reason for his added satisfaction.

I, too, had nothing but admiration for Planinca. He was never going to blitz a field or win in a canter. But when the pressure was on, you always knew that Planinca would not give up, and would be the one who keeps giving maximum effort right to the finish.

At the close of the 1984-85 racing season I won my first ever trainer's award, the Jumps Trainer's Premiership sponsored by Florsheim shoes. I don't recall getting a pair of shoes as a prize but they did give me a plaque (I had to buy the frame though). That plaque remains proudly hanging on the wall of my living room to this day.

It was one of the rare times in that period that the Jumps Trainers Premiership had been given to someone not named J J Houlihan. For three decades, the great Jim Houlihan dominated jumps racing in Australia. Jim would have to be the archetypical 'late bloomer.' He had been a builder by trade in country Victoria, did a bit of part-time preparation of trotters, and was also a noteworthy semi-professional punter. Then in 1970, when he was fifty-seven years old, he retired from building and became a full-time horse trainer. He had success over the flat, but specialised in jumps, and for three decades was the colossus of jumps racing. His record speaks for itself: eight Australian Hurdles titles, seven Grand National Hurdles, four times winner of the Grand Annual at Warrnambool. Jim was a real character too, and a lot of trainers looked up to him. In 2004, he was admitted to the Racing Hall of Fame, and he was also awarded the Order of Australia. He remained active into his early nineties, and died only a few years ago, aged 93.

My success with the jumpers in 1984-85 meant that I finished the season with 17 city winners. Although eight of those wins came from Fast Food and Planinca, it nevertheless meant I had climbed the Victorian Metropolitan Trainers Premiership and finished in seventh place, ahead of around 1,400 other registered trainers in Victoria, so that was something to be proud of. Ahead of me were some great names: Geoff Murphy, George Hanlon, Bart Cummings, Jim Moloney, Bob Hoystead and, miles in front of everyone, Colin Hayes. All great trainers and every one of them in their late 50s and early 60s. This generation of trainers wasn't going to stay on top forever, and I was ambitious enough to believe that soon I might replace them.

* * *

Foxseal was spelled for a few months after his Brisbane Cup triumph, before we launched him on a campaign to have another crack at the Melbourne Cup — or should that be the 'Foster's Melbourne Cup' as it was called that year for the first time, much to the dismay of traditionalists everywhere?

Foxseal started the Spring campaign well with a second in the Group One Metropolitan Handicap up in Sydney, beaten narrowly in a thrilling finish. He also ran well against the best middle-distance horses in the land in the W.S Cox Plate, finishing sixth. The Melbourne Cup was actually a half-hearted goal, as Foxseal, despite what his Group One Brisbane Cup victory might suggest, was never a genuine two-miler. To be frank, that Brisbane Cup field had been a weak one, and against the cream of the Australasian stayers that the Melbourne Cup attracted Foxseal was always going to be up against it.

And so it proved to be. His Royal Highness, Prince Charles, was there to present the Cup, but, unfortunately, not to me. Foxseal had finished a disappointing twenty-third in a field of twenty-three. My only consoling thought is that we brought some relief to the thousands of people who drew Foxseal in their office sweeps and picked up a booby prize for finishing last.

Although there was no fairytale finish for Foxseal, the Dodsons, Greg Hall on board or myself, another Cup fairytale had been played out. The winner of the one-million-dollar race, Just A Nuisance, had been purchased in New Zealand for just $20,000. His initial staying efforts were less than impressive and trainer John Meagher had considered abandoning the flat and turning him into a jumps horse instead in the hope of better results. But he persevered over the flat, and the horse rewarded him in the greatest fashion possible.

I had once believed that to dream of training a Melbourne Cup winner was not a foolish, hopeless one. Because it was a race that so often rewarded the dreamers with their unfashionable horses purchased for a few thousand dollars, the battlers saddling up their long-shot runners. The invasion of the top foreign horses, an invasion that has been encouraged by the handicapper with the generous weights given them, has, of course, changed all that, and sadly the Melbourne Cup is out of reach for most Australian trainers. The Cup is now a race for the world's elite stayers, but at the expense of some of the Cup's romanticism.

Foxseal came back in the autumn of 1986. We placed him in the better-class races, and though his sole win was a listed race at Morphettville, he performed heroically on several occasions. In the Futurity Stakes, Foxseal in his inimitable style came flying home and I was sure another Group One success was in our grasp. But then he was badly blocked in his run halfway down the straight, and could only finish fifth, though just a length behind the winner, the champion sprinter Campaign King. He also finished third in the Group One Sydney Cup, and was just a stride away from scoring back-to-back Brisbane Cup victories.

Although Foxseal brought a lot of joy to myself and the

Dodsons, he also, unfortunately, caused me a lot of grief with the race stewards. There had been the constant run-ins with the stewards over the positive dope swabs when I was in Bendigo. More recently, I had found myself in hot water for speaking my mind. I had argued that the authorities should introduce the allocation of barrier draws by computer. I believed it would allay any suspicion of interference in barrier draws, but the authorities didn't see it that way — they must have thought I was implying the racing clubs were involved in corrupt practices. In any case I was privately warned not to speak out of turn.

The last thing I wanted, therefore, was to get offside with the authorities again. However, Foxseal's style of racing would invariably bring him to the stewards' attention. We had to carefully manage when the horse made his runs in races because of his problem with wind being sucked up the back passage. Sometimes the timing didn't work — he'd take off, his back passage would fill up too early and his run would quickly peter out. Other times he wouldn't be able to go at all because of the pace of the race. To the stewards it might have looked on occasion that Foxseal wasn't being allowed to run on his merits — a cardinal sin in racing.

Melbourne's Chief Steward at the time was Pat Lalor. One jockey, after copping a suspension from Lalor, nicknamed him the 'Smiling Hangman.' and it was a name that stuck. Lalor had a distinctive, thin-lipped smile with which he would greet you, but he combined his pleasant, amiable nature with a strict, zero tolerance administration of his job. I had always found him firm but fair, although he was probably a bit cool towards me, no doubt wondering why controversy and I were never too far apart.

From memory, Foxseal was the subject of four separate steward inquiries. Each time I would patiently explain to Lalor and the other stewards Foxseal's peculiar problem. Immediately after one race, to demonstrate this to the stewards, I brought Foxseal around, lifted his tail and, on cue, the horse released a magnificent and prolonged trumpet blast of flatulence and you could have dropped a golf ball in his arse. On other occasions, I would pointedly issue pre-race riding instructions to the jockey, usually Greg Hall, within earshot of the stewards so that they were forewarned of our riding tactics. In spite of this, they continued to haul me into the stewards' room whenever Foxseal either died on a run or unleashed it too late, when the race was as good as over. I would then need to once again explain to their satisfaction that we had given Foxseal a genuine run.

Lalor was a former jockey, and this background would have provided some useful insight into the decision-making processes jockeys engaged in during the running of a race. I remember one Foxseal inquiry after a race at Sandown, and Pat Lalor was questioning my riding instructions.

'You've left the run way too late, giving your horse no chance, Mr Hore-Lacy.'

Again, I explained to Lalor Foxseal's condition and the difficulties this presented in terms of timing his runs.

'But you were a former jockey, Mr Lalor,' I said to him, changing tack. 'Where would you have taken off on Foxseal if you'd been riding him?'

For a moment Lalor looked taken aback. The Stewards room was a place where the stewards asked the questions of the trainers, not the other way around. Nevertheless, I think he was a little flattered that I would be seeking his opinion as an ex-jockey.

'Where would I have let him go if I'd be on him?' He considered for a moment. 'Well, I would have started jogging around them at the eight hundred mark.'

Directly behind the chair where the Chief Steward sits, hanging on the wall, was a large map of the Sandown track. I gestured towards the map behind him.

'Mr Lalor, just have a look behind you.' Lalor turned in his chair. 'You'll notice that the eight hundred metres at Sandown is on a turn. So you would have started your run around a turn would you, Mr Lalor?'

Lalor immediately realised his mistake, his face turning a bright red. But before he could say anything I added, 'If so, Mr Lalor, I'm glad you never rode a horse for me!'

The other stewards had diplomatically raised hands to mouths to mask their smiles, while Lalor quietly fumed. I suspect that that was one of the rare occasions when a trainer had stood up to him in the Stewards room.

I never begrudged Lalor's suspicions towards me — he was only doing his job. This was at a time when there was a pall of suspicion over the racing industry. The Fine Cotton ring-in scandal had been just a year or two earlier, and some people believed that was only the tip of the iceberg. The media had been reporting the involvement of underworld figures who were being tipped winners by trainers and jockeys and fixing races. Bookmakers who were the victims of massive betting plunges tended to be the noisiest alarmists, funnily enough.

The racing industry gets a bad rap at times, and I'm not denying that there are some shifty characters hanging around our racetracks. But to suggest that the whole racing industry is rife with corruption and criminal behaviour is both ludicrous and insulting. It really annoys me when I hear a judge, journalist or academic making sweeping generalisations about the industry I love, when they have no idea how the industry actually operates.

In my forty-odd years as a horse trainer only once did someone approach me and indicate that a horse should not be given a proper run. This individual, a Greek man, co-owned a horse with me.

'Look,' I said to him in the lead-up to a race our horse was in, 'the horse might find the others in the race a bit above him in class. Honestly, I don't think he has much chance of winning.'

'He better bloody not win,' the owner snapped back at me. 'I don't want him doing well in this one.'

I gave this exchange some thought, and it made me uneasy. I've no doubt got my faults as a trainer, but one thing I always strived to do is have my horses perform at their best. I'm as competitive as they come and I frankly see no point in not trying your best every time.

The next day I gave the Greek owner a call. 'I'm not sure if it's a good idea that I continue to train for you. You better buy my share, or I'll buy yours.'

And so the Greek guy and I parted company. He bought me out and I never had any further dealings with him. And that was the only occasion that someone has asked me to not allow a horse to run on its merits.

* * *

Foxseal had been my most outstanding horse up until then, but that status was about to be challenged by a filly called Canny Lass. Canny Lass was another of Alec Dodson's horses that he had bred himself. He had bought a mare called Jesmond Lass for a decent amount of money, with the intention of keeping her as a broodmare. He sent her to the newly-crowned leading sire in Australia, Bletchingly, and Canny Lass was the result.

Canny Lass had shown promise as a two-year-old — her first race was in the Debutante Stakes, a listed race, at Caulfield, and she was precocious enough to finish second. She won only one race as a two-year-old, in the 1984-85 season, though she was always up against the best two-year-olds. The problem wasn't her lack of ability — she had plenty of that — but her feeding habits.

She was a terrible eater after a race. Sometimes she would go off her food for up to a week, which played havoc with my attempts to maintain her condition.

In the winter of '85 I sent her up to Queensland to spell, and when she came back as a three-year-old she was so much stronger — she looked a three-lengths better horse. Her appetite had also improved and after a race she would clean out her feeder every time.

She started to live up to her potential in the spring of '85, winning the then Group Two Veuve Clicquot Classic at Moonee Valley over 1200 metres in September. I could also see she was not just a sprinter and was confident that she could do well over the longer distances.

At that time I was campaigning with Foxseal all over the country. As Canny Lass didn't mind the travel I would bring her along as we criss-crossed the nation. The two horses ended up becoming great travelling companions, to the point where one would fret if the other wasn't there. Alec Dodson remarked that they would have made a wonderful couple for breeding purposes... if it weren't for the minor obstacle that Foxseal was a gelding.

As a three-year-old Canny Lass ran in five Oaks races around the country — the Victorian, the AJC Oaks, the Australasian, Queensland and WA Oaks — and was placed in three of them, including a very unlucky second in the Australasian Oaks. She finished her three-year-old season with four wins, the Veuve Clicquot being the biggest.

Again, in the winter I sent Canny Lass to Queensland to spell. She spent about a month there in a nice, grassy paddock enjoying the Queensland winter. And again, her time up north worked wonders and she really bloomed. She came back to Melbourne a big, strong four-year-old, and when I saw her gleaming coat and how well she had filled out I thought, 'This might just be her spring.'

Not for the first time I was criticised by some experts for the spring campaign I had mapped out for Canny Lass. Never mind that we ended up winning two Group One races with her that spring of 1986 — the Marlboro Cup over 1400 metres and the Elders Mile. The Marlboro Cup (in the days when it was okay to name a race after a cigarette brand) is now known as the Sir Rupert Clarke Stakes, and at that time was Victoria's richest sprint race of the season. It became my second Group One success, and was a particularly impressive victory. Canny Lass won by an easy three lengths and could have won by more but jockey Greg Hall eased her towards the finishing line.

The ultimate goal that spring was the Caulfield Cup, as Canny Lass had been given the lightweight handicap of 49 kilograms. Unfortunately for Hall, he was never going to get that weight, so I offered the ride to the then best lightweight jockey in the business, John Marshall. Marshall was based in Sydney where he was stable rider for Bart Cummings. Although he had first choice on the early Caulfield Cup favourite, Drought, he had no hesitation accepting the ride on Canny Lass.

Marshall rode Canny Lass in the Group One Elders Mile (now called the Toorak Handicap), carrying the ludicrous weight of 55 kilograms. I was publicly critical of the severe weight given to my mare, but as it turned out, the handicapper got it right again. Canny Lass had a relatively comfortable victory. Prior to the Caulfield Cup I raced her in the Rupert Steele Stakes over 1200 metres. It was this race that attracted all the criticism regarding her preparation, especially when she failed to sprint in the race and came a distant 14th. When she lined up for the Caulfield Cup it was her fourth race in twenty-three days, and over a big range of distances. The critics were baying that I was racing the horse too hard.

This was a ridiculous assertion. In fact, I've often been critical of other trainers' methods where they work their horses too much by overdoing the track work. I certainly didn't want to overwork a top horse like Canny Lass because, frankly, she and Foxseal were the only class horses then in my stable — why would I want to kill the golden goose, so to speak? I don't gallop my horses too hard on the track, and instruct the track work riders to keep the horses under a tight hold. Rather than wasting my time getting a fully fit horse even fitter, I was teaching them to relax in their races. Canny Lass, in fact, did most of her work without a rider, being led from a pony, or going to Mordialloc Beach.

Despite the criticism of her preparation, Canny Lass went into the Caulfield Cup as favourite. I thought she was as close to a good thing as you can get in racing, but in a race over 2400 metres a lot can go wrong and, unfortunately for us, a lot did. No doubt her failure only gave more ammunition to the critics, though I'd like to think that not long into the following Autumn Carnival I had shut them up again.

Normally you would like to bring a horse back into work a couple of months before a big race, six weeks at a minimum. However, Canny Lass picked up an injury after the Spring Carnival, a swelling in her off foreleg. It wasn't until Boxing Day 1986 that I was able to work her again, and her first scheduled race, the Group One William Reid Stakes over 1200 metres, was just a month away. It was a race against time to get her ready, and she went into that race overweight and only about 80 per cent fit. She was also up against the previous year's Horse of the Year, Bounding Away, and the boom South Australian colt, Rubiton.

Before the race I gave Greg Hall, now back on board her, his riding instructions. 'Park yourself in behind and wait for a split. When it comes, dash her through and she will do the rest.'

Canny Lass was normally a slow starter in races, and when they came to the Moonee Valley turn she was about eight lengths from the leaders and caught on the rails. The front-runners were starting to slow and Canny Lass was making ground but remained blocked in. For an agonisingly long time it looked like she would never get clear, but then the opening appeared, Greg steered her through, and she took off — exactly as planned. She ended up winning by two lengths.

When Greg Hall returned to scale he was shaking his head in both bewilderment and elation. 'Coming around the bend,' he told me, 'I thought we're not going to get a clear run, but when we got a little bit of space she took over and off she went. What a freak she is!'

I suppose most mornings can tell a similar story about the one that got away, but it taught me lesson there is not much point in being the underbidder and as any trainer will tell you Rick is always hard to outbid when he gets on one.

The favourite Rubiton didn't run a place, and I was very relieved. A couple of years earlier I was at the Adelaide sales and spotted a big leggy dark brown by Century. He was the last lot in the sale that day and it was getting dark. Anyhow, I started bidding. I had no client and no money and my legs were shaking when I put in a bid of $42,500. Imagine my relief when a little fellow three from the front and wearing a green beret, put in a bid of $45,000 and secured the colt.

Anyhow, I went back to Melbourne and a couple of days later I told Alec Dodson what I had done and how relieved I was when I was outbid. Alec replied, 'You should have bought him, I would have taken him!' I then told Alec that that bloody yearling would come back to haunt me. We heard nothing for about 18 months. Meanwhile, the big brown horse had been named Rubiton. He won a minor mid-week handicap at Morphettville and was brought over to Melbourne and I can still hear the race caller, Bill Collins, saying 'Oh, this is a super horse' as he went over the line 6 lengths clear when winning the C S Hayes Stakes at

Moonee Valley! Rubiton went on to win the Cox Plate, Futurity Stakes, Underwood Stakes and the Mackinnon Stakes and won $1,360,330 in prize money which would be equivalent to three million dollars on today's prize money levels!

Canny Lass raced in the top races that autumn but was unable to get another victory. Nevertheless, I thought she might be a good chance to win Horse of the Year after collecting three Group One victories that season. Instead it went to the New Zealander Bonecrusher, no doubt on the back of his famous Cox Plate victory, the slog-fest down the Moonee Valley straight with Our Waverly Star.

* * *

The 1986-87 racing season was my most successful yet. In 84-85 I had finished seventh in the Victorian Trainers Premiership, in 85-86 I had crept up to fourth spot (and had also captured my second consecutive Jumps Trainers Premiership). In 86-87 I increased my number of winners by fifty per cent to 34 winners and finished second, behind the great Colin Hayes. Or perhaps it would be more accurate to say that C.S Hayes was first, Daylight second, and I led the field of also-rans. Hayes did have a couple of things in his favour, however, including more than five times the number of horses in his care than I had. If I was to challenge for the top position, either Hayes would have to scale back his team, or I would need to increase mine.

Colin Hayes was a phenomenon as a horse trainer. Although nothing would have pleased me more than to knock him off the top perch, I was full of admiration for what he had achieved. Like me, he hadn't come from a racing family. Another similarity was that he too was not afraid to do the unconventional, to be innovative, do things his way rather than follow the herd. Although all the most successful trainers had been city-based, Hayes made the centre of his empire the country property of Lindsay Park in South Australia's Barossa Valley. He created an idyllic environment for schooling his horses — he was arguably the best in the business when it came to getting his young horses ready to race.

Hayes was also renowned for his understanding of his horses and treating them as individuals, which is something I, too, have always tried to do. I think some trainers forget horses are individuals and treat training as some kind of assembly line process. Just because it's Tuesday or Thursday doesn't mean a horse has to be given fast work. In the same way, while a two-hour grooming session might be fine for some horses, the ones who love to be pampered, it will only unsettle others.

Hayes was not university educated, but was very articulate and had the knack of mixing easily with all levels of racing society, from English lords and Arabian princes to the humblest stablehand and farrier. He was known as Sugar Lips because of his ability to charm and endear himself to others. In this regard we were very different, and it may well have been a reason why he had more success than me. Certainly, he was much more effective in attracting the richest owners, whereas I have felt uncomfortable fawning to rich patrons, particularly those whom I don't care for. I've knocked back a few partnership opportunities simply because I didn't respect the other person — the names of a few politicians come to mind here.

Despite the advantages Colin Hayes had over me, I was determined to one day unseat him from his position at the top of the Trainers Premiership. Only a couple of years earlier everyone believed that T J Smith's tenure as Sydney's number one trainer was unassailable. But, then another trainer with a double-barrelled surname, Brian Mayfield-Smith, came out of nowhere and took the Premiership. I've always been a believer in setting myself goals, and my main goal was to emulate Mayfield-Smith's achievement. Moreover, I had carefully devised a bold and ambitious plan to do exactly that.

I was pretty chuffed when Colin Hayes rang me himself and congratulated me on my training effort in coming second in the Victorian Trainers Premiership that year with only a handful of horses.

CHAPTER 7

Success breeds success — that would be the best explanation for my rise up the training ranks. Alec Dodson opened his wallet to me and I was able to build up a good team of horses. Then once the winners started to arrive on a regular basis, other influential owners began engaging my services. Sir Rupert Steele, then Chairman of the VRC, sent some horses my way, as did Kingston Town owner David Hains. Prominent VRC Committee Member, Kevin Heffernan, was another who gave me some horses to train.

I also had a clear strategy to get me to the top. At Epsom, I had forty-five horses in training and was adding ten more boxes to further increase my capacity. What I needed though was additional land to be used for spelling and pre-training work — the Colin Hayes model. To this end I was negotiating the purchase of a block of land at Cranbourne in Melbourne's outer-east. In those days, there were bold visions of making Cranbourne a future state-of-the-art training centre, and I hoped to be one of the pioneers.

Once the additional stalls were in place at Epsom and if a training centre at Cranbourne was operational I would have capacity for about 100 horses — not quite in Colin Hayes' league, but getting closer to it. A pre-training complex would also allow me more time to spend on actual training. At that time, I was working 12-hour days, and a good proportion of that time spent on young horses' basic education: such as putting them through the starting stalls, and getting them comfortable racing in the midst of other horses. The aim of the Cranbourne pre-training complex was to have the schooling done before they came to me at the track, and the main stable would be supplied with horses well forward in their preparation.

I also began to re-align the balance of my stable: away from the tried horses I had enjoyed success with in the past, and towards a greater proportion of two-year-olds. The set-up of Australian racing in terms of prize money and feature races favours sprinters, particularly two- and three-year-olds. It also makes economic sense for a trainer to focus his or her efforts on the younger horses. The ideal, in business terms, was to get a classy sprinter precocious enough to race as a two-year-old, pick up a few black-type races then, after the three-year-old season, send the horse to stud. The horse, particularly if it's male, can then provide a steady and highly lucrative stream of income through stud service fees. On the other hand, stayers tend to be late bloomers that in most cases are a drain on resources in their early years. Training costs had become so expensive that a lot of owners could no longer afford to wait a couple of years. There are also fewer rich staying events and, with a couple of exceptions, prize money for the longer races has failed to keep pace with the sprints.

I already had a good stable of handicappers, welter-types and winter campaigners, but was light on two-year-olds. To right this I had spent a cool $1 million at the main yearling sales in Australia and New Zealand in 1987. Unlike some fortunate trainers whose owners provide an open cheque-book before the sales, I have usually had to buy the horses myself, then get on the phone and try and sell them. Although I've always had a knack for salesmanship and I've never had a fear of cold-calling people to try to sell them a horse, it is very time-consuming. My time would be much more productively spent on looking after the horses already in my care.

The cost of thoroughbreds, like so many other asset classes in the eighties — shares, property, commodities — were spiralling upwards to dizzying heights. And a growing number of owners were finding the purchase of a new horse now out of their grasp. I came up with an idea to syndicate horses in partnerships of six people. It was a radical idea as most horses up until that point had been owned by one person with maybe a mate or two. I believed my idea had legs — that syndicates or partnerships were the future for horse ownership, allowing a group of owners to split the purchase and upkeep costs amongst themselves. And so the Rick Hore-Lacy Racing Partnership '87 project was born.

The concept behind the Racing Partnership project was quite simple. I had purchased 24 yearlings at four major yearling sales in 1987, spending around $1 million in total. My idea was to offer four syndicates, six horses in each syndicate. I would sell a sixth-share in each syndicate. This way instead of having twenty-four owners each owning one horse, I'd still have twenty-four owners but each with a share in a syndicate. It also increased an owner's chances sixfold of owning a good one. Each syndicate would have at least one horse that had been purchased at the Magic Millions sales, giving them eligibility for the newly created and lucrative Magic Millions race.

* * *

Alec Dodson bought Jesmond Lass (dam of Canny Lass) in the early 1980s after seeing it advertised in a small classified ad in the Sporting Globe. By the late 80s that method of buying a horse seemed quaint and old-fashioned. Things were now done on a more grandiose scale — simple advertising had morphed into elaborate and large-scale marketing and public relations campaigns.

The great circus owner and promoter P T Barnum once said,

'Without promotion something terrible happens — nothing!' Subscribing to this view, I decided to launch Racing Partnership in the boldest possible fashion. We organised a large do, a black-tie event, to be put on at Huntley Lodge Stud in the country town of Sunbury, just north of Melbourne. No expense was to be spared — marquees were set up outside, silver service catering had been hired, and crates of expensive champagne ordered. Invited were prominent owners like David Hains, Sir Donald and Lady Trescowthick and Bill Lanyon. We had also identified and invited a host of potential new owners from the business, legal and medical professions. In all about 150 potential clients gathered for the launch that June 1987 evening. The theme of the evening, which was to become the Racing Partnerships slogan, was: 'It's fun to race horses with nice people.'

When everyone was seated at their tables, I stood up on stage before them, microphone in hand.

'Ladies and gentlemen.' The buzz of conversation died down. 'This is a big night for me. I've got a million bucks worth of horses here which I haven't paid for!'

It got a laugh, but like a lot of humour there was a frighteningly large amount of truth in that line. I had taken a massive gamble buying one million dollars' worth of horses upfront. If this event failed to do what it was intended to do — sell horses — then I risked losing just about everything.

The twenty-four yearlings were paraded before the assembled guests while they sipped on their French champagne and dined on hors d'oeuvres, and I provided commentary. After the parade of horses, dinner was served — an impressive array of dishes. Dinner was accompanied by a video showing my training highlights — perhaps a little on the short side at that stage of my career. For the benefit of any of my detractors who might have gate-crashed the event, each clip of a big race win was given an additional voice-over, 'Fluke, fluke, fluke.' There were still plenty of people who couldn't believe the unconventional training methods I employed could possibly work, thus preferred to attribute my successes to blind luck.

The evening at Huntley Lodge went reasonably well. That night and the following few days we ended up selling almost half the shares, and the general reaction overall was a positive one. It wasn't a bad effort, as it's never easy when you are doing something for the first time, introducing a new concept in horse ownership.

'It's fun racing horses with nice people,' that slogan was deliberately chosen. I wanted others to share my own love of racing. I also knew from Alec Dodson's experience the immense pleasure and enjoyment horse-racing brought to him through his ownership of Foxseal, Canny Lass and Planinca. It was almost as if those horses gave him a new lease of life. I remember one day Alec saying to me, 'Rick, I don't understand these old fellas who lose interest in life. Why don't they buy a horse or two?'

Encouraged by the partial success of the evening I announced that it would become an annual event. I was still confident of selling the remaining shares in the coming months, and we only needed to get one or two very good two-year-olds from that initial batch and support for the concept would continue to grow. I had no doubt that syndicates were the future of horse ownership — this, at least, turned out to be prophetic.

Already I was planning my raid on the next year's yearling sales. After months of negotiation a firm of underwriters had agreed to finance, to the tune of $2 million, my next season's yearling purchases. With this amount of spending money, I would be joining the likes of Tommy Smith and Bart Cummings, the acknowledged heavyweight spenders at yearling sales. The future was looking brighter and brighter, and my confidence in overtaking Colin Hayes as premier trainer in Melbourne was never higher.

If William Shakespeare had been writing about Rick in the 1980's, instead of Macbeth, he might well have penned the line: 'Unfortunately, Rick's ambition overleapt itself.'

* * *

Plans to purchase property at Cranbourne for a pre-training complex failed to materialise. Myself and real estate deals have never enjoyed great success together. It was a minor setback — far more calamitous headwinds were about to hit. The racing authorities announced a policy change that was to have a massive impact on the industry in general, and myself in particular. As from August 1, 1987, horses would be routinely tested for steroids under the category of a prohibited substance. The decision meant the effective banning of steroids from horse racing.

Steroid use was a common enough practice in the racing industry in those days. I would have thought that as much as ninety per cent of stables were using steroids at some time. For me they had been a major contributing factor towards the success I had achieved up to then. Yearling prices had been rising at astronomical rates during the eighties, so my main strategy had been to find the horse bargains, horses with unfashionable bloodlines that nevertheless looked like athletes. Then, with a combination of the right feeding, proper preparation and steroids to build them up, these horses could be improved by several lengths. That was my method, and my results, second in the most recent Victorian Trainers Premiership, spoke for themselves.

I was one of the most outspoken opponents against the steroids ban. Obviously, there was an element of self-interest involved, but I also genuinely believed at the time that steroids were beneficial to the both the racing industry and the horses themselves. They increase a horse's appetite, its sense of well-being, they assist with the body's synthesis of protein and help prevent dehydration and, I suspect, they break down less. Geldings in particular thrived on steroids, giving them the confidence and determination that came naturally to a stallion.

I've experienced racing first-hand in four continents and, in my opinion, Australian racing is the best in the world. Two factors give our racing its unique character and identity: our handicap system provides opportunities to racehorses of all abilities, and the prominent place geldings hold in our industry. In Europe and the United States, they race colts which have a handful of starts and are then retired to stud. In contrast, Australia had horses that would race season after season after season; their longevity, their ability to win races year after year were what made them champions. Think of Phar Lap, Bernborough, Kingston Town and Manikato — all champions over many seasons and, not coincidentally, all geldings.

The ban on steroids would hit smaller operations, in particular, those battlers who rely on a handful of runners competing in as many races as possible. Without steroids those horses would not be able to back up as frequently. For the larger owners and trainers, it wouldn't matter because they have so many replacement runners, but for the smaller operations it would make a serious dent in their earnings.

I also believed that the steroids ban would be the first nail in the coffin in which country racing would inevitably be buried. With horses making fewer appearances, both the size and quality of the fields at a country meet would be heavily affected.

The decision to test for steroids was a simplistic and inflexible one, the result of a puritanical stance that racing should be drug free. Of course, we all want racing to be fair, with all horses having the same chance. However, banning steroids, I argued at the time, would have the opposite effect to that which was intended, making racing more elitist and hitting the smaller trainers and owners hardest.

That decision was made twenty-five years ago. Almost in spite of the decision, the Australian racing industry has continued to do alright, so my criticisms of the decision might now appear alarmist. I think that racing proved to be more resilient than I had expected. Nevertheless, the face of racing has been permanently altered because of the decision. Racing *has* become more elitist, and it *has* become harder for smaller operations to compete and for country racing to attract good fields. Too many top colts rarely race beyond their three-year-old season — they become bright but fleeting shooting stars rather than the durable champions of yesteryear. And champion geldings are now the exception rather than the rule.

* * *

Alec Dodson sold Canny Lass to breeding billionaire Robert Sangster in 1987, a decision I fully supported. Although it meant the end of her racing career, the economics of the decision were too compelling to ignore. Alec would have been a fool — a romantic fool perhaps, but a fool all the same — if he had continued to race her. She certainly provided him with plenty of thrills and excitement. She won five group races, three of them Group Ones, and collected over $560,000 in prize money. If she had been running today her stakes wins would have been well and truly over the two-million-dollar mark. And with a bit more luck, she might have been even more successful — she finished second in Group One races on two occasions (the SAJC Oaks and the Lightning Stakes), plus four seconds in Group Two and Three races.

Foxseal was also coming to the end of his grand career at that time. He raced until he was a nine-year-old, still winning races at that age. He had 94 starts in total, and won 16 races, earning

$655,000 in prize money. His biggest win was the Group One Brisbane Cup, but he also won two other group races, and picking up nine placings in group races. He became a two-mile cup specialist, racing in distance cups eleven times, which might well be a record in itself! Even in retirement he was a durable old bugger. He lived for twenty-six years before old age got him, just fell over one morning in Alec Dodson's paddock on the Mornington Peninsula and never got up again.

Despite the retirement of my two champions, 1988 was meant to be the year that I consolidated my position as Colin Hayes's challenger for the title of Victoria's Premier trainer. However, those ambitious plans quickly began to unravel. With the implementation of the steroids ban I had to readjust my training methods, not an overnight process. At the same time, a much more menacing external influence was looming on the horizon — a series of shocks to the economy.

In October 1987, after a prolonged period of phenomenal growth, billions of dollars were lost on the world's share markets in a dramatic few days of trading. I wasn't a share market player, but several clients and potential clients were. Seeing their wealth evaporate in the course of a few days, they understandably lost their appetite to invest money in another asset class that was vigorously overheating — thoroughbred racehorses.

Australia was also starting to be hit by some unintended effects of the economic reforms introduced by the Hawke Labor Government in the 80s. Deregulation of the financial industry had transformed the business landscape. The Hawke Government had allowed the entry of foreign banks to operate in Australia, while relaxation of the regulatory environment in the banking sector had suddenly seen a host of merchant banks pop up and flourish. The traditional banks, their market share eroded by these newcomers, responded by throwing out their former prudent and conservative lending practices. They began lending money to just about anyone who asked for it, including me. 'Leveraging' and 'negative gearing' were the new buzz words, and everyone was doing it. It was quite a contrast to the 60s when I was trying to establish the import business. Back then if I had the temerity to ask for a business loan, I would just get bank managers' doors slammed in my face, their 'No bricks and mortar, no loan' mantra ringing in my ears.

The official inflation rate at that time was around seven per cent, which was high enough. But for some asset classes it was way above that. The cost of a family home, for example had increased some 40 per cent in a two-year period. Interest rates were also relatively high, 11 per cent in the first half of 1988. But then the economic policy makers, almost by stealth, began to raise interest rates. By the end of 1989 the official rate was 18.5 percent, and the banks' rates were obviously even higher.

The intended effect was to slow down the economy — and mission well and truly accomplished there. The economy slowed down, came to a stop, then started going backwards, and we were in 'the recession we had to have' — the name given to it by then Treasurer, Paul Keating.

Anybody who had borrowed money was suddenly in deep strife: home owners, businesses, investors. For me, it was a double-edged sword. I had 'leveraged' with the best of them, taking out loans to finance my yearling sale buying sprees, and was now hit with spiralling interest rate bills. At the same time, owners, with their own financial woes, had put away their cheque books, so I was left holding a lot of expensive horseflesh.

I have always taken big gambles — in fact, I don't believe you can have great success without taking great risks. The Racing Partnership concept was a huge gamble; I had bet the proverbial farm on the idea. Unfortunately, of the twenty-four yearlings I had offered to syndication, less than half of them had been sold. For the remaining horses, the only other option I had was to get into bed with various finance companies and lease the horses through them. It seemed like a deal with the devil; even today I shudder when I think about it. Those lease payments, coupled with out-of-control interest rates, were crippling. It was like being in financial quick sand, sinking deeper and deeper into debt.

It wasn't all the economy and evil financiers driving me to economic ruin. Some of my financial problems were self-administered after I let early success go to my head. I drove a near new Mercedes, owned a sprawling beach-side home (or more accurately the bank owned it), and sent my three children to expensive private schools. The 1980s were notorious for their conspicuous consumption, and I guess I reflected that period only too well.

At the same time, I had allowed horse training to take over my life, unfortunately at my family's expense. The twelve-hour days, seven days a week, didn't leave me much time to spend with my family. Although my wife Maria did a superhuman job bringing up the children, they suffered from having an absent father. Days would go by without the kids seeing their father; I was always down at the stable, out at the track, or on a plane somewhere on my way to interstate race meetings or far-flung yearling sales.

My son Ricky undoubtedly suffered more than the girls with no strong father figure in his life watching over him, guiding him. I had always resented growing up with a father who was a virtual stranger, yet here I was repeating the sins of the father. Ricky was in the difficult teen years at that time. He wanted to follow in my footsteps and be a horse trainer, but I wouldn't have a bar of it. I believed he would be much better off concentrating on his studies, going to university and eventually getting a profession. A horse trainer's life was filled with hard work, struggle, uncertainty and, unless you were one of the lucky few, poverty. So I did everything possible to push him away from the stables.

I don't believe in regrets — because you can't go back and undo past mistakes. The one exception, however, the one real regret I have, is that I didn't spend more time with my boy when he was growing up. If I had made that effort, and spent just a little bit of time with him each day, kicking the football around, a game of backyard cricket, taking him to school sports, things might have turned out quite differently for him.

Instead Ricky was left to his own devices. His grades began to suffer at school, and despite my efforts to discourage him from anything to do with horses, he would still sneak down to the stables regularly. The racing world is the archetypical school of hard knocks — it attracts more than its share of misfits, school drop outs and runaways. And Ricky seemed to be drawn to it, hanging out with the stablehands and track work jockeys. It was around this time, and in that environment, that Ricky had his first taste of marijuana.

* * *

1989 started off with the greatest of promise. I had hoped that at least one of the yearlings offered at the Racing Partnership launch in 1987 would turn out to be something special. A colt by Proud Knight out of a Bletchingly mare had shown plenty of early promise, and we set him for the major two-year-old feature races in the Autumn '88 Carnival, including the Blue Diamond Stakes and the Golden Slipper. The colt was named Clay Hero — an anagram of Hore-Lacy.

Clay Hero was a brilliant sprinter, but unfortunately, he had problems with hard tracks. The east coast of Australia was in the middle of a mini-drought at the time, and the rock-hard surfaces were tough on his joints, leaving him sore after each run. As a result, I could never give him the right preparation. He also had the misfortune of coming up against two outstanding two-year-old sprinters, the Victorian colt Zeditave and the brilliant filly Special. They were the undisputed starts of the Autumn '88 season, with Clay Hero relegated to bridesmaid role.

Clay Hero maintained his form as a three-year-old, and his persistence finally paid off. Both Zeditave and Special were still racing well. Special, if anything had become even better. But both horses by-passed the Group One Oakleigh Plate and Clay Hero, without his two nemeses, went into the race favourite. Darren Gauci was Clay Hero's regular rider but had been suspended. So I employed a jockey who, although still an apprentice, had done well for me in the past, John Didham. John was the son of the legendary Midge Didham; he was destined to live in his father's shadow but was an exceptional rider in his own right. He rode a brilliant race to guide Clay Hero to victory, John's first Group One winner. In doing so, Clay Hero became the third of my horses, following Foxseal and Canny Lass, to enjoy Group One success.

Meanwhile, on Alec Dodson's Mornington property, a young colt out of Bletchingly and Jesmond Lass was just being broken in. Alec and Ethel would often go out to the property and check on their horses. Driven around by the foreman, they felt a special tinge of excitement watching this young colt developing. Alec had a feeling it might turn out to be something special. A full brother to Canny Lass, he named the colt Canny Lad.

But Alec, 83 years old, was in deteriorating health. He had suffered from emphysema since I had known him, a legacy of decades of chain-smoking. I've had a lifelong hatred of smoking — I've been known to admonish house guests that if they had their way with my wife I might, over time, forgive them, but if they ever lit a cigarette in my house I would cut them out of my life forever!

Alec's condition had now deteriorated to the point where it became a struggle for him to even breathe. In March 1989, he was admitted to Cabrini Hospital in Melbourne's inner east, and I visited him every day. He was more than just a generous benefactor and wise mentor. I saw in him the father I had never really had. We both knew his time was quickly running out — in the hospital he was hooked up to an iron lung, the only way he could continue to breathe.

Then one day when he came to visit him, he took my arm and said to me, his voice reduced to a weak rasp, 'Rick, what do you want? I think I can still sign a cheque.'

'I don't want anything.' I told him, and the tears were welling in my eyes. 'I just want you to live.'

The next day Alec Dodson passed away. He had had a long and successful life, a life that was truly well-lived. He had worked his way up from nothing, had great success in business, and through the right combination of daring and prudence had enjoyed great wealth. Business success had opened doors into the diplomatic circle. During the Second World War he liaised with the Portuguese government, providing them with valuable information regarding Japanese activities in and around Portugal's colonies. The Portuguese were so grateful for all his assistance, they made him an honorary consul, a title he proudly retained to his final days.

Business success was also his entrée into the racing world, and in typical style he put back into racing just as much as he took out. He was generous to the racing and breeding industries, providing finance and sponsorship, especially to his beloved jumps racing.

More importantly, Alec was a wonderful man who won the respect of all those who knew him. I don't think he had a single enemy — a rare feat for a wealthy successful person. He was gentle and kind-hearted, modest to a fault and loyal. He gave me a lot of advice and sometimes, but not often enough, I even followed it.

I am sometimes asked if I might have regretted my response when, on his deathbed, he offered me whatever I wanted. I could have said, 'Well, Alec, could you leave me the horses I've been training for you.' If I had asked, he would have granted it, and it would have saved me a lot of financial worry. I remember when I told him that all I wanted was for him to live, his eyes shone with gratitude and happiness. It was confirmation to him that our relationship wasn't built on what I could get out of him, and that I loved him like a father.

* * *

Alec Dodson knew Canny Lad would be a beauty when he was still being broken in. I was sure he was something special too, and his first barrier trial confirmed it. He had given the leaders five lengths on the turn, then cruised up to them and won like a ready-made racehorse. The jockey that rode him that day, Harry White, told me I had a good one. He also said he would be keen to get the mount for the upcoming Spring Carnival.

Unfortunately for White, when it came time for Canny Lad to have his first run, in the 900 metre Maribyrnong Trial Stakes in October 1989, he was out serving a suspension. And so Harry's loss became Shane Dye's gain. Dye was down in Melbourne for the Spring Carnival, and was doing track work for me. With Dye on board Canny Lad won the Maribyrnong Trial, breaking the Flemington track record.

At the presentation of the trophy, my excitement was kept in check by an overriding sadness. In my presentation speech, I referred to what was weighing on my mind. I told the crowd that Canny Lad had been bred by Alec Dodson. 'It's a great pity Mr Dodson isn't here to see him win. He would have been very proud.'

Canny Lad's next race was the Debutante Stakes, then called the Florentino Stakes. It was a roughly run race with Canny Lad bumped and ridden on, and then forced to go six-wide at the turn into the Caulfield straight. Nevertheless, he got up on the line and when Dye led him back he said to me, 'Geez, he's good!'

At the presentation ceremony Dye went even further. 'He's better than Courtza,' the two-year-old Dye had ridden to a Blue Diamond-Golden Slipper double six months earlier.

Canny Lad made it three from three with victory in the Group Two Maribyrnong Plate. Again, not everything went his way, and on a couple of occasions in the race it looked he was beaten, but he showed guts and fought back. After the Maribyrnong Plate, I spelled Canny Lad to get him ready for the Autumn Carnival when the big two-year-old races were run, including the most prestigious prize of all, the Golden Slipper.

He returned in the autumn fitter, stronger and a more mature racehorse. His first race back was the Blue Diamond Prelude, and he maintained his unbeaten record, winning by half a length. That was Canny Lad's style: he was never going to blitz a field; he only did what he had to.

Then things started to go wrong. He pulled up sore after the Prelude win, which meant I would have to alter his preparation work and give him a lighter load. A few days later, when I went down to the stalls in the morning to check the horses, a sick feeling arose in my stomach. Canny Lad could barely put any weight on one of his forelegs he must have injured himself the previous night in his box. If it had been any of my other horses that would have been the end of the autumn campaign, the horse would have been sent off for a spell. But I knew Canny Lad was a potential champion and as good a chance as any I was likely to get to win a Golden Slipper. I also knew that he was as brave and courageous as they come, so I wasn't ready to give up on him quite yet.

Over the next few weeks I had to nurse him and handle him with kid gloves. He had a build-up of fluid around the joint of one of his forelegs. I would give him the occasional light run, then immediately we would place his legs in knee-high plastic boots packed with ice. He was given treatment with a laser machine, and a clay paste concoction I had picked up from America, which helped reduce the swelling and heat around the injury. Most of his preparation, however, involved swimming and beach work. I'd take him down to Mordialloc Beach which was five minutes away and exercise him on the sand and in the water.

Victoria's most lucrative two-year-old race is the Group One Blue Diamond Stakes in the first week of March. The bookies, unaware of Canny Lad's troubles, sent him out a 13-4 favourite. He suffered his first defeat, coming second to Mahaasin, but considering all he had gone through it was another gutsy performance.

Another reduced preparation followed for the VRC Sires Produce Stakes over 1400 metres a few weeks later. I had no doubt he would be suited by the extra distance — the question was whether the reduced preparation would be enough to win. I shouldn't have doubted the horse's will to win though, as he won again in another close finish.

The ultimate goal, of course, for Canny Lad was the Golden Slipper in Sydney which, along with the Melbourne Cup, is Australia's richest race. The Slipper was four weeks after the Sires Produce, but I was nervous about giving him a run beforehand, worried that his tender leg wouldn't be able to withstand the rigours of another race. So instead his Golden Slipper preparation was a mix of gentle runs, ice baths and swims in the bay. No one else knew how precarious Canny Lad's condition was, even Shane Dye was in the dark. There was more than one occasion when I considered abandoning the Golden Slipper quest when his injury showed next to no improvement.

Our Golden Slipper hopes then took another blow, this one delivered by Sydney's weather. In the week leading up to the race, Sydney suffered through torrential downpour day after day. By the Thursday before the race the Rosehill track had been downgraded to a Heavy rating. With the forecasters predicting further rain, it was obvious that the Slipper would be run in a bog. It was disappointing because wet weather always turns a race into a raffle. Canny Lad had never raced on rain-affected tracks so I had no idea how he would handle the conditions but, ominously, his sister Canny Lass hated the wet.

I delayed Canny Lad's trip up to Sydney to the very last moment, flying him in on the eve of the race. There were three reasons for the decision to delay. Sometimes it's better to arrive later rather than earlier because it lessens the chance of something going wrong for the horse in the unfamiliar environment. I also wanted to avoid the wet training tracks up at Sydney, worried a slip on the uncertain surface could put an end to everything. Finally, I was a little anxious about security. I wouldn't say I was paranoid about someone getting to my star galloper, but I think there are times when you can never be too careful. My experience at Bendigo had taught me that the hard way.

The Golden Slipper might not have the international reach of the Melbourne Cup, and lacks the rich tradition of that race, but to me a sprint between the best young horses in the land is much more reflective of our racing industry than a two-mile handicap race. If you can win the Golden Slipper, well, you have reached one of the pinnacles of the training profession.

I went into the race with mixed feelings. In terms of natural ability, I had the best horse in the race. But I also knew that Canny Lad had had, to put it mildly, a less than perfect preparation — he hadn't raced for four weeks whereas most of his opponents had benefited from a much more conventional Slipper build-up, racing the week before. And the track remained heavy — rain being the great leveller in racing.

If I was nervous before the race, Shane Dye was his customary cocky and confident self. He had no doubt that he was going to win the Slipper for a second consecutive year. Perhaps if he had known the injury concerns around Canny Lad he wouldn't have felt so certain. But self-confidence was the Shane Dye trademark, and no doubt a key ingredient to all the success he has enjoyed. The horse, too, seemed relaxed and at ease before the race which was a good sign. Before the Blue Diamond he was jumpy and reluctant to get into the stalls; possibly he knew that he was in no condition to run at his best that day.

The bookies assessed Canny Lad as only an 11-2 chance, with three horses — Triscay, Draw Card and a colt from Western Australia called Paklani — ahead of him in the betting. Despite the lingering doubts I had about our chances, 11- 2 was too good a price to knock back. Sydney's biggest bookie, Colin Tidy, was generous enough to lay me $30,000 to win $160,000!

As soon as the starting gates sprung open, most of the jockeys veered their horses to the outside of the track where the going was judged to be firmer. But Dye opted for the direct route, keeping Canny Lad about three or four wide from the rails for the early part of the race. Although he settled well back in the field, it meant that when he did make his run, at the home turn, he had a relatively uncongested passage. Using the favourite Paklani as his pathfinder, Dye followed him to navigate his way through the the half a dozen horses ahead. With just two hundred metres to go, Canny Lad had gone past Paklani and was two lengths behind the leader, With Me.

Dye had Canny Lad under the whip, and in the muscle-burning mud it became a test of power and will-to-win. They are qualities Canny Lad had in abundance; he drew up alongside With Me, got his head in front and as the winning post flashed past was drawing away to win by three quarters of a length.

How did I feel having just trained the winner of Australia's richest race? Having achieved a dream, a goal that I had been working towards ever since I took out my trainer's licence? I was shaking, I felt unsteady on my feet, but it was out of relief more than exhilaration. All those hours of nursing Canny Lad through his ailments, the sleepless nights of worrying, my mind constantly trying to think up new ways to get him right for the race. It had all paid off, and I felt relieved.

The Prime Minister, Bob Hawke, — a man who loved his horse-racing, and probably loved his punting even more — presented the Slipper trophy to me. The gold-plated trophy with its diamond-encrusted slipper bows is one of our sport's more unusual looking ones. In my acceptance speech I honoured the jockey because he deserved it: Shane Dye was the best wet-track rider in the business, the best jockey in Australia, and his Golden Slipper ride had proved it. It wasn't a flashy ride, but it was perfection all the same, a flawless display of timing and judgement.

Amidst triumph, the occasion was also tinged with sadness. I had to get away from the throng of media, well-wishers and backslappers for a few moments. Feeling reflective I sneaked away to a quiet corner of the Members' Bar in the ultramodern Rosehill grandstand. A few years earlier, when Alec Dodson and I were first starting to taste success together with Foxseal, Alec said to me, 'There are two dreams I have in racing. To win the Melbourne Cup and win a Golden Slipper.'

Well Alec, your horse just won the Slipper; it seemed very unfair that you hadn't lived to see it.

Swimming Redoute's Choice at Mordialloc beach.

© Vince Caligiuri

Pinnacles with Chris Symons

© Taron Clarke

Redoute's Choice (above and next page)
Courtesy of Arrowfield. © Bronwen Healy

Sculpture of Redoute's Choice

Toorak Toff and Craig Williams

Toorak Toff and Damien Oliver

Toorak Toff with Damien Oliver aboard

Rick with Toorak Toff

Rick walking Redoute's Choice at Mordialloc Beach
© Vince Caligiuri

CHAPTER 8

Alec Dodson's death was a personal body blow, but it also had a massive impact on my training fortunes. After he passed away, ownership of his horses moved to the faceless executors of his estate. Overnight I went from over fifty horses to just eleven in training. It was like starting out in the business all over again. Walking around the stables was a depressing feeling. All those empty stalls around me, the bustle of activity replaced by an eerie quiet. I pleaded long and hard with the managers of the estate that I at least be able to keep training Canny Lad. Fortunately, they agreed.

Despite owing the banks and finance companies large amounts of money, I was emboldened to start expanding my training operations again. It was around this time that I made serious inquiries into leasing stables in Sydney. Bart Cummings had stables in two cities, Sydney and Melbourne, and Lee Freedman, whose career was just beginning to take off after winning the Melbourne Cup with Tawriffic, also had a two-city operation. With my recent success in the Slipper, there was no problem in getting approval from the relevant racing authorities. What held me back and ultimately derailed the expansion was a personnel issue. If I wanted to succeed in Sydney I would need a top-class stable foreman to oversee the operations, someone who was not only highly competent, but also a person in whom I could have unqualified trust. But I was just unable to find the right person.

If you look at the really successful trainers of that period, many of them were family affairs. Colin Hayes had his sons David and Peter as his right-hand men and heirs to the operations. T J Smith's brother Ernie and daughter Gai provided vital assistance. Bart Cummings was from a family of trainers and his son, Anthony, served under him before branching out on his own. The Freedmans were a team of brothers with Lee as the frontman. They were family businesses whereas I was more of a sole operator, which made it hard to expand into new frontiers.

Although the Sydney expansion proved to be a no-goer, I was still determined to establish a pre-training complex in Melbourne. I was also starting to build my stable numbers up again by buying more and more yearlings, which in turn made the need for pre-training facilities even more imperative. David Hains, the millionaire investor, breeder and owner with whom I had developed a good working relationship, rented out to me 17 hectares at his Braeside property, not far from my Epsom stables. It gave me access to first-class schooling and agistment facilities: thirty boxes, a 1600-metre training track, sand rolls and treadmills, agistment yards and two staff houses. The intention was to use the Braeside facilities for light work, spelling and, most importantly, getting the young horses ready for full training.

Yearling sale splurges, attempts to expand interstate, a financial commitment to an ambitious pre-training complex. No doubt I was starting to wade into the deep waters again. I would have been better served if I had learned from the lessons dished out to me in the past, the ones about biting off more than one can chew. But my success in the Golden Slipper perhaps had blinded me, deceived me into thinking that I was bullet-proof. There have actually been scientific studies done with athletes and share traders as the guinea pigs. The studies show that success has a physiological effect on men in particular. It alters our chemical makeup, makes us more confident, but also more reckless and prone to take greater risks. I'm sure if a bunch of horse trainers were submitted to the same tests the results would go off the charts!

* * *

In Ernest Hemingway's novel *The Sun Also Rises,* the central character is asked how he went bankrupt. The hero of the story replies: 'Two ways. Gradually, then suddenly.' And with those five words Hemingway seemed to perfectly sum up my own financial difficulties.

For some reason, despite a couple of spectacular past failures, I had yet to rid myself of the urge to dabble in property speculation. Alec Dodson, observing somewhat disapprovingly my hand-to-mouth existence, had always urged me to invest in property — a highly lucrative source of wealth for himself. But property failed to ignite my enthusiasm the way buying horses did. Property investment seemed designed to make me poorer and some other lucky bloke richer, and so it proved again in 1990.

A friend and I decided to buy a 26-block of land in Hallam on the outskirts of Melbourne. The land had recently been re-zoned for residential development, so we bought with the intention of subdividing it and selling off lots to meet the demand for new housing from Melbourne's ever-expanding population. These investment ventures always look beautiful on a spreadsheet, rows and columns of neat figures multiplied by rates of return promising mouth-watering profits. Unfortunately, the Hallam investment failed to go according to plan. Our spreadsheet failed to calculate the bureaucratic delays, the cost overruns, the economy's slide into recession, the spiralling interest rates. The venture quickly turned from guaranteed get-rich-quick scheme into a financial millstone around my neck.

At the same time as my real estate venture was going down the gurgler, I had just spent $200,000 at yearling sales on behalf of a new client. Not long after I had purchased the horses I got a phone call from the client.

'I'm sorry, Rick,' I'm not going to be able to come up with the $200,000.'

Another victim of the recession we had to have, he mournfully advised me that he wouldn't be able to go through with the deal.

My debts were already in the millions of dollars, so what's another $200,000 — you might think — to add to the pile? But the reneged yearling deal along with the failed Hallam property venture, proved to be the tipping edge for Rick Hore-Lacy and his parlous financial state.

I had leasing arrangements with five separate finance companies. It had always been a battle meeting those monthly repayments, but for three years I had been prompt and reliable, even when constant interest rate hikes — interest rates were 21 per cent at the time — were making it even more difficult. Then it just came to the point where I could no longer make the payments. One finance company, Elders Pastoral, was owed $185,000 — of my debts to the five finance companies theirs was the second lowest. But they ended up being the one to pull the pin and take legal action against me to recover their money.

I don't begrudge Elders for taking me to court. They are a business who were owed money and had lost confidence in my ability to pay. I think they, better than most firms, knew all too well the dangers of over-leveraging. In the mid-980s, John Elliott had taken control of them, and had saddled them with huge debts while he went on a company takeover frenzy. That, of course, turned out badly for everyone, and particularly Elders.

My financial situation was laid out bare for all to see in the Bankruptcy Division of the Federal Court, and it wasn't pretty viewing. I owed the AGC Finance Company $1.25 million (from the ill-fated Hallam property deal). Prime Finance was owed $450,000, Pegasus Leasing around $315,000, Citicorp $32,000... on top of the Elders Pastoral debt. The total amount added up to a tear-inducing $2.2 million!

Furthermore, my private company, Racebreed Pty Ltd, was insolvent with a deficiency of $155,000 in shareholders' funds. My only major asset was my house in Parkdale, but even the bank owned most of that. All the horses in my name were leased, so technically the finance companies owned them too.

Set out in black and white like that, it looked a horrible financial mess, and a damning indictment on my financial management. And I'm the first to admit that when it comes to business sense I've made some remarkably stupid decisions. However, I was hardly alone amongst horse trainers in having financial difficulties. Bart Cummings and T J Smith were two other high-profile trainers who were about to plunge into debt-fuelled financial crisis. Tommy's publicly listed company had hit problems when his business partner turned out to be a shonk, and the company had to be rescued by an American billionaire. Bart was let down badly by some big-name accountancy firms who left him carrying millions of dollars in debt. Cummings had to sell his Vaucluse home and Castlereagh farm. At least Bart was able to quip after losing his house that it needed re-painting anyway!

I had a succession of lengthy meetings with my creditors where they painstakingly picked over my bones. In the end, we reached an agreement: I would pay them $100,000 before the end of the financial year a few months away, which would then get me full and final release of my debts. The creditors would also recover a proportion of the money through the sale of my assets — the land at Hallam and my shares in horses. They were estimating that this would recover for them another $1 million or so. Of the five creditors, only Elders voted against it, so the arrangement was passed by the requisite majority. And so I became bankrupt under Part 10 of the Bankruptcy Act.

Bankruptcy, of course, is a terrible thing; in fact, the whole thing was emotionally draining. However, I've probably always had a somewhat cavalier attitude towards money and/or the lack of it. I wasn't quite sure where I would get the $100,000 from, but I was confident that a good horse and my share of its prize money earnings would quickly sort out the problem. My attitude towards life's blows is that they're not going to kill you. They might knock you down, sit you on your bum, but you just have to get back up and start all over again. And that's what I did. The next yearling sales on the calendar I was there, jotting down notes in my notebook, bidding for young horses that caught my eye. Nothing had changed...though now I come to think of it, perhaps the bloodstock agents were a bit colder towards me when they saw me taking an interest in one of their horses.

You can't be a horse trainer without a resilient character. Without resilience, the first inevitable bad break — your best horse goes lame, a jockey's brain fade costs you victory in a major race, an owner takes a good horse off you after you've done all the hard work turning it into a racehorse — would break you.

* * *

I had been focussing my efforts on two-year-olds for just a few years, and quickly discovered that this part of racing was highly addictive. Training horses is an adrenalin-producing business, and training two-year-olds provides the biggest adrenalin shots. It's exciting because no matter how much pre-sale due diligence and research you do, no matter how good your horse selection judgement is, you never really know how that raw, undeveloped yearling is going to turn out. You buy on potential, the potential you glimpse in the bloodlines, the shape of the limbs, the way the horse carries itself, a nice loose walk that captures your attention as it parades around the ring. Sometimes, and I swear I've seen it in yearlings, it can be nothing more than a glint in the eye, the suggestion of intelligence and determination — two vital ingredients in good racehorses.

Clay Hero, bought back in 1987, had been the first young horse to vindicate my judgement in the yearling sales ring. Canny Lad, of course, came to me through Alec Dodson, but at the same time as Canny Lad I had another very good two-year-old called Unspoken Word. I bought Unspoken Word at the New Zealand Magic Millions Sales for just $19,000.

As a two-year-old, Unspoken Word was always in Canny Lad's shadow, yet won three Group races — the Myer Fashion Stakes, a Blue Diamond Prelude and the Black Opal Stakes in Canberra. He was also runner-up in the inaugural New Zealand Magic Millions (a race in which I trained the second, third and fourth placegetters).

Unspoken Word had a change of ownership after his two-year-old season. The new owner was a Western Australian who shall remain nameless. This gentleman was one of those nightmare owners that all trainers dread — arrogant, demanding, the ones who think they know everything about training. I was very excited about Unspoken Word's three-year-old prospects and I thought I could develop him into a champion. Unfortunately, I never got the chance. The Western Australian owner decided that only the best would do for his horse, and I wasn't the best. He took Unspoken Word away from me and gave him to Bart Cummings. Unspoken Word did go on to win a couple more Group races, but I remain unconvinced that Bart did a better job that I could have done.

Another promising two-year-old I had around that time was a Straight Strike colt which I bought for a bit more than $50,000 at the Inglis Classic Sale in 1990. I sold it to the wife of the Sydney bookmaker Harry Barrett, and it raced under the name Diddy Do It. The horse, a striking grey colt, was a real handful to train. He raced in the Blue Diamond Stakes, was going beautifully and his jockey Jim Cassidy believed that barring some unlikely mishap the race was his. Well, mishap struck — with the race at his mercy the colt threw Cassidy from the saddle.

In the Golden Slipper Diddy Do It blew the start when he jumped away awkwardly and was never in the race, finishing ninth. A few weeks later we had him in the Champagne Stakes, and as soon as the starting gates flung open he tossed his jockey, Larry Olsen this time, to the turf.

It was frustrating because there was no doubt Diddy Do It had enormous ability. While we spelled him to get him ready for the three-year-old season I spent a lot of time trying to get him to relax. We set him for the Sandown Stakes over 1000 metres, and I remember getting a call from Harry Barrett on the morning of the race.

'How do you think he'll go today?' Harry asked me.

Diddy Do It was, of course, always an uncertain proposition, but I had schooled him as best I could. On potential alone he was as good a chance as any.

'Have a small bet on him,' I advised Harry.

From the moment, the starter gates flew open 'Diddy Do It' was up to his usual tricks and jockey Kevin Forrester had his hands full. At the home turn the horse was a clear last. I remember thinking, 'Oh gawd, not only is this horse as unruly as ever but if Harry Barrett has listened to me he's going to be cranky as hell.'

But then Forrester started to weave his way through the field, the horse got clear, reached the leaders fifty metres from the post and, much to my relief, went past them to win by three-quarters of a length.

I understand that Harry Barrett did take my advice and had a small bet, though a small bet for Harry was a large bet by everyone else's standards. Bookmaker, Colin Tidy, later told me that Harry went up and down the ring and 'didn't miss anyone out.'

Apart from promising two and three-year-olds like Unspoken Word and Diddy Do It, the star of my stable remained Canny Lad. His three-year-old season didn't quite reach the heights of his two-year-old campaign, but he still picked up a few more Group wins. His first start back he was beaten in the Group Two Ascot Vale Stakes by Bureaucracy. I could have trained the quinella that day, because I had almost purchased Bureaucracy as a yearling at the New Zealand Magic Millions sales. On that occasion, I probably outsmarted myself — the vendors wanted $30,000 for the colt, which had been passed in on my bid of $20,000, but I thought I could get him for a discount and offered $22,500. Then Harry Lawton, a great judge of racehorses, jumped in, offered a bit more and I missed out.

Canny Lad's next start was the Group Two Moonee Valley Stakes which had just been renamed the Bill Stutt Stakes. Shane Dye was again on board Canny Lad, and at the halfway mark Canny Lad was six lengths off the lead. By the time the field reached the turn into the straight, Dye had worked the horse up to the lead, drawing him alongside none other than his old rival, Bureaucracy.

Well, those two horses fought it out all the way down the straight, neck and neck. The Moonee Valley straight is only a short one but that afternoon it seemed endless. It was one of the most exciting duels I've seen on the racetrack; I barely escaped a heart attack watching it unfold! At the finish line Canny Lad lunged forward, like a hundred metres sprinter, to just get his nose in front of Bureaucracy. (The official margin was a short half-head). The winning time was the second fastest in the history of the race.

The main target for Canny Lad that spring was the Cox Plate, worth $1.7 million and Australia's premier weight-for-age event. Three-year-olds didn't have the greatest record in the Cox Plate, I think there were only three in the previous twenty years — it's a tough and demanding event that only champions win.

The pace in the Cox Plate was hot from the start. Stylish Century, the previous year's VRC Derby winner, did what he always did and shot off at a lightning pace that spread-eagled the field. By the halfway mark he was ten lengths in front; Canny Lad was probably fifteen lengths back. Inevitably the rest of the pack caught Stylish Century at the turn and he was swamped by runners. Sydeston and Canny Lad forged to the front on the turn past the tiring Stylish Century and looked like fighting it out until the horse that had been rested back in the field, Better Loosen Up, flew home and beat them both. Exciting stuff! Michael Clarke on Better Loosen Up had been biding his time at the tail of the field. He came from nowhere, around the outside of the field and took off after the two leaders. This time the Moonee Valley finish line flashed up too quickly; Better Loosen Up had won by half a length from Sydeston, Canny Lad finishing third. When the race time came up, 2:01.5, Better Loosen Up had set a course record. Canny Lad had been beaten by two champions, but had made them work all the way. Better Loosen Up, incidentally, is one of the best horses I've seen in the last twenty-five years, an international star who would go on to win the Japan Cup.

The autumn of 1991 was to be Canny Lad's final campaign, and he started it in impressive fashion winning the Group Three Tattersalls Stakes. I wasn't surprised by the win, but was a little taken aback by the ease of it. He won by three and a half lengths and seemed to be in second gear. It was completely out of character for Canny Lad who up until then had never won by more than a length and seemed to relish the close finishes.

After Canny Lad's Tattersalls Stakes win I had bold plans for the rest of the Autumn Carnival, and even entertained hopes that he could be kept in racing for his four-year-old season. But, unfortunately, his form petered out and the Tattersalls was to be his last victory. At the end of the season he was sold to one of the biggest breeders in Australia, the Woodlands Stud, where he would become a top sire.

Canny Lad would be up there as one of the best horses I've trained, certainly in the top three. He brought me a lot of joy — not just the Golden Slipper win but also his early two-year-old victories when he had us jumping out of our skins with excitement at his potential. And his win as a three-year-old in the Bill Stutt Stakes remains one of the most exciting races I've seen.

He also brought me a lot of stress — he literally worried me sick at times. I'd get these intense stomach cramps just from fretting over his health or some other misfortune befalling him. But that's the way of horse racing for the majority of trainers — your entire livelihood and welfare can become dependent on the fortunes of a single horse. And when you think about the myriad of things that can go wrong — a fall at the track, a mysterious virus, crooks and their nefarious activities, an innocuous accident in the stables — it's a constant reminder of how precarious the business is, and how we trainers are mere playthings in the hands of fate.

* * *

Canny Lad and Diddy Do It had been retired to stud, and Unspoken Word had been taken off my hands. But I was fortunate enough to have a few young racehorses in my stable that had the potential to replace them. The two best ones could not have offered a bigger contrast in styles.

I purchased Kenny's Best Pal as a yearling just a few days after Canny Lad's Golden Slipper win. I think it's fair to say that there's a bit of a rush of blood after such a major win, an unshakeable optimism that may cause trainers to spend a little bit more than they had intended. However, when I saw a Bletchingly yearling with an ideal comportment and length about him, I couldn't help but think, this might just be another Canny Lad.

I was in the unfamiliar position of already having an owner lined up — it was just a matter of finding the right horse. Normally for me it had been the other way around. Ken Jones was an American businessman based in the Pacific island territory of Guam. He had a strong Southern drawl, and although in his seventies when I came to train for him, still handsome. Ken had made his fortune selling American-made produce to American servicemen in Guam during the war in Vietnam, but had made the majority of his wealth through property development. He also had a stud farm in one of the heartlands of American racing, Kentucky.

I wasn't the only one to like the look of the Bletchingly colt. A bidding war broke out and as the colt's price climbed I needed to make a quick call to Jones to check if he wanted to stay in the bidding race. He did, and finally, for $200,000, Kenny's Best Pal was sold to me. It was the most amount of money I had ever paid for a horse before. At least this time it wasn't my money I was gambling with!

The other promising young horse in my stable at that time was named Yachtie. In contrast to Kenny's Best Pal, Yachtie failed to even reach his reserve, a paltry $20,000, at the 1991 Magic Millions. I was at those sales and had looked closely at the strapping colt, by the first season sire Broad Reach. I was buying on behalf of another of my clients, Chris Marks. We had already purchased one yearling at the sales and Chris had flown back to Melbourne because of business commitments. Yachtie was one of the last lots offered on the final day. I really liked the look of him, but because of my recent... ahem... financial problems, had my hands tied and couldn't bid. With no other serious interest, the colt returned unsold to his breeders, Widden Stud in the New South Wales Hunter Valley.

Then several months later Widden Stud, remembering my interest in their colt, got in touch with me to see if I was still interested. This time I was able to convince three of my clients, including Chris Marks, to buy the horse. There was reluctance because Broad Reach was an unproven sire, an unknown quantity. I eventually had to rope in my wife, Maria, to make up the shortfall but the deal was done.

The 1991-92 season was twelve months of frustration for me. The size of my stable had been more than halved, there were the financial storm clouds hanging over me, and I was enjoying little luck at the track. The ambitious goal for Kenny's Best Pal was the Golden Slipper which would give me a second winner in three years. I knew that if I could pull that off, the owners would return in numbers, bringing with them the good horses, and I would be back on track to a Racing Premiership. But Kenny's Best Pal struck shin soreness, a common problem for two-year-olds, and I was unable to give him any preparation. He just wasn't mature enough at that stage and I had no choice but to spell him until his three-year-old season.

Yachtie in contrast was going beautifully. He ate well, was a delight to train, nothing seemed to faze him. The Gold Coast Magic Millions was his immediate goal, but with less than a month to run he had failed to earn enough prize money to qualify.

I was a little bit desperate, but I ended up taking him across the country to Perth in December to run in the listed Karrakatta Plate at Ascot. The cross-country travel didn't faze Yachtie and he finished second. The prize money earned him a spot in the Magic Millions, so — mission accomplished — it was off to Queensland.

The Magic Millions was won by a brilliant two-year-old called Clan O'Sullivan, incidentally also owned by Ken Jones. It was Yachtie's misfortune to constantly run up against the best and just be outclassed by them. He came second to Riva Diva in the Blue Diamond Stakes, second to Clan O'Sullivan in the Black Opal, and second to Burst in the Champagne Stakes. In Australian Rules parlance, I was kicking a lot of behinds, but no goals.

We decided to give Yachtie the opportunity to run in the Golden Slipper, even though it meant paying a late nomination fee. The Herald Sun, one of Melbourne's leading dailies, made me look an idiot by reporting that I had forgotten to nominate for the Slipper, costing the owners tens of thousands of dollars for the late fee. Newspapers with their blatant disregard for facts can sometimes leave me shaking my head. The truth was that I hadn't even purchased Yachtie when Slipper nominations closed. The Herald Sun a few weeks later published a tiny, three-by-two-inch correction hidden deep inside the back pages of the paper. In the race itself, Yatchie finished out of the placings, but a creditable fifth.

The following season, 1992-93, started off with yet more misfortune and near-misses. Yachtie continued his interstate travels, and so, unfortunately, did his bridesmaid's role. In the Peter Pan Stakes at Rosehill he was beaten by the narrowest of margins in a photo finish with Play or Pay. His record at that stage from 15 starts was just two wins, but 12 placings. So he was nothing if not consistent. Yachtie did what Shakespeare would refer to as a tragic fault — he couldn't sprint or quicken at the end of his races.

Meanwhile Kenny's Best Pal, who we had also taken up to Sydney, picked up a stomach bug there. That was the end of his Sydney campaign before it even began. Back in Melbourne, it poured rain through most of the Spring Carnival and Kenny's Best Pal was proving to be useless in the wet. He had been one of the most anticipated three-year-olds that season but was failing miserably because of the wet tracks.

When it came to Cox Plate day there was a break in the bad weather. Kenny's Best Pal was entered in the Group Three BMW Vase over 2040 metres. The punters had long given up on him and he went into the race at odds of 40 to 1. However, with champion Sydney jockey Mick Dittman on board, Kenny's Best Pal caused an upset to win.

Dittman, nicknamed The Enforcer because of his hard-riding, gave Kenny's Best Pal the perfect ride, willing the horse on to victory. At the finish, the horse was ahead by a length and still powering away from the field. It was only his second victory. He carried 55.5 kilos yet ran a time just two-tenths of a second slower than that recorded by Super Impose a couple of races later over the same distance in the Cox Plate. If Kenny's Best Pal had been in the Cox Plate he would have carried seven kilos less than he did in the Vase. Racing throws up a lot of hypotheticals, and this was another case of my wondering, What if...?

Kenny's Best Pal now looked an ideal chance for the VRC Derby over 2400 metres a couple of weeks later. We had always believed he would be best suited over the longer distances because of his bloodlines. Unfortunately, it started raining again, and kept on raining! Kenny's Best Pal could only finish fifteenth in the wet going and was spelled after the race.

It's frustrating but it's also the nature of racing — even though you know you have a good one on your hands, a Group One winner waiting to happen, things go wrong, they don't pan out the way you plan, and all the hopes and dreams you had for the horse remain unfulfilled. Every trainer has had a horse or three like that — and if you can't deal with that frustration, if you continually lament your bad luck, then you need to quickly get out of racing or it will do your head in. I just had to persevere with Kenny's Best Pal, get him right for the Autumn carnival, and hope my luck would turn.

The Group One Australian Guineas at Flemington is run over 1600 metres, and is the premier mile race for three-year-olds. Mick Dittman had ridden Kenny's Best Pal to both his previous two victories but was unavailable to take the ride in the Guineas. So I engaged Greg Childs, one of the top Melbourne jockeys and a rider I considered to be a Flemington specialist. After all the setbacks Kenny's Best Pal had endured he looked as fit as he could be, the track was firm and we were all feeling confident. Ken Jones was in Guam but with the marvels of what then passed for modern technology, was able to listen to the race through a Radio Australia satellite hook-up.

Childs got caught three-wide throughout most of the race, tried to make a run, but the gap closed before he could get through and the horse was pushed even wider. Watching from the stands I could feel frustration rising inside me, a growing despair that again it was not to be. As they came to the turn Childs and the horse were still four-wide, but with the long Flemington straight in front of him Kenny's Best Pal just took off, reeled in the leaders and drew away to win. The race was just a second outside the course record set by the champion Vo Rogue.

At last the horse had fulfilled his potential and won a Group One race. The $350,000 prize money had more than paid for his purchase price. The win also couldn't have come at a better time for me professionally. With the long drought of Group One winners, I was on the verge of becoming yesterday's man. I'm not a religious man, but when I went up to the presentation stand to collect the trophy, relief and jubilation overcame me and I shouted into the microphone, 'Thank God for Kenny!'

The tide had turned for Kenny's Best Pal, I was sure of it. I knew he was tailor-made for a Derby. The AJC Derby at Randwick was approaching a few weeks away, and I was rubbing my hands in anticipation. Alas, the Guineas victory was a false dawn. Two weeks after that win the horse broke down and his autumn was over. I tried desperately to get him right for the next season, but Kenny's Best Pal never raced again.

Kenny's Best Pal's Australian Guineas win was a lone highlight in a fairly dismal season for me. At one point, a bleak four-month period from April to July, I didn't train a single city winner. In times like those, you begin to wonder where the next winner is going to come from.

The Australian economy was still trying to crawl out of recession, and owners had yet to regain the confidence to start spending money on horses again. I had two choices: I could sit on my bum, waiting for things to improve, or I could go out and do something. I chose the latter, and applied for a trainer's permit in Singapore.

I had been training horses for almost fifteen years and though I loved my job and would never have considered any other occupation, the unchanging routines that training revolves around were making me feel stale. I had visited Singapore, Malaysia and Hong Kong several times, searching for new owners, and had enjoyed my brief stays there. Singapore, in particular, is a clean, safe, well-ordered city with a great standard of living — ultra-modern, but also with plenty of old world charm courtesy of its British Colonial and Chinese influences. The training facilities were good, the Bukit Timah racecourse was top-class, and the racing industry was relatively well administered.

I submitted my trainer's application to the Singapore Turf Club, and was reliably informed by my contacts there that mine was the best-credentialed of the submissions to take over the available stable space at Bukit Timah. In anticipation of my forthcoming move I started reducing my stable until I was down to just eight horses. It was a far cry from the golden days of the mid-eighties when I had over fifty horses in work and more in the spelling and pre-training paddocks.

'Guanxi' is an important part of Chinese culture and society — it means 'relationships' or 'networks.' In Chinese societies, including places like Singapore and Hong Kong, it is almost impossible to succeed in business without having the right 'guanxi.' Another important part of dealing with any kind of authority in Chinese societies is a generous amount of greasing the bureaucratic wheels, offering exorbitant gifts, exchanging favours and, it has to be said, a brown paper bag generously stashed with bank notes might sometimes be in order too.

I, of course, was blissfully unaware of these niceties of Chinese business-dealing when I submitted my application, confident that as a multiple Group-winning trainer from one of the world's strongest horse- racing nations, there would be little obstacle to the granting of my Singapore trainer's permit. So it came as a major surprise when I was eventually informed by the Singapore Turf Club that 'unfortunately Mr Hore-Lacy, your application on this occasion has not been successful.' or words to that effect. The vacant stable space instead went to a local trainer. This trainer had a mediocre record with horses but, I'm led to understand, he did have very good 'guanxi.'

The rejection from Singapore meant that I had to basically start from scratch again. In fact, with just eight horses in work, I actually had less horses than when I first took the plunge and became a trainer back in the late '70s. It was a massive fall in fortunes for me. Not only was I just a small-time operator, I was also technically a bankrupt. Now breeders, who had once feted and fawned over me, watched me nervously whenever I made an appearance in the yearling sales yards.

I am not one to see a glass half-empty, so I just needed to revise my goals. Once I had set myself to be Victoria's number one trainer with a huge machine-like training operation to drive it. But then I had been overly ambitious and bitten off more than I could chew. Learning from my mistake, I simply scaled back my goals. Twenty city winners a year, a team of 30 to 35 horses in work and a similar number on my books, and an annual buying budget of half a million dollars for yearlings: that would be enough for me to make a good living, be successful and happy.

Unfortunately, a gathering storm cloud on the home front was about to upturn all those plans, and change my and my family's life forever.

CHAPTER 9

Training a Melbourne Cup winner is an incredibly difficult task. Like the majority of horse trainers in this country, I haven't yet managed to do it. Training a Golden Slipper winner is just as difficult, and only accomplished by a select few. I did it, once, many years ago, and it took all my craft and training know-how, plus countless hours of preparation to get it done. In fact, just running a moderately successful training operation takes long hours, a lot of hard work, sweat and tears, the capacity to multitask and high-level management skills, plus a generous helping of good fortune.

On the other hand, when I was new to marriage and parenting, I thought raising a family was just a natural skill, something we're all born with. I didn't realise that successful parenting — like horse training, or running a business — takes hard work and constant effort.

Ricky was our first-born child. He arrived in the world on November 9, 1971, the proverbial little bundle of joy. Much as I loved my two daughters, I always felt a special bond with Ricky — the first child, the son. The only problem was that I didn't take the time to cement that bond.

I don't really recall what expectations I had as a first-time parent. I tended to leave a large chunk of the parenting responsibilities to my wife, Maria — like most fathers in that day and age (and I expect it remains the case for many men today). Maria was the one who read the parenting books, who discussed parenting strategies with other mothers, who devoted every waking hour to caring for our new family member. I saw my role as financial provider, the one who went out and earned the money that paid for the food on the table, the clothes on our backs and the roof over our head. Possibly I performed this role a little over-zealously, devoting long hours to first the import business and then establishing myself as a trainer.

Not that I was a cold and distant father. I loved the time I spent with my children, watching them grow up. I experienced the same joys and thrills as any other parent when our babies say their first words, take their first unsteady steps. It's just that I didn't make enough time for sharing these moments with my children.

Ricky grew up around horses and he loved the animals. As soon as he was old enough he was up in the saddle, riding the ponies on our property at Gisborne, and his earliest dream was to be a jockey. Even though he was of medium height he was slightly built so he had the physique for it. But I wouldn't have a bar of it, and did everything in my power to discourage him. I knew how tough a jockey's life can be, that only a tiny minority make a good living from it, leaving the rest to fight over the scraps. Ninety per cent of those involved in our industry, including jockeys, are eating the paint off the walls.

Most jockeys sacrifice schooling to learn the horse-riding trade, but a majority never graduate past the apprenticeship stage. They are then left without a job, without a proper qualification and without an education — a sure-fire recipe for poverty. And, of course, there's the ever-present spectre of serious injury, or worse, that hangs over a jockey each time he or she climbs up on a horse.

I wanted Ricky to get a good education and to eventually enter a profession. It's ironic really — my mother pushed me towards becoming a lawyer and I rebelled, yet here I was doing exactly the same thing to my own son. I saw the racetrack as a temptation and so I did everything to keep Ricky away from it. Although my intentions were good, it meant that — seeing as I spent most of my time at the track — I was essentially shutting my son out of my world.

Ricky was initially a good student at school. We sent him to Mentone Grammar, a well-regarded and upmarket private school in Melbourne's south-east. He wasn't what you would call brilliant academically, but as long as he put the work in he was intelligent enough to finish in the top twenty per cent of his classes. And for a while he performed to those expectations.

However, by trying to keep Ricky away from the world of racing, perhaps I inadvertently turned it into the forbidden fruit. Whatever the case, Ricky found the lure of it too strong. As a teenager, he would hang out with the young apprentices, the track riders and the stable hands — they became his mates.

I wrote earlier how I regretted not spending time with Ricky kicking the footy around or playing games of backyard cricket. My parenting principles might seem old-fashioned now, but I strongly advocate the importance of sport in a child's life, particularly a boy's. It's healthy, it's character-building, and it keeps them busy. I didn't take the time to foster that love of sport in my son, and as a result he began to hang out with a bad crowd — the lazy kids, the troublemakers and no-hopers.

Growing up in the early fifties at Geelong Grammar I had no first-hand experience of drugs. I don't even recall any second- or third-hand experience. I was blissfully ignorant of marijuana, cocaine and heroin. I went to university in the late fifties and early sixties, and still drugs remained an unknown in my world. Like most Australians, drugs only appeared on my radar with the Vietnam War where Australian and US soldiers on leave introduced the exotic drug into our sheltered society. I can honestly say that I've never taken an illicit drug in my life — the strongest mind-altering substances I've ever taken were a few too many glasses of red.

Ricky grew up in a much different environment. I don't know the statistics on how many teenagers in the 1980s had experimented with drugs, but I suspect it would have been quite high. We first discovered Ricky had been smoking marijuana when he was 15. Maria urged me to sit down and talk to Ricky, give him a stern lecture, which I attempted to do. I can hardly say I was an expert on the subject; I really knew nothing about it, just a vague idea that drugs were dangerous. So, instead, it was Ricky who ended up giving me the lecture.

'Dad, I don't know what you're getting upset about. Marijuana's completely harmless. It's less harmful than a glass of wine.'

'That may be the case son, but I don't want you ending up a drug addict. I've read that's how heroin addicts start off, marijuana's just the first step.'

'That's rubbish, Dad. Legal drugs like alcohol and tobacco do far more harm and damage than smoking the occasional joint.'

Now I was on the back foot; my son was making me seem like some old wowser, a hypocrite to boot. Happy enough to indulge in a relaxing glass of wine after dinner, but up in arms if his son enjoyed a bong!

To my eternal regret, I let it go. I made it clear that I didn't approve, but I was hardly going to disown him over it. If I had my time over again I would have set very strict boundaries. I would have educated him about the dangers of drugs as soon as he was old enough to understand. I would have monitored his friends, and come down hard if he stepped out of line. That might sound unfashionably harsh and restrictive parenting, but I've had the wisdom of experience — you can't let your children set the perimeters when they are still too young to make wise choices, or they could live to regret it.

Here's what marijuana *can* do to you. I'm not saying it definitely *will* do it to you, just what have been some of the observed and documented adverse effects on those taking it.

- Heightened anxiety or fearfulness, panic attacks
- Impaired judgement, loss of coordination
- Increased heart rate and a decrease in the heart's pumping efficiency
- Long-term adverse effects on brain systems, including vision control
- Increased memory loss, and impairment of the ability to form new memories
- Destruction of brain cells
- Reduced immunity to infection
- Decreased lung efficiency and efficiency of the respiratory system
- Increased risk of lung disease (marijuana contains carcinogens)
- Increased risk of bronchitis
- Decreased sperm cell counts in men, and increased risk of impotency
- Decrease in the brain's problem-solving skills
- Impairment of foetal development in pregnant marijuana users
- Increased risk of major psychological disorders such as depression, psychosis and schizophrenia

* * *

The first noticeable effect we saw in Ricky from smoking marijuana was apathy. He would spend all his free time just lounging around on the living room sofa or cooped up in his bedroom. He stopped helping out around the house, and could barely bother with his homework. Then his grades at school started to deteriorate. When he was younger, he was constantly curious about the world and always a hive of activity. But overnight both his curiosity and energy seemed to vanish.

At first, we were inclined have the view that this was fairly typical, if not exactly welcome, behaviour for an adolescent boy, part of being a teenager. However, instead of just growing out of it, his apathy worsened — he would spend half the day sleeping and the only activities he seemed to have any interest in were lying around watching TV or listening to music. It was as if our happy-go-lucky, good-natured son had been taken away, then returned to us brainwashed and lobotomised.

Maria and I thought hard about getting some kind of medical help for him, sending him off to a counsellor or psychologist. But, then he suddenly seemed to improve, and he assured us that he was no longer smoking marijuana. Although he still had bouts of despondency, they would be interspersed with bursts of energy, and he would be sprouting bright ambitious plans. With the benefit of hindsight, those swings in mood were too dramatic and his energetic moments almost manic — a professional might have recognised something more sinister at work. But we were just relieved to see the old Ricky back, and that he was beginning to mature and get his act together.

Even his studies improved. At this time, he was in his final year at Mentone Grammar. The end-of-year VCE exams were looming, and Ricky had knuckled down to his studies. Although I would have liked to see him go on to study Law, he had decided on this new thing called Science and Information Technology. I had no idea what that was, except that it had to do with computers. Even a Luddite like myself knew that computers were going to be the Next Big Thing, and so I was pleased that he found an area of study that not only interested him but would lead to a promising career.

One weekend, when he was seventeen years old, several weeks before the VCE exams, Ricky went to a 21st birthday party in the inner city. He went with some school mates, but there were also a few older ones there, in their late teens and early twenties. There were also large amounts of booze and drugs present.

One of the older boys was the son of a former well-known VFL football player. This lad had recently broken up with his girlfriend, or rather, she had dumped him. The footballer's son, like many a famous person's child, had grown up with an exaggerated sense of entitlement, and wasn't used to not getting his own way. He had taken the girl's rejection badly; he had also taken his pent-up anger and frustration to the party.

The footballer's son had inherited his father's athletic build. Ricky in contrast was medium height with a slim physique. Unfortunately, it made him a tempting target for insecure bullies. The footballer's son caught sight of Ricky across the room, began to glare at him. When Ricky glanced across and their eyes met, the footballer's son immediately challenged him.

'What are you looking at?' he called out to Ricky.

I imagine Ricky was immediately appeasing, offering a nervous apology. Although he'd done nothing wrong, he knew better than to get into an argument with a bigger bloke. But the footballer's son was up and striding across the room towards Ricky.

'I said, what are you staring at? You want a fight, do you?'

Ricky kept telling him he didn't want to fight, the bigger boy kept challenging him. Ricky decided the best course of action would be to ignore him, and turned away to talk to his friends. It was at that moment that he was king-hit, floored by a punch to the side of his head.

The police report said that the footballer's son laid several blows to Ricky's head with his fists and his steel-capped boots. It was a pretty quick fight, over in an instant. Ricky had gone down straight away, blood pouring from his mouth, his jaw smashed in three places. Perhaps it was another example of my neglect as a parent; I had never taken the time to teach him some basic self-defence skills — although how do you defend yourself from a punch from behind?

Ricky was taken to hospital immediately. There they operated on him, re-setting his jaw and wiring it back together again. Maria and I headed straight to the hospital when we got the news. The doctor on duty told us that, with the severity of the damage, Ricky would be on a liquid diet for at least three months.

In the eyes of the police it was a clear-cut case of assault. They suggested that we consider pressing charges. The father of the aggressor, the ex-footy star, became involved. I think he was as much concerned about the negative publicity for him if the incident found its way into the media as he was with Ricky's welfare. I remember having a couple of meetings with him and he tried to negotiate his way out of a court appearance for his son.

I was concerned by the unprovoked attack on my son, and had no intention of letting it be swept under the carpet. If nothing else, that young thug needed to be taught that punching an innocent person in the head should not go unpunished. And so the matter went to court, many months after the event. We did eventually negotiate a settlement, with the footballer's son to pay Ricky five thousand dollars — spare change really for an ex-footy star. If we tried to get more it would have involved an even lengthier and more expensive court case, with the risk that the court in its wisdom might decree Ricky was entitled to no more compensation than his medical costs. I've studied law and I've been in court, so I know full well that it isn't always justice that is served, but he who has the deeper pockets.

And so we settled for compensation for the medical fees. The footballer's son might have copped a good behaviour bond, I don't recall the details. And Ricky, well, he paid his medical bills and even had spare change to buy a second-hand car. But, as things were to turn out, he copped the worst of the deal.

* * *

Ricky had a determined character — even as a kid if he fell off a horse he quickly got back on again. After the assault, his jaw was wired shut, and he lived on a diet of soup, Sustagen and painkillers for months. Yet he was determined to sit his VCE, determined to get a good enough mark to get into the Science and Information Technology degree he had set his sights on.

He had his study timetable all set out, the Mentone Grammar headmaster himself taking the time to help Ricky with his planning — an hour on this subject, another hour on that subject. Ricky tried to stick to his study plan, but he wouldn't be ten minutes into the study session and the pain from his jaw would overwhelm him. I can remember seeing him emerge from his bedroom in tears, from the pain and from the frustration that he could see all his hopes of passing the final exams evaporating. The painkillers were clearly inadequate, and eventually he found something that was more effective than the drugs prescribed for him. He started smoking marijuana again.

The VCE results were released early in the New Year. In what was an annual ritual, thousands of young school-leavers awaited the postman's arrival with hope or dread, depending on how well they'd applied themselves the year before. But even the best students couldn't help feeling slightly anxious, that something might have gone wrong on exam day, derailing all their hard study. It was as if these young adults' whole future rested on that letter from the government, on that final exam score. Do well and your life would be one of boundless possibilities, bomb out and your future was about to embark on a downward spiral.

Ricky had long before resigned himself to the worst. The pain of his broken jaw had ruined his exam preparations, while getting high on marijuana instead hardly helped his cause. So he felt no shock or surprise when his results confirmed the worst; he had failed to make the entry score for his Science and Information Technology course. The only surprise was that he had missed out by just three marks, tantalising close to success but not quite.

We tried to cheer him up. I had my own experience to share; you didn't necessarily need a university education to embark on a career you loved and in which you could enjoy some success. It didn't matter what we said, however; Ricky was beyond consolation. In fact, his emotional state had taken a worrying turn. The events of the previous few months had given his self-confidence a heavy battering; he considered himself completely worthless. Depressed, he would just sit around all day, doing nothing, achieving nothing, which only reinforced his sense of worthlessness. And so the vicious cycle began.

A friend of mine, Kevin Weight, a horse owner, was also an accountant with his own successful practice. I had spoken to him about Ricky's situation.

'How about if I found him some work with me?' Kevin offered. 'Would your son be interested in that?'

It was a great opportunity, and Maria and I encouraged Ricky to take up the offer. Ricky agreed to give it a go, and we even saw a renewed sense of hope in his manner.

After a week at the new job Ricky was despondent again.

'How's the new job going?' I asked, concerned about the return of his black mood.

'It's hopeless, Dad,' he confessed to me. 'I can't do anything right there.'

'You've only just started. You can't be expected to know everything about the job straight away. And I'm sure Kevin feels the same way.'

'You don't understand, Dad. I'm completely useless at it. I don't understand anything, I keep making mistakes. I'm sure I'm about to get fired.'

Ricky didn't wait to get fired, and instead resigned from the job not long after. Again, he was inconsolable about this new failure. It wasn't until later down the track, and a conversation with Kevin about Ricky, that another side of the story was revealed. I told Kevin how down on himself Ricky had been over his performance in the job. Kevin appeared surprised.

'I don't remember having any problems with his work. I thought he was doing well, and was actually surprised when he announced he was quitting.'

It showed just how much of a battering Ricky's self-confidence had taken.

Ricky spent a lot of the next year or so unemployed, interspersed with the occasional low-paid and dead-end casual job. He was a regular marijuana smoker by then. I imagine that just about every day he was smoking the stuff, 'getting off his face' as they say.

What does a parent do in this situation? I admit there were times when I was angry with him, that he seemed to be throwing his whole life away without even trying. There were times when I would have gladly put him out on the street. If he wasn't going to follow the rules of the house (no drugs) then he could find somewhere else to live. And there were times when I had to access the deepest wells of patience and tolerance, trying to be as supportive as I could while my son worked his way through what were obviously troubling issues for him. As a parent, you just try and do your best, but you can never be guaranteed success.

Perhaps there were parallels with my own misspent youth, but the big difference was that I didn't have to face the destructive force that marijuana has on the personality and character of its users. I spent my university days enjoying myself, though wasting a lot of time and money in the process. But, then there came a moment when I decided to grow up and become an adult, which I was able to do without too much trouble. My son, in contrast, had his spirit crushed and his character altered beyond recognition by drugs. For him there was to be no second chance.

I am fervently anti-drugs and I believe I have strong reason to be. If I come across here as some kind of shrill moral crusader, well so be it. And if ever the day comes when those drugs are legalised, I fear it might very well be the writing on the wall for our society. People like to advocate that marijuana is harmless. Well, I'd hate to live in a society where a large proportion of the population are regularly getting stoned. If you think that mental health problems have been increasing in our community in the last few decades, a by-product of the fast-paced and stressful times we live in. Just see what happens if marijuana is legalised. Mental illness will become an epidemic. And don't even get me started on what it would do to the economy's productivity if large numbers of the workforce were turning up to their jobs with marijuana in their system.

* * *

I wish there were a happy ending to this part of the story, just as throughout the ordeal I had hoped, more than I had hoped for anything before, that somehow things would turn around, that we could get our son back so that our family life would return to normality. Isn't it what all parents hope for? There are a small minority of parents who will settle for nothing less than exceptional success for their children, and another tiny minority who perhaps give up caring anything for their kids. But most parents just hope that their children will have happy, healthy, normal lives. It seems such a small thing to ask for, so surely we wouldn't be denied it.

One day, Ricky came to me, very worried.

'Dad, do you think it's possible for Martians to have put something in my head, and are now controlling what I do?'

'Well, son, I suppose it's *possible*. But I'd think it extremely unlikely.'

He seemed reassured by that, at least for a short time. But then the voices in his head came back again. It would be the beginning of a nightmare period for our family, both saddened and burdened by what was going on in Ricky's mind.

There were increasing signs that he was beginning to lose all touch with reality. His plans for the future became ludicrously ambitious, the TV was sending him messages, songs on the radio contained codes that only he could decipher. The spells where he was living in some kind of altered universe became longer, and his moments of lucidity briefer. Most painful of all, when he was close to his old self, it was as though he realised that he was going insane. He'd be distraught, shedding tears of fear and confusion. Maria or I would find him lying on his bed in his room, his eyes red from crying. 'I just want to end it all,' he told us.

Both Maria and I felt powerless to help him. We did convince him to talk to our family doctor, who found that Ricky had all the symptoms of schizophrenia and recommended immediate admission to a psychiatric hospital. The problem was that the only person who could admit Ricky was Ricky himself. At least Ricky, in his moments of clarity, recognised that he had serious mental health issues. Eventually he agreed to go to the Kingston Centre, a State-run mental institution in the nearby suburb of Mordialloc, for treatment.

I'm sure the staff in these places do the best they can, but I found the Kingston Centre a grim and depressing place. From the moment we stepped inside, the environment seemed to drain all hope from us, as if we had entered a point of no return. When Ricky admitted himself there for an indefinite stay he was locking himself up alongside some frightening headcases. I saw some people wandering the corridors who looked as if they'd happily knife you in your bed given the opportunity. I remember on more than one occasion while visiting Ricky of being unsettled by a maniacal scream from some other part of the building.

Ricky had locked himself up because he feared taking his own life, but now felt in even more danger inside, in danger from his fellow inmates. Needless to say, after just a couple of days there he was demanding to be let out again. And under recently introduced legislation, no one but Ricky had the power to stop him from leaving.

Maria, in particular, was concerned that Ricky was being released too quickly. She cornered one of the doctors.

'It's not long enough. Why can't you keep him here until the drugs have completely left his system?'

'No ma'am,' the doctor proclaimed. 'We've fought a hundred years for the patient's freedom not to be locked up against their will.'

I guess, when thinking about the treatment Ricky should receive, I had in mind one of those places in America where celebrities and the rich book themselves in, like the Betty Ford Clinic. Ricky would spend however long it took there to receive treatment, get the marijuana out of his system, and learn how to overcome his addiction in the future.

Well, I don't even know if Australia has a Betty Ford-type clinic — certainly the Kingston Centre's treatment was far removed from my perhaps idealistic hope. In any case, when Ricky came out he was no better than before. The majority of the time he would behave like a crazy person. There would be brief periods of clarity where he would realise what was good for him and re-admit himself to Kingston. Then a few days later he would be back on the streets again. There was no improvement in his condition, in fact, it was only getting worse.

Sometimes Ricky would disappear for weeks on end, and Maria and I would fear the worst. Both of us would be on edge, waiting for the knock on the door, the police on our doorstep with grim expressions on their faces. One time, Ricky headed off to Cairns in Far North Queensland. He had some grand ambitions of working on a fishing trawler where, he believed, he could earn a small fortune while also enjoying the health benefits of an active, outdoor work environment.

For weeks we heard nothing from him, he could have been on the other side of the world by that time for all we knew...or worse. At last he made contact with us. He had shacked up at a cheap boarding house in Cairns, but had fallen in with a bad crowd. According to Ricky these people were in even worse shape than him, crazy, volatile types capable of almost anything.

He then got into a dispute with some of them. Maria received a spate of phone calls, every ten or fifteen minutes, each progressively shriller and more alarming.

'They're going to kill me,' he told Maria in one phone call.

The next phone call, the situation had escalated. 'They're all psychos! They have bombs, and they're planning to kill a lot of people.'

By that stage it had become impossible to tell with Ricky what was real and what wasn't, but there was no doubt that he had been terrified by the experience. The next day he left Cairns and came back to Melbourne.

On 10 May, 1996, I turned fifty-seven. I had long ceased

to celebrate my birthdays, which were more a reminder of my decline towards old age rather than an occasion to be feted. Maria and I had a quiet lunch with our two daughters, Kate and Emma. Ricky, who literally lived at no fixed address, was a no-show.

Ricky called me in the afternoon from a public phone box. He seemed despondent, not unusual for Ricky, but also calm. It was one of his lucid periods. We chatted briefly, and then he said, 'I've got to go now. Goodbye, Dad.'

I said goodbye, too, hung up and immediately wished I hadn't. Something in his tone, so solemn in its finality, made me break out in a cold sweat. He hadn't said 'See you later' or 'Bye' but 'Goodbye.'

Early that evening, there was a knock on the door. Instinctively Maria and I looked at each other, fear on our faces. I even remember saying to Maria, 'I've got a horrible premonition this is going to be terrible news,' as we both went to the door.

The two grim-faced police officers were standing on our doorstep, just as I knew they would arrive one day. Fifteen minutes after his birthday call to me, Ricky had walked to Parkdale station, only a couple of kilometres from our house, and had thrown himself in front of a train. He died instantly.

Our boy was gone, and devastation like a wave swept over me. No matter how much I had expected this moment to arrive, had tried to prepare myself for it, it still struck like a hammer blow.

Yet even in that moment when we first received the news, I felt a brief flicker of relief, a feeling that was to grow stronger in the ensuing days. Relief that all the pain and suffering that Ricky had been enduring, and the pain and suffering he had been inflicting on those who loved him, was over. For the last five years there had been a constant misery in our lives — sometimes almost unbearable in its intensity, but more often than not a dull, unremitting pain somewhere deep in the heart. But perhaps now Ricky would at last find some peace.

CHAPTER 10

Fifty years earlier, death had taken from my mother a son, Nigel, in tragic circumstances, and it destroyed her. After Ricky's death I, too, found myself staring into a dark, bleak nothingness. The morning after his death, I woke up after a fitful sleep, and it was as if overnight every last ounce of happiness, hope and energy had been drained from me.

I lost interest in everything, including horses. I remained a trainer, but really was just going through the motions. The fact that my training fortunes had sunk to one of their lowest ebbs only eroded my enthusiasm for horse training further. After Ricky's death, I went through a thirteen-month drought in which I didn't train a single city winner. Oddly enough, despite my lack of motivation and lack of success, I never contemplated throwing it in — probably because I had no alternative career to fall back on. I was fifty-six years old, an age when many men's thoughts occupy themselves with dreams of retirement, midweek days spent on the golf course instead of the office. As a recent bankrupt, however, retirement was never an option for me. Then again, if my lack of success on the racetrack continued much longer, the decision to retire would probably have been made for me...by clients voting with their feet.

Fallout from the bankruptcy episode continued to cloud the state of my finances. I had always managed to survive as a trainer by trusting my judgement in the yearling sales ring. I'd buy a promising youngster, school it and get it race-ready then on-sell it when it was close to making its debut. But now, with no money in the bank, I couldn't even do that. But then, from the most unexpected source, a lifeline was thrown my way, a lifeline that literally saved my training career.

* * *

The Inglis family has been involved in the horse-racing industry for generations. The family began selling horses in 1865, when William Inglis opened his 'horse bazaar' in Pitt Street, Sydney. By the time Reg Inglis became involved in the business, William Inglis & Son was the largest bloodstock and auctioneer firm in Australia. The Inglis Sales held at Easter in Sydney were amongst the premier yearling sales in the thoroughbred industry.

Reg was an imposing man, but he was also honest and fair, the type that people used to refer to as a true gentleman. The firm had always staked its reputation on integrity, and Reg upheld that tradition.

In early 1995, while my son Ricky's life was spiralling out of control, the business of horse-training ground on. After the premature retirement of Kenny's Best Pal I had no more champions to replace him. In fact, I had let most of my horses go in preparation for the move to Singapore that never eventuated. My stables had been reduced to a small team of plodders whose best hopes of victory lay in restricted races at country meetings. Knowing the talent in my stables was threadbare, I was desperate to replenish it at the new season's yearling sales. But how, when I was penniless? I decided to swallow my pride and go to Reg Inglis and ask for a line of credit. Reg, who perhaps knew I was going through a particularly rough trot, paused for a moment, then smiled. 'Sure Rick, I'll let you have $100,000.'

Racing's a tough game at times, and the people in it are accustomed to making tough decisions which can appear heartless. It also loves its successes and can cruelly turn on the failures. But, despite its flaws, it's also full of good people who look out for each other, who can show kindness at the most unexpected times. Reg Inglis's magnanimity that day was just such an occasion. (I wasn't the only one to benefit from his generosity — he also helped out Bart Cummings when he faced financial ruin).

I always feel a twinge of nervousness in the sales yard when I'm appraising the young horses. So much rides on the decision to bid for a horse, including, of course, large amounts of money. If your judgement lets you down and you choose wrongly, it can turn out to be a very expensive mistake. At the Easter Sales in 1995 I felt this pressure weighing on me especially so. If I got it wrong, not only would I be in debt to one of the most influential men in racing, I'd probably be unofficially barred from future yearling sales for years after.

I'm a strong believer in buying types as yearlings, that is, looking primarily at their conformation, their physique, as the basis for my decisions. Pedigree's secondary to me — just as well because I've never had the funds to buy the fashionably-bred ones. At these Sydney yearling sales one colt immediately caught my eye, an athletic-looking chestnut colt by Snippets. Snippets was a former Golden Slipper winner, but at that stage of his bloodsire career, a still unknown quantity. So I was able to get the colt for a modest $45,000.

Being flat-footed, and slightly pigeon-toed, prospective owners weren't exactly queueing to purchase a piece of Spartacus. I managed to convince a few owners to buy in; friends of mine, including Kevin Weight — the accountant who had tried to help

Ricky with a job a few years earlier. When the colt turned two I checked with horses' names to see which had become eligible for re-use. One of those names seemed ideal for a young horse I felt just might become a champion. Without hesitation, I selected Spartacus for our horse's name.

I'm often asked which of the many horses I have trained has been my favourite. There are a few that stand out for me — Foxseal, Canny Lass and, later, Redoute's Choice. However, Spartacus would have to be right up there with them. As a sprinter, he was like a powerful machine, plus he had incredible courage and determination whenever he raced. But when he wasn't racing, he had the sweetest, gentlest nature — there was something almost kindly about his disposition.

When he was a two-year-old I was going through an all-time low, trying to deal with Ricky's death. I felt dispirited, depressed even. My only moments of solace were the daily walks I shared with Spartacus each afternoon. Around the track at Epsom we'd stroll, enjoying the quiet and tranquillity. Every day we did our ten laps of the stabling area of the training track, and this gentle rhythm, the soft clip-clop of the horse's hoof steps the only sound breaking the early afternoon hush, seemed to restore me. It brought me peace and calm for the first time since Ricky's death — I couldn't have chosen a better therapy to repair my broken spirit if I had tried. I'd sometimes become so removed from myself on these walks that I'd lose all track of time. I'd turn to do an eleventh lap of the track — but if I wasn't keeping count of the laps, Spartacus always did — and he would give me a gentle nip on the shoulder. It was the only trouble he ever gave me, and even then, he was just reminding me to keep my mind on the job. If someone tells you horses can't count, don't believe them! They are creatures of habit and Spartacus knew exactly when it was time to go home.

As a two-year-old Spartacus was raw and still growing into his massive frame. His first race was in the Criterion, a listed race at Caulfield. He missed the start, ran wide and almost off the track, fought his rider all the way, and still managed to come third. I knew then that I had a good one on my hands.

August 1997 marked the beginning of a new racing season and the beginning of a new start for me. The preceding season had been my most dismal since becoming a full-time trainer — not a single city winner. Spartacus took his place in a run-of-the-mill handicap race at Caulfield, and won in a canter. Hooray, the drought was broken! It was obviously a huge relief, but I also felt the excitement of anticipation. It's a wonderful feeling to have your hands on a top horse again.

His next start was in a Group Three race, the C S Hayes Stakes, and he was barely troubled to win by almost two lengths. He stepped up another grade to contest the Group Two Chirnside Stakes, but raced greenly to finish fifth. Spartacus redeemed himself at his next outing, the Group Two A J Moir Stakes at Moonee Valley. Coming from a wide barrier he burst out of the gates and led all the way to win.

We continued to place Spartacus in the major sprints in the Victorian Spring Carnival, culminating in the Linlithgow Stakes where he came up against the star three-year-old sprinter of the season, Mahogany. I was eager to see how Spartacus would match up against this new champion, trained by Lee Freedman and owned by two of Australia's richest men, Lloyd Williams and my cousin and old sparring partner, Kerry Packer. Mahogany was to emerge victorious; Spartacus finished fifth, pulling up lame, and so we sent him for a spell to get him ready for the new year.

The Autumn Carnival actually begins in the middle of summer, with the weight-for-age Group Three Rubiton Stakes held in January at Caulfield. On board Spartacus that day was

Greg Childs, former leading jockey in Victoria who had just returned from a successful two-year stint riding in Hong Kong. Once again Spartacus used his blistering early acceleration to go straight to the lead, and when they reached the finish line he was still there, to pick up his third Group victory.

The Group 1 Australia Stakes (also known as the William Reid Stakes) was held on Australia Day at the tight Moonee Valley track. Spartacus was up against Mahogany again, Greg Childs once more on board. The last time I had won a Group One race was back in 1993, four years previously, when Kenny's Best Pal won the Australian Guineas. Coincidentally, Greg Childs was the winning jockey then and he, like me, hadn't had a Group One winner in Australia since. (Unlike me, however, he'd had about three or four over in Hong Kong).

Everyone thought Mahogany was a good thing — after all, he'd already won seven Group 1 races in his short career. Spartacus's only chance was to race to the front and hope he could hold off the others. Things went exactly to plan as Spartacus scorched them at the start, playing catch-me-if-you-can. Well, that's exactly what Mahogany decided to do. The champ looked like a Ferrari up against a bunch of family sedans as he cruised away from the pack and began to run down Spartacus. In the straight it was a two-horse race, Mahogany clearly the better. One moment Mahogany was four lengths behind, then it was two lengths, then it was one length, half a length. Then he was neck and neck with Spartacus, and the finish line still 150 metres away. The race was lost.

Then Spartacus surprised everyone, including myself. We all knew he was a brilliant sprinter, but that day he showed he was a gutsy street fighter as well. Mahogany was giving everything he could to bridge the narrow gap between them, but Spartacus refused to let Mahogany go past and held on to win. My first thought, oddly, was to check the race time. Spartacus had just smashed the Moonee Valley track record for the 1200 metres.

The Mahogany-Spartacus re-match came the next month, in the Lightning Stakes at Flemington. That summer had been a particularly hot one, and I was worried about giving Spartacus too much work in the lead-up to the Lightning, when we had a run of 100-degree days. Then in the days before the race, Melbourne got some rain, not large amounts, but enough to soften the Flemington track and take away the firmness that sprint machines like Spartacus love.

On the day of the race I checked Spartacus in the mounting yard. He would need to be in absolute tip-top shape to match Mahogany. Sadly, I could see that I'd been too easy on him and he was carrying a bit of weight. And so it proved. Spartacus was missing his customary dash and never felt comfortable on the soft ground, and finished third. His run was dismissed as a failure by the racing experts, however. I felt that, all things considered, third in a Group One race was still an admirable performance.

Next up was the Group 1 Oakleigh Plate, run over 1100 metres at Caulfield. Despite his 'failure' at Flemington, and despite the fact that he would need to equal the weight-carrying record for a three-year-old if he were to win, I felt supremely confident about his chances. For the Oakleigh Plate we had something else in our favour; Australia's then premier jockey, Darren Beadman, was on board.

The punters didn't seem to share my confidence — he opened in the betting markets as 3-1 favourite (Mahogany wasn't racing), but with no one wanting to back him, drifted out to 5-1. It always used to amaze me some of the prices you could get for Spartacus. I think his shortest price was 7-2. The day he won the C S Hayes Stakes in a canter he was 10-1, the A J Moir Stakes it was 8-1. I couldn't understand it; he either ran a track record or close to it, yet he was always good odds. Perhaps people didn't think I still had what it took as a trainer.

Spartacus liked to lead all the way, but he was up against another noted front-runner, the equal favourite Cangronde. Cangronde, from the New South Wales Central Coast, had been given the nickname 'the Bush Express' by the media and had arrived in Melbourne for the Autumn Carnival with big wraps on him. His record going into the Oakleigh Plate was 16 starts, 14 wins. One of the defeats had been at his last start, in the Lightning Stakes, where he had finished second to Mahogany and just ahead of Spartacus.

Cangronde tried to go hard from the start, but Beadman and Spartacus went harder. The two sped away from the field, the others floundering in their wake. By the 900-metre mark the pressure was beginning to tell, but only on Cangronde. As the Bush Express started to lose steam, Spartacus pressed an accelerator pedal and shot away from him. The other equal favourite, Rock You, tried to give chase, but Spartacus was too fast, too strong, and won by one and a quarter length. I had become accustomed to checking the race time after each Spartacus victory. The semaphore confirmed by suspicion — another track record broken.

Returning to the mounting yard, Beadman — always a bit of a showman — leapt off Spartacus à la Frankie Dettori. To the media gathered around him he compared Spartacus to two Olympians. 'He comes out of the blocks like Ben Johnson, then settles like Rob de Castella.' (This quote, I hasten to add, was before the Canadian sprinter's name had been forever tarnished for drug-cheating. Today, of course, you'd be serving defamation writs if someone compared your horse to a Ben Johnson or a Lance Armstrong).

The Oakleigh Plate was Spartacus' fifth win as a three-year-old. He had won five Group races, two of them Group One's and three of them weight-for-age, and accumulated almost $700,000 in prize money — a good return on my original $45,000 investment two years earlier. If only my real estate ventures had been as successful, I'd have been a billionaire by now!

Unfortunately, due to the nature of modern racing, Spartacus, though only three years old, was actually drawing closer to the end of his career rather than launching the start of one. A multiple Group-winning colt was hot property as a breeding prospect. After the Oakleigh Plate, I was fielding enquiries from all the top stud farms. The best offer was from Yallambee Stud, owned and run by Peter and Rick Woodard, and we sold a share in Spartacus to them.

Ironically, after all Spartacus' achievements, it was in our interests that he do as little racing as possible. He had already established his reputation, and every time he went to the starter's gate we ran the risk of eroding that reputation with an inglorious display. So Spartacus was given a lengthy spell to return in the spring as a four-year-old for one last campaign.

Spartacus came back in August. In the early weeks of the Spring season the most suitable races for him were up in Sydney. We took him up to race in the 1100 metre Missile Stakes at Rosehill, a Group Two event. Spartacus wasn't one hundred per cent fit, was in need of a run, and finished a narrow second to the reigning Golden Slipper winner (now a three-year-old), Guineas.

For his next start, we returned to home turf, Melbourne, and his favourite track, Moonee Valley. Moonee Valley is a small course with tight corners and many horses struggle on it, but not Spartacus. For some reason, he seemed to revel in careening around the turns, yet oddly for a powerhouse sprinter of his kind, he never raced as well at Flemington down its famous 1200 metre straight.

The Manikato Stakes, run over 1200 metres, is the first Group One event of the Spring season. The race is named after one of the greatest sprinters I had the pleasure of watching and a horse that Spartacus was sometimes compared to. Same massive build, and both had the prized ability to run at top speed yet stay relaxed. In the Manikato Stakes, Spartacus was up against Guineas again, as well as another champion three-year-old, Paint (the Blue Diamond winner and Golden Slipper runner up), as well as Poetic King, who had won the event the previous year. Spartacus had drawn an outside barrier, but I felt no concern, confident he would jump straight to the lead or be right up outside the leaders anyway.

Paint was the early front-runner and Spartacus, with Darren Beadman again on board, matched him for early pace, sitting on his outside all the way. Once they reached the straight the horses were hit with a gale-like head-on wind, and the younger horse began to tire. Spartacus just kept going and drew away. For a moment, the experienced Poetic King looked like he might challenge, but Beadman urged Spartacus on and the horse responded to hold on and win by a length and a quarter.

It was his third Group 1 success, and his seventh win from thirteen starts. Shortly after, the horse was crowned the 1996-97 Horse of the Year for his three-year-old season. This sudden change in fortunes was hard to take in. Less than eighteen months earlier I had been at my lowest ebb, both personally and professionally, and now I was the 50%-part owner and trainer of the best three year old horse in the land. It just goes to show the importance of persevering, even at the deepest and darkest point in the tunnel. You just never know if a small rise in the path lies a little ahead to reveal the light of success at the tunnel's end.

After Spartacus' triumph in the Manikato I faced a bit of a quandary. Looking at the racing program ahead for the rest of the Melbourne Spring carnival there were few suitable sprint races for him. I also had to hope the good weather Melbourne had been experiencing would continue to hold. But, as any Melbournian will tell you, it's always a risky proposition relying on favourable weather in our fair city.

Because of the dearth of top sprint races, I made the decision to try Spartacus over the longer distances. Darren Beadman agreed with me that he had the stamina and courage to do well over 1400 metres or even a mile. The most suitable race was the Group Two J J Liston Stakes over 1400 metres. Normally held at Sandown, that season it would be held at Caulfield, a track Spartacus had always done well at.

Although Spartacus had never raced further than 1200 metres, I didn't think the extra distance would trouble him too much. Also, he would be up against a relatively weak field — a mix of winter horses stepping up in class and stayers resuming for the Spring Carnival. He wasn't going to find an easier 1400 metre weight-for-age race to win. The weather forecast, however, was for showers, then rain, and possibly hail. My memory is we got all three, and that was the end of Spartacus' chances. He came third to Happy Star!

Poor weather dogged Spartacus for the rest of the spring. He came back in autumn 1998 for a couple more runs, but failed to add to his winning tally. By this time, co-owners Yallambee Stud believed that Spartacus would be more valuable on the stud farm rather than running around racetracks, and so in March his retirement was formally announced.

It's always sad when one of your good horses retires, knowing you'll never get the thrill of watching the horse race again. I was especially emotional when Spartacus finished. Of course, I was proud of his achievements and he single-handedly restored my training reputation. But more than that, it was his nature, so gentle and kind off the track, such a tenacious fighter on it that endeared him to me. When I was at my lowest point and my life seemed bleak and meaningless he brought me hope and excitement again. If Spartacus hadn't come along, I shudder to think how I might have ended up.

Not long after Spartacus' retirement, the Epsom training complex where I had my operations was closed down, with the land sold off to developers. That, too, was sad — Epsom was a great facility, well-located near the beach where I could take the horses swimming, one of my signature training methods. Some trainers had been at Epsom for generations, when it was a rural setting on the city boundaries. It was especially difficult for these old-stagers to uproot and start again somewhere else.

I was more fortunate in that I had arranged to take over stables at Caulfield. The only problem was travelling to the track every day from my house in Parkdale. It was less than twenty kilometres away, but not a journey I particularly cared to make at three o'clock every morning. I looked at the new stables at Caulfield, its ideal location adjacent to the track, and the idea occurred to me — why not build a house on top of the stables? Jesus was born in a stable, and I could live ten metres from one!

The Melbourne Racing Club, who owned Caulfield, agreed to my plan, and so I added living quarters above the stables at my own expense. The house was spacious, and I had a balcony that overlooked the track, from which I could stand and watch my horses do their track work. It was an ideal spot for entertaining owners and potential owners with a barbecue on race days. And, of course, it was bloody convenient. I lived there until I retired from training. I named the place... Spartacus Lodge.

* * *

If there was a Trainer's Prayer, it would go something like this: 'Lord, just give me one good horse. One good horse, and I will do the rest.' Because in racing that's all that's needed to get you going. People see you up on the winning dais, collecting another Group 1 trophy, and lo and behold, the phones start ringing again, people start telling you about the yearlings they have in the paddock that just need a good trainer.

Spartacus put my name in the paper again and almost immediately my fortunes took a turn for the better. But even in my wildest dreams I couldn't have possibly imagined what was in store for me.

In autumn 1998, around the time that Spartacus's retirement was announced, I was sitting at a table in the on-course restaurant at Flemington, The Terrace. At the table next to mine were a couple, a gentleman of South Asian appearance in his mid-fifties and a slightly younger woman. Neither of them were known to me, though I thought I might have seen them around the tracks previously. Unbeknown to me, a very attractive widow I had been seeing, who had a figure to die for, had befriended the Asian gentleman and his lady friend when I was not there.

We struck up a conversation about racing, and it was clear the two knew their stuff. They introduced themselves. The gentleman was Muzaffar Yaseen, a Sri Lankan businessman. He owned a successful clothing business — he is one of Sri Lanka's richest men — including operations in Australia. He was also a racehorse owner, and the woman with him, Iris O'Farrell, turned out to be Yaseen's racing manager in Australia.

Iris O'Farrell was running a TAB agency just near the MCG in East Melbourne when she met Yaseen in the early eighties. Yaseen was staying at the nearby Hilton Hotel, and the two struck up a friendship. In 1992 Yaseen called her for advice on buying a horse, and with that Iris became his bloodstock manager.

Yaseen had attained some notoriety in the racing industry when he was one of the biggest spenders at the Melbourne

Premier yearling sales for a short period from 1993 to 1995. This was at a time when the racing industry was still licking its wounds after the excesses of the eighties and buyers were short on the ground. Yaseen showed he was a canny businessman by picking up yearlings when they were relatively cheap. Unfortunately, none of his purchases had found much success on the racetrack.

At that Flemington luncheon, they made me an offer I couldn't refuse.

'We have a big Danehill colt in the paddock. Would you be interested in training him?' Yaseen asked.

The colt had been bred by Muzaffar Yaseen himself. One of those Premier Yearling purchases had been a filly by Canny Lad. He had paid $220,000 for it, the most expensive buy at that sale. Yaseen called the filly Shantha's Choice, Shantha being the name of a beautiful Indian girl who was very friendly with Yaseen and who had selected the Canny Lad filly at the Victorian Yearling Sale. It won on debut, a country maiden, raced one more time but that was it. Total career prize money would have been less than $10,000, so on face value a colossal waste of money. But Yaseen and O'Farrell had other plans for the horse, putting it on breeding duties on their property in Seymour, north of Melbourne. They booked her in with leading sire, Danehill, a so-called 'shuttle stallion' who served southern hemisphere mares in their breeding season, and then when the season was over, went off and impregnated northern hemisphere mares in Ireland.

Out of that mating between Danehill and Shantha's Choice, a colt was born. Yaseen wasn't exaggerating when he said the young horse was big. Although not yet two he had the size and girth of a three-year-old. He was impressive to look at, but what also impressed me the first time I saw him was his nature — he was intelligent and he was very relaxed. Big, smart, poised — I thought: This colt had the makings of a champion. The colt's name was Redoute's Choice.

Big means strength and power, highly desirable attributes in a two-year-old. Unfortunately, it also made them prone to shin-soreness — the condition afflicting young horses that was the bane of all trainers' existence. My view of shin-soreness was that it's a necessary evil that should be dealt with early on. Subject the shins to hard work from the start so they are strengthened and don't become a problem that disrupts the horse throughout its career. Redoute's Choice also had a pronounced gait; when he ran he hit the ground hard — again though good for power it was tough on his shins. Predictably enough his shins would flare up after each training run. The fact that he was a bit straight in front only exacerbated the problem.

Redoute's Choice had just turned two, the Spring Carnivals were about to begin. Last season's champions were preparing their returns, while a new batch of champions were about to emerge. Redoute's Choice, however, would have to remain behind in the paddock.

I had been singing the praises of their horse to Yaseen and Iris O'Farrell, so no doubt they were as disappointed as I was that the horse's debut would be delayed until the following autumn. But, as I told them, it was necessary to take these things slowly or risk doing permanent damage to the horse by rushing its preparation. I'm not sure all owners understand a trainer's caution, but it is because we have the horse's' best interests in mind.

December 1998 and Redoute's Choice had received virtually no race preparation at all, because of the tenderness of his shins. To say he was 'green' as far as racing smarts go would be an understatement. In early December, I brought him in from the spelling paddock to give him some track work. These training gallops are conducted in the early hours of the morning, under cover of darkness, so there was just myself and a couple of track riders to witness him in work. I had put him up against an older horse of mine, a city winner, and Redoute's Choice more than matched the other horse. I got him back to the stable, put ice on his shins, wordlessly praying that they wouldn't flare up after the run. My prayers weren't answered — perhaps no more than I deserved being a non-religious man. Anyway, it was back to the spelling paddocks for Redoute's Choice. I'd give him another three weeks to see how he went.

We brought him back just after Christmas and he continued to work very well. I remember one early morning run in the barriers for the first time, up against five other young horses. When the gates opened he just stood there for a moment, giving the others three or four lengths start. Then he took off, rounded them up after about 300 metres and eventually finished five lengths clear.

My initial goal for Redoute's Choice had been the Blue Diamond Stakes, the 1200 metre Group One event in late February run at his home track Caulfield. We entered him for the Blue Diamond Colts and Geldings Prelude that is held two weeks before the main event. However, it was no good — the shins were still too tender to run him. Yaseen was over in Sri Lanka, so I would communicate with him via fax through Iris O'Farrell. I sent off my latest report: 'I think we are going to have to bite the bullet and put him out for a spell. We can console ourselves with the knowledge we have a potential champion three-year-old.'

Both Yaseen and O'Farrell thought that we should give Redoute's Choice every opportunity to prove his fitness. Owners want to see their horses run, but I was cautious. I felt that if something was to go amiss and this horse, this precious jewel in my stable, went lame because of our impatience, I would never forgive myself. Try as I might, I couldn't convince myself it was in the horse's best interests to continue. I arranged for him to be spelled.

On the morning that he was due to leave the stable for the agistment paddock, I had one more squeeze of his shins. There was the slightest of improvements, so I decided to hold off spelling him for a few more days.

There was one more lead-up race available before the Blue Diamond Stakes, the listed Veuve Clicquot Stakes over 1100 metres the week before. Redoute's Choice's shins continued to improve, and I gave him a pre-dawn gallop a few days before the race, putting him up against the other top horse in my stable, Theatre. Theatre was being ridden by champion jockey Damien Oliver in preparation for the upcoming Group 1 Newmarket Handicap.

Theatre had a strong gallop but Redoute's Choice was even stronger. Oliver had never seen the young colt before and when he returned from the run to give me his report on Theatre, his first words instead were, 'What the hell was that?'

'That' was Redoute's Choice, and I felt almost gleeful. I felt even better when I saw how well the horse recovered from the run, with not a hint of shin-soreness. He was ready to go.

Despite never having raced before, Redoute's Choice opened at conservative odds of 6-1 with the bookies. That price quickly tumbled to 5-1, 4-1 before settling at 7-2. It's hard to keep a secret in the racing world — obviously the word was out that Redoute's Choice was a horse to look out for.

Jim Cassidy was on board Redoute's Choice, and he had to be at his best that day. Because of his shin problems, Redoute's Choice had been given virtually no track work, only swimming, to get him race ready. When the starting gates sprung open, Redoute's Choice missed the start and immediately fell behind the pace. Two-year-old races tend to be roughly run affairs, as the young horses with their lack of race experience run erratically and don't always do what their riders would like them to do. Cassidy had to steer Redoute's Choice through the field, a stuttered run as the colt received several checks on the way. At one point, he got hit with a heavy bump that slammed him into the running rail. But Redoute's Choice never let his head go down, kept on going, barging his way past the other horses, and eventually powered away from the field for a comfortable win. To win, he had to beat another very good two-year-old, Testa Rossa, who went on to win four Group 1 races.

It was a terrific performance by the horse, but much credit should also go to Jim Cassidy. I was keen for Jim to ride him again in the Blue Diamond Stakes; because of the horse's greenness he would need to have a top line jockey on board. Unfortunately, Jim had already committed to another horse in that race, so I was forced to look elsewhere.

Once it became known that I needed a jockey there was no shortage of candidates to choose from. The phone rang hot with jockeys pressing their claims. It felt good to be popular again!

One of those who called me up was Danny Nikolic. I knew Danny from when he was just a kid, a fourteen year old who used to sometimes skip school at the upmarket Catholic school De La Salle College to hang out at the Caulfield track a couple of suburbs away. He rode for me when he was an apprentice in the early nineties — he would have ridden dozens of winners for me at that time.

Controversy and Danny Nikolic have never been too far away from each other throughout his career. Despite his undeniable skills as a jockey he has always been a bit wayward and even in his early twenties trainers were starting to overlook him. A jockey's reputation is everything and once trainers started to steer clear of him he struggled to get rides. In 1998 he made the decision to move to Sydney, to start anew as it were. The fresh environment was clearly good for him as he quickly enjoyed success in the new city. All he needed was a big race win to cement his place in the top echelon of riders. He was so keen to ride Redoute's Choice in the Blue Diamond that he was willing to give up a full card of rides in Sydney that day. I knew what a good rider Nikolic was and so I told him the ride was his.

Even in those early days I felt Redoute's Choice would prove to be the best horse I've ever trained. But I certainly didn't go into the race over-confident. There was the problem with his shins. In the week between races, we nursed them in ice-buckets, and took him to the beach. He still raced greenly and so was prone to make mistakes in a race. He would also be up against another top two-year-old prospect called Testa Rossa, who had won the Magic Millions in impressive fashion. Redoute's Choice would be backing up after only a week's break, hardly the ideal preparation, and also would have to make history by winning the Blue Diamond at just his second start. Then the barrier draw was announced and Redoute's Choice drew the worst possible gate. And, if that weren't enough, he would also have to overcome the Rick Hore-Lacy Blue Diamond Curse.

Despite having some top two-year-olds in my time, I had yet to train a Blue Diamond Stakes winner. I had, however, had plenty of near misses. In 1990, I had Canny Lad in the event. Shane Dye was the jockey, and being a careful observer of racing patterns, he had noted the horses weren't coming from behind at Caulfield that day. He persuaded me to let him drive Canny Lad into a handy position off the lead. But, when the race was run, Canny Lad got boxed in and couldn't get a run, while the winner Mahaasin came from well back and around the outside, exactly where Canny Lad would have normally been. When he eventually got out he flew home and ran second, a certainty beaten. Of course, Canny Lad went on to win the Golden Slipper a month later.

The next year I had Diddy Do It, who was in great form going into the race, and had Jim Cassidy on board. Jim told me after the race that Diddy Do It was going beautifully, was just about to take off and make his winning run when the horse in front of him stumbled and fell, and Diddy Do It fell straight over the top of him. In 1992, I had Yachtie in the race. When they reached the home turn and Yachtie put down the accelerator and raced to the lead I thought, 'Yes! This time it's third time lucky!' Only to see the Bart Cummings-trained Riva Diva come from nowhere to grab him on the line.

Would fate intervene again in the race? I felt it was the only thing that would beat Redoute's Choice.

Punters weren't as confident as me. Redoute's Choice opened at 6-1 then drifted out to 8-1. All the money was on Testa Rossa, who started 2-1 favourite. As the horses waited in the starting gates I held my breath — would my horse blow the start again? The gates opened and Redoute's Choice made a clean start; and he needed to because the field flew out of the gates. The front-running Northeast Sheila sprinted away to a three lengths lead, with Testa Rossa in the box seat behind her. Danny Nikolic was doing a good job positioning Redoute's Choice from his wide barrier to a position closer to the inside.

With 200 metres to go the front-runner was beginning to tire and Testa Rossa took over. The favourite backers might have felt their money was safe, but Redoute's Choice began to give chase. Testa Rossa was starting to struggle, Redoute's Choice was getting stronger. He raced past the favourite to win by over two lengths.

It looked to have been a sensational run and when the winning time came up, it confirmed it — the second fastest in the history of the race. In fact, the record time by Hurricane Sky had been hand-timed because of a clock malfunction. In the days after Redoute's Choice's win people began to question the validity of

Hurricane Sky's time. Already Redoute's Choice was generating a kind of aura around him — longtime racing fans who had just witnessed his stunning Blue Diamond win found it hard to believe any two-year-old horse could have run faster.

After the Blue Diamond win the next obvious target was the $2.5 million Golden Slipper. The only problem was that, because of all the trouble we had getting Redoute's Choice to the track, we had never seriously entertained the prospect of running him in that race. So Redoute's Choice, who had just stamped himself as the best two-year-old in the land, wasn't even entered in the Golden Slipper. Which meant there was the small matter of a $100,000 late entry fee if he wanted to run.

Despite this hefty late fee, I don't think his owner Muzaffar Yaseen thought twice about coughing up the money. Although, as everyone knows, there are no certainties in racing, this was as close to a good thing as you could get. His main rival, Testa Rossa, who he had just easily disposed of, was heading for a spell, and the Sydney two-year-olds weren't exactly a vintage crop that year.

Although Redoute's Choice had recovered well from his Blue Diamond win, I took a cautious approach with his preparation and decided not to race him before the Slipper. No horse had ever won the Slipper at just his third start, but we already knew Redoute's Choice was no ordinary horse.

I planned to fly Redoute's Choice up to Sydney at the last possible moment. The horse had such a poised and self-assured manner that I held no fears that he might be spooked or off-put by a new environment. Besides, the longer we were in Sydney and away from our normal surroundings, the greater the chances of something going wrong. It was the same preparation I had successfully used with Canny Lad's successful Golden Slipper tilt.

Danny Nikolic's ride on Redoute's Choice in the Blue Diamond had been faultless, and obviously he was keen to go around again in the Slipper. What a great story it would have made — forced to leave Melbourne because he wasn't getting rides, and six months later he was in touching distance of one of the biggest prizes in Australian racing.

A great story, but the twist was that another jockey was also keen to get on board Redoute's Choice, the legendary Shane Dye.

Shane Dye is one of the best jockeys I've seen. And he had won a Golden Slipper for me before, on Canny Lad. His four Golden Slipper wins equal the record for winning Slipper rides, and if anyone knew what it takes to win the race, it was Shane Dye. I had to make the hard call, phoning Danny Nikolic up a couple of weeks before the race.

'Sorry Danny,' I told him. 'You did a good job for me in the Blue Diamond, but I'm going to use Shane in the Slipper.'

Danny was upset, understandably, but that's racing. We all love the romance of the track, the stories that pull on the heart-strings, but more often than not racing is a hard-nosed business where decisions are made from cold logic rather than sentiment. I have no qualms about dropping a jockey for someone I think might do a better job. I can think of plenty of times when a jockey has let me down, pulled out of a ride at the last minute because they received a better offer. That's just part of the business, everyone's looking after their own interests.

The Sydney-based Dye flew down to Melbourne a couple of times to ride Redoute's Choice in track work. We ran him the clockwise direction to get him used to the Sydney way of running. After his first ride on the horse, Dye came back with his assessment, 'Gee, he's lazy. Only does what he has to.'

'And that's why he's such a good colt,' I told Dye. 'Only does what he needs to.'

Shane Dye might have been underwhelmed by his track runs, but I could barely contain my growing excitement. The horse was showing no signs of shin soreness, his blood levels were perfect, he was eating right.

The barrier draw was held and I braced myself for bad news. Instead we got barrier four — I couldn't have drawn him better myself! Suddenly Redoute's Choice went from a 4-1 chance to a raging 6-4 favourite.

We flew up to Sydney with Redoute's Choice late on the Thursday night before the Slipper, arriving in Sydney before midnight and getting to his Rosehill stable around one o'clock in the morning. Plane trips can upset horses, but this flight was probably the smoothest I'd ever had. Seven hours later Redoute's Choice got his first look at the track as I walked him around it. The AJC Chief Steward, Ray Murrihy, approached me, accompanied by two veterinarians from the Thoroughbred Racing Board.

'Rick, we'd like to take a look at your horse if you don't mind. All these reports about his shins, we wouldn't want to have him run around tomorrow if he wasn't race fit.'

I shrugged my shoulders. Let them test him, they'll soon find there's nothing wrong. Instead of asking him to run on the track Murrihy and the vets asked us to take him out on the road and trot him on the bitumen. It was an unusual request, but again I had no problem with it. If they wanted to test his shins, then a run on a hard surface like a road would be the ideal test.

By this time a sizeable crowd had gathered. Most of them had come out to watch Redoute's Choice gallop and had followed us out on to the suburban street where Murrihy had chosen to run the shin test. Amongst the crowd I saw my old friend, Harry Barrett, Sydney's biggest bookie, who had become unofficial leader of the Redoute's Choice cheer squad. Harry's interest in the horse wasn't purely out of an appreciation for the colt's skills. About a year previously I had attended the wedding of Harry's daughter, had a bit to drink and, my tongue loosened by alcohol, had told Harry that I had the 1999 Golden Slipper winner on an agistment paddock just outside Melbourne.

Harry, of course, was keen to find out the horse's name, but I clammed up. A short while later Harry asked my wife Maria for a dance, and no doubt using all the charm he could muster had extracted the name from Maria. To be a successful bookmaker, information is everything — and Harry was a master of being better informed than anyone else.

He never told me how much he had riding on Redoute's Choice in the Golden Slipper or what price he had got. I remember telling him that I had managed to get 25-1 early on, and was looking at a payout of $250,000.

'Good for you, Rick, good for you,' Harry smiled. But I could see from the glint in his eye that he had done much better.

After Redoute's Choice's road test the vets gave him the all-clear. The horse seemed to have adjusted well to his new surroundings, just as I had anticipated he would. He found himself the centre of attention but appeared unfazed, as though the gaping crowds and the flash of cameras was all just par for the course.

In fact, everything was falling into place perfectly, everything was going to plan. And then the plan went horribly wrong!

CHAPTER 11

Saturday, 27 March 1999, Golden Slipper day, was shaping up to be one of the best days of my life. It's the trophy I've always coveted the most, even more than a Melbourne Cup win. And I wasn't going to get a better opportunity; Redoute's Choice only needed to keep out of trouble in the race and victory would certainly follow.

Despite it being well into the first month of autumn, Sydney was still sweltering through a hot, humid stretch. For a southerner like me it felt almost tropical. I went down early to the Randwick stables where Redoute's Choice was stabled, and greeted the security guard we had employed expressly to keep Redoute's Choice safe from foul play. The guard reported a dull, uneventful night — all good there.

I ordered another blood test of the horse, his third in two days. There had been a slight irregularity in his blood count the previous day, nothing too concerning, but on this day, nothing would be left to chance. The morning's blood count seemed okay. His temperature was 38 degrees, also normal. My stable vet declared the horse fit and ready to race.

Shane Dye arrived shortly after. He was full of high spirits, confident that in six hours' time he would extend the number of his Slipper wins to five. Perhaps we were tempting fate, but we joked about where we would go to celebrate that evening. At about 9:00 am I made my way back to the hotel.

I was feeling good, a marked contrast to my state of mind in the build-up to my first Slipper win with Canny Lad nine years previously. In those days, I fretted so much about everything that all the enjoyment of the big occasion was sapped out of me. Instead the worry made me sick, literally. My stomach was probably a minefield of ulcers, but worse were the headaches. I'd get a knot in the muscles at the back of my head that felt like a giant eagle digging its talons into me.

In recent years, however, I had learned to relax much more, and was determined to enjoy the day as much as possible. Although I was more relaxed, it was impossible to cure the nerves completely. In my hotel room, I felt lost for what to do. Actually, there was nothing to do but sit and twiddle my thumbs, or get up and pace the room. After a couple of hours of this I'd had enough. I decided to go down and give the horse a shampoo, so that he'd look the part come race-time.

A lot of trainers would get someone else to groom their horses, however, I've always been a very hands-on trainer. Plus it seemed a good way to kill some time. As it turned out, it was extremely fortunate that I did decide to do so.

Redoute's Choice was standing in the back of his box; what I saw sent an icy chill of dread down my spine. His ears were down, head bowed, looking listless. I called out to him and his ears pricked up.

'That's better,' I thought, but almost straight away the ears dropped again. Up closer I could see his eyes were dull, a little unfocused, and I knew for certain that something was not right.

Then I took his temperature, and it was up to 38.9 — a horse's temperature should be 38 or less. I could feel this overwhelming weight starting to press down on me; I just wanted to sit down somewhere, as though my legs wouldn't support me much longer.

Howeve, there was no time for this — I had to act quickly. I got on the phone to the Chief Steward, Ray Murrihy.

'Ray, it's Rick Hore-Lacy here. We've got a problem with Redoute's Choice.'

Murrihy heard the worry in my voice. 'I'll be there right away.'

The Chief Steward arrived with two TRB vets. I'd just taken the horse's temperature again — 39.1 degrees and rising. The first time I'd taken the temperature I knew the horse couldn't run that day, the Golden Slipper dream was over. But that second temperature reading was even worse — if we didn't stabilise the temperature immediately there was a strong chance Redoute's Choice would die.

The vets took only a moment to assess Redoute's Choice's condition, and gave him some antibiotics. The horse was then rushed to the veterinary hospital at Randwick so that he could be properly monitored and cared for. Meanwhile, Murrihy made the announcement that shocked thousands of racing fans. The Golden Slipper favourite had been scratched.

My immediate thought, and I'm sure the thought of a lot of others too, was that my horse had been nobbled. Redoute's Choice had been heavily backed throughout the lead-up to the race, and bookies faced an estimated $5 million payout if he won. Memories of Big Philou, sensationally scratched just before the start of a Melbourne Cup after crooks nobbled him, sprang to mind.

The vets were circumspect. They diagnosed travel sickness, a fairly common complaint for horses. When travelling horses have their heads up for hours on end — in the back of a trailer or in the hold of a plane — they can't clear their throats. Mucus builds up and infection can result.

Murrihy still had to investigate. The security guards confirmed that nobody had got near the horse who shouldn't have. Murrihy scrutinised the records that all trainers must keep of their horses' health. He looked at the previous day's blood tests, the blood count just outside normal range.

'Why didn't you alert us to this earlier?'

'I thought it might be just from the stress of the new surroundings. And the vet had given the all-clear.'

'You should have still told us.'

Stewards are a bit like cops, I guess, in that they have to be suspicious of everything. I was used to these grillings and, to be honest, I was more concerned about the horse's health than a mild tongue-lashing from the stewards. Once Murrihy had finished his questioning, I asked to be excused. I wanted to get to the hospital and check my horse.

The antibiotics had an immediate effect, and Redoute's Choice's temperature began to gradually drop. That night I didn't get a lot of sleep, fretting over the health of my horse. The next morning when we returned to the hospital the temperature was down to 38.3; by midday he could walk around and have a bit to eat. It was clear that travel sickness — a respiratory bug — was the culprit, not foul play.

I suppose that was the silver lining — the horse was making a good recovery when we could have easily lost him. It was lucky that I had gone down to the stables to give him a grooming. Otherwise we might have taken him to the track without noticing anything awry, attributing the bowed head and quiet manner to shyness from all the noise and commotion of a big race day. But if he had run in the Slipper, the stress and exertion under race conditions would surely have killed him.

I was in no mood, however, to count my blessings at that time. Instead I felt absolutely devastated. The owner, Muzaffar Yaseen was even more shattered than me. I had already experienced it on numerous occasions; the jolt of shock as racing pulls the carpet out from under you, leaves you sitting on your bum, a look of dumb disbelief on your face. But for Yaseen it was a new experience.

Even today, seventeen years on, the wound hasn't quite healed and I still flinch a little at the memory of an opportunity blown. Redoute's Choice was an absolute certainty that day. It was one of the weakest fields in Golden Slipper history; the eventual winner, Catbird, was a welter-class horse, I don't even think it won another race. Only one, a welter in Canberra!

Redoute's Choice made a quick recovery. Two days after the drama of race day he was right as rain. This was obviously a great relief, yet at the same time a little galling — as if reinforcing the cruel trick fate had played on us. Just two days after being hospitalised, Redoute's Choice was declared fit to travel again. This time we went home by road — possibly the longest Sydney to Melbourne road trip ever, stopping the car every couple of hours, letting the horse out for a stretch and a walk around.

Back in Melbourne he was sent off for a well-earned spell, to be readied for his three-year-old season. I was certain that the disappointment of the Golden Slipper would fade from memory once he showed the racing world what he was capable of in the spring.

* * *

The $200,000 Manikato Stakes, run over 1200 metres at Moonee Valley, is the first Group 1 race of the spring. The obstacles facing Redoute's Choice in that race were high. He would be facing weight-for-age horses — that is, the best of the best — at only his third start, on a track he had never raced at before. He would be up against probably the best sprinter in Australia at that time, Isca. Furthermore, Redoute's Choice, coming back from a spell, was not quite at peak condition, and had been drawn awkwardly in barrier eight. There was also the prospect of a wet track, and the horse had never raced on soft ground before.

I first offered the ride in the Manikato to Jim Cassidy a few weeks before the race. Jim had also been offered the choice ride on the hot favourite for the rich Sydney Magic Millions, which would run on the same day as the Manikato Stakes. But Jim showed his faith in my horse by electing to ride it instead. Having missed out on Redoute's Choice's Blue Diamond win because of other commitments he didn't want to miss out again.

The only problem was that under weight-for-age conditions Redoute's Choice had the light weight of 50.5 kilos, and Jim hadn't ridden at that weight since his apprentice days. I don't think the public quite appreciates what jockeys have to go through to get themselves down to a light weight. Some jockeys might literally not eat for three or four days. They spend hours in the sauna, sweating off any excess fat. I've even heard of jockeys putting on layers and layers of clothes, then sitting in the car with the heater on full blast. The physical toll that 'wasting,' as it's known, takes on some jockeys is frightening. They are constantly fatigued, experience dizzy spells and powerful mood swings — and then they're expected to control a 500-kilogram animal running at speeds of 60 kilometres per hour!

Isca was Redoute's biggest threat in the Manikato. Going into the race she had won her last five starts. She had been on course to take out Melbourne's unofficial Triple Crown of sprint races, winning the Lightning Stakes and Newmarket Handicap, and only missing out on the Oakleigh Plate due to injury.

My instructions to Cassidy before the race were simple. 'Ride him up with the leaders, and make them do the work. Our horse has got seven kilos less than the others, when he should have seven more! So get out there and make them chase you down the straight.'

Cassidy followed the instructions to a tee. He sat the horse just outside Isca to the home turn, then gave Redoute's Choice a flick of the whip. Redoute's Choice accelerated past the leader and cleared away from the pack to win by one and a half lengths.

The next race on Redoute's Choice's program was the Group 2 Ascot Vale Stakes. I had won the Ascot Vale the previous year with Theatre. As Redoute's Choice always easily beat Theatre on the training track I was again full of confidence about his chances. The only problem was that Melbourne's miserable late winter weather was only getting worse. Redoute's Choice had won the Manikato in soft conditions, but I didn't think he looked comfortable in the going. He was a naturally long strider which caused his hooves to skid on the greasy surface.

Redoute's Choice would be up against his old foe, Testa Rossa. While Redoute's Choice was getting all the plaudits and fanfare, Testa Rossa had started his autumn campaign up in Sydney, winning two Group races there. The Ascot Vale Stakes was billed as a match race between the two; the Herald Sun even ran a full-page feature on it and labelled the race 'The Showdown.'

Unfortunately, the rain continued to tumble down, and the match race never eventuated. Testa Rossa ran second, while my horse struggled all the way to finish a disappointing fourth. Of course, the conditions didn't suit; nevertheless, as I made my way down from the stands after the race, I felt a little shell-shocked. It was the first time he had tasted defeat and perhaps I had believed the horse was indestructible, capable of anything — I felt empty.

He would get another crack at Testa Rossa a couple of weeks later, this time on his home track of Caulfield in the Group 1 VicHealth Cup, previously known as the Sir Rupert Clarke Stakes, over 1400 metres. However, the wet weather continued and neither Redoute's Choice nor Testa Rossa had been given any favours by the handicapper. Then Redoute's Choice drew a wide barrier, gate sixteen, to make his task even harder.

Despite Cassidy's best efforts, Redoute's Choice was forced to race wide all the way. To put that in perspective, it's like asking the horse to race a longer distance than his opponents — they might as well have started him ten metres behind the others. And yet once he hit the Caulfield straight he flew home, trying desperately to reel in Testa Rossa, who had had the much easier run. The winning post arrived too soon and Testa Rossa had added another Group 1 victory to his list, while we had to settle for third and the hard luck story of the day.

The next race on his schedule, the Caulfield Guineas, is one of Australia's classic three-year-old races. Run over 1600 metres, the Group 1 race is particularly prized by breeders. Guineas winners of the mile distance have a proven reputation for going on to breed both sprinters and longer distance gallopers.

In the Caulfield Guineas, it would again be Redoute's Choice versus Testa Rossa, and once again the race was heavily promoted as a match race between the two. The two horses had raced each other three times and Testa Rossa had finished ahead twice. Nevertheless, bookmakers, judging that Redoute's Choice had been unlucky not to win the previous start and better suited over the longer distance, sent my horse out as favourite.

In the build-up to the race I began to feel a mounting pressure on me, the first time in years that I really began to experience the stress of training once again. Part of it was my own doing; I had built the horse up as a champion, yet it had been defeated in its past two starts. Another loss and people might start blaming the trainer! Perhaps the horse's owner, Muzaffar Yaseen, might even take the horse away from me. That's the nature of racing. It doesn't matter if it rains, or the horse draws an unfavourable barrier — you're the trainer and the buck stops with you. How many times had I seen the blank look on connections faces when I have patiently explained why their horse was beaten, knowing that they don't believe a word I'm saying?

I was also concerned about Redoute's Choice's still troublesome shins, and had again designed his preparation mainly around beach-work rather than gallops on the training track. Not everyone was enamoured with my reliance on beach-work, claiming it was a far from ideal preparation. Horses have long been taken to the beach, but mainly as a kind of warm-down exercise after track work. They'd stand in the therapeutic salt water nursing their aches and pains for a short while. But this wasn't what I was doing with my horses down at Mordialloc beach. With Redoute's Choice I would work him from a stormwater pipe at one end of the beach to another pipe almost two hundred metres away. He would stride through the water for one lap, until he was huffing and panting, steam rising off his coat. The return leg would be at a gentler pace. It was the equivalent of an athlete's interval work, and I'd repeat this three or four times so that he was working for 750 to 1000 metres, walking for 750 to 1000 metres — a pretty solid workout.

Despite the worry about the horse's shins, Redoute's Choice's preparation for the Guineas had been ideal. All we needed now was a good barrier draw and a dry track. And the gods, too, were benign — Redoute's Choice drew gate number one and the Melbourne skies stayed clear and sunny, beautiful spring weather.

As soon as the race began Jim Cassidy took immediate advantage of the inside draw and raced Redoute's Choice straight to the front. As they approached the turn Redoute's Choice held the lead, his immediate challenger, Align, was starting to struggle, but Testa Rossa was nicely placed just behind them.

They entered the straight and, suddenly, disaster struck. From the stands, it looked as if Redoute's Choice misjudged the turn, lost his bearings, almost drunkenly veering across the field, going sideways as the other horses straightened. Damien Oliver on Testa Rossa seized the moment and dashed his mount clear, while Jim Cassidy worked furiously to rebalance our horse. By the time Redoute's Choice had refocused, Testa Rossa had shot a length clear. It was obvious the race was lost — Testa Rossa was too good a horse to be run down from there.

As I watched in stunned disbelief it was like a dark cloud had blocked out the sun, the day suddenly turned chill and gloomy. All the hard work, all the preparation, had been for nothing. And after all my bold claims of what a champion Redoute's Choice was, the best horse I'd trained. Yet the facts were that he had raced Testa Rossa four times, and now was getting beaten by his smaller rival for the third consecutive time. There comes a time when the excuses have to be shelved — I had to admit that Testa Rossa was the better horse.

I began to make my way down the stairs of the Caulfield grandstand, a grim look on my face, steadying myself to face the inevitable criticism. And I'd be lying if I said that self-doubt hadn't entered my mind at that moment. Was I to blame for the horse's defeat, had I wilted under the pressure?

And then someone was grabbing me by the arm, directing my attention to the race still in progress. Redoute's Choice was chasing after Testa Rossa, gaining ground with every stride. The race had transformed into a two-horse battle down the straight, shades of Bonecrusher-Our Waverley Star in the '86 Cox Plate. Testa Rossa was fighting bravely, but Redoute's Choice was now like a machine that just kept going and going. And then the winning post was only metres away, the two were neck-and-neck, and despite the roar of 25,000 spectators I will forever remember racecaller Greg Miles' triumphant shout: 'Redoute's Choice lifts! And got up!'

I have never felt such emotion, such joy, as I did that moment. Even today, eighteen years on, I still can't find the words to describe the excitement, the adrenalin rush, the pure bliss that

that victory gave me. As I made my way through the crowd, well-wishers swarming around me (my back would be red from the backslaps that rained on me), I saw an arm push through the wall of people. Then Dean Lawson, Testa Rossa's trainer, with outstretched arm offered me his handshake.

'Well done, Rick, congratulations. We've been beaten by a champion.' and he even gave me a warm smile, absolute grace and good sportsmanship, because I knew the hurt he must have been feeling to have certain victory snatched away from him.

I wondered how Muzaffar Yaseen must have been feeling. At this time of year, the busiest time for his clothing business, he was unable to make the trip to Melbourne. Instead he was holed up in the Sri Lankan capital, Colombo. However, he had set up, at enormous expense, a satellite system so the race could be beamed live into his Colombo home. How thrilled he would have been to watch his horse win what people were already claiming to be one of the great races in living memory. That $200,000 investment in Shantha's Choice all those years ago was now proving to be a remarkably canny one. Unfortunately for Yaseen, his $50,000 investment in the satellite service was not so fruitful — as I was later to learn, the system crashed just moments before the race start and he had missed the whole thing!

Immediately after the race, Redoute's Choice was installed as favourite for the W S Cox Plate, Australia's premier race that always attracted an elite field of middle-distance runners. Only one three-year-old had won the Cox Plate in the previous fifteen years — that had been Octagonal in 1995, when he'd beaten Mahogany by the barest of margins. Plenty of three-year-olds had tried and failed: Our Maizcay, Stylish Century, Courtza, Tristanagh, Zabeel, Almurtajaz, Our Poetic Prince, Beau Zam, and my own Canny Lad. In fact, in the last ten years only two other three-year-olds had even run a place, Canny Lad one of them.

This time Jim Cassidy wouldn't be on board — it would have been physically impossible for him to get down to the 48.5 kilos Redoute's Choice was allotted to carry as a three-year-old. Instead I turned to Sydney jockey Chris Munce, who had won the Melbourne Cup the previous year. Munce said he could probably make 49.5 kilos.

'Not good enough.' was my terse reply. Redoute's Choice, despite his strength and physical maturity, would need every ounce of advantage if he were to beat the crack field of gallopers lining up to take him on. Munce's manager called back a couple of days later. Yes, Chris had promised to lose the extra kilo.

The field for the Cox Plate was, as always, an impressive one. Sky Heights had just won the Caulfield Cup, Tie the Knot and Intergaze were both multiple Group 1 winners, Testa Rossa would be there. The Cox Plate would also have its first internationally trained runner, Dermot Weld's Make No Mistake. But the biggest danger was the New Zealand mare Sunline, arguably the best mare in Australasia, even at that early stage of her career. (At that time, she had only two Group 1 wins — she was to go on and win a sensational thirteen Group 1's). Sunline was a great front-runner and many keen judges felt she would be exceedingly difficult to run down.

There were ominous signs in the lead-up to the race. On the Tuesday before the big race, Moonee Valley held its Cox Plate Breakfast with the Stars where four or five thousand hardy race fans turned up at the barbeque breakfast to get a chance to mingle with connections and watch the Cox Plate runners work out.

Redoute's Choice decided to treat his gallop as a stroll in the park, literally, and barely raised a sweat. His lacklustre display had my blood pressure soaring. Basically, he had just wasted a morning's work, throwing his tightly planned training regime out of schedule. Fortunately, I was able to find another galloper, a visiting

New Zealand horse, to run alongside him. We got permission from the Moonee Valley Racing Club to give him another run, and this time Redoute's Choice, with a training partner alongside him to get the competitive juices flowing, put in a much better gallop.

In the race itself Sunline, as expected, went straight to the lead and Munce had Redoute's Choice nicely positioned just behind her. With 600 metres to go I thought the Cox Plate was mine. Redoute's Choice with his lighter weight would be able to run the older mare down. But I underestimated Sunline; as they reached the turn Sunline suddenly surged away, and my horse couldn't go with her. Sunline seemed to get stronger and stronger down the straight and won by one and a half lengths. Although not as impressive as her famous seven lengths victory in the Cox Plate the following year, it was still a masterclass display. Redoute's Choice in contrast had failed to run the distance and ended up finishing fifth.

Not only were my hopes for a first-time Cox Plate dashed, but that run also meant the end of our ambitions for a Victoria Derby win. Clearly the horse had had enough this campaign and so we sent him off for a spell.

One month later, while Redoute's Choice recuperated in the spelling paddocks, Muzaffar Yaseen sold a half-share in the horse to one of the biggest names in Australian breeding, John Messara. Messara ran Arrowfield Stud in New South Wales' Hunter Valley. The stud had just lost the services of its most valuable stallion, Danehill (sire of Redoute's Choice), and Messara saw Redoute's Choice as the ideal replacement. Messara had always been an astute judge of stallion potential, and his decision to buy Redoute's Choice would turn out to be one of his most prescient purchases. He paid $5 million for his 50 per cent stake, which meant I now had in my care the most valuable horse in the history of Australasian racing.

With a new co-owner on board I felt the dynamics in the stable immediately change. Yaseen was very much a hands-off owner. Although I found him personable enough he was also somewhat aloof, with a reputation in both business and racing circles as being a bit of a recluse. He and his racing manager, Iris O'Farrell, certainly had opinions on what races they hoped to see Redoute's Choice contest, but overall, they allowed me to do my job and train the horse as I saw fit.

Messara was a different kind of owner. He had a live-wire personality who seemed to run on nervous energy. And even though he had bought Redoute's Choice for the colt's future stud career, that didn't mean he hadn't strong views on how Redoute's Choice's racing career should be managed.

I would have liked to have seen Redoute's Choice race as a four-year-old, but it was made clear to me that the upcoming Autumn Carnival would be his last campaign. Messara and I eventually decided to run him in five races, all of them Group One's, starting with the Australia Stakes at Moonee Valley on Australia Day. His preparation had an immediate set-back when he developed an abscess on his hoof. Although he could still run, we couldn't use the traditional nail-on horseshoes, instead putting glue-on shoes on him for the first time. We also decided to try him in blinkers, in the hope that would cure him of his tendency to race wide.

The Australia Stakes was to be run under lights for the first time — an innovation, incidentally, that I had put forward years earlier. Redoute's Choice was odds-on favourite, but he didn't take to either the glue-on shoes or the blinkers and finished a disappointing second to another emerging three-year-old, Miss Pennymoney. As trainer of Australia's first ten-million-dollar horse, I must admit that I began to feel the pressure after the surprise defeat. Messara too, was disappointed, but I reminded him that victory is never guaranteed in any race you enter, no matter how good your horse is.The next race on the schedule Messara and I had devised for him was the C F Orr Stakes, run at Caulfield over 1400 metres. The week before the race, Jim Cassidy got himself suspended for a couple of weeks, so a new rider had to be found. Messara wanted Darren Beadman, who had just returned to racing after a two-year retirement. Beadman, a deeply religious young man, had famously given up racing when he was at the peak of his career, Australia's number one jockey, to answer a call from God to become a church minister. But now, presumably, God had called him back to racing.

In the lead-up to the Orr Stakes I gave a lot of thought to riding tactics for Redoute's Choice. The blinkers would go, as would the glue-on shoes. I also wanted to try running the horse from further back in the field, rather than as one of the pace-makers. My instructions to Beadman as he saddled up were clear: allow the horse to drop back and let someone else lead.

When the barrier gates sprung open, Redoute's Choice missed the start slightly, which suited my tactics perfectly. But over the first couple of hundred metres it became clear that no one in the race wanted to lead, so the field was moving in a leisurely canter. Beadman then decided to ignore my instructions and took Redoute's Choice to the front and set the pace. For one-kilometre, Redoute's Choice raced alone out in front, but then in the straight Miss Pennymoney loomed up beside him and edged her head in front. At that stage, I was beginning to rehearse the spray I would give Beadman for ignoring my riding instructions. However, Redoute's Choice was up to the challenge thrown him by Miss Pennymoney, got his nose in front again and held her off over the last two hundred metres. It was his fourth Group One victory in just nine starts, and he had re-established his reputation as a champion. The win also made him my most successful horse in terms of number of Group 1 wins.

The Futurity Stakes would be Redoute's Choice's next challenge, where he would meet Testa Rossa for the first time that autumn. Jim Cassidy had served his suspension and was ready to resume his role as preferred rider for Redoute's Choice, and I could see no reason why he shouldn't. John Messara, however, was of a different mind. Now I don't know the details of what had happened between Messara and Cassidy, but it was clear that Messara wasn't the Pumper's biggest fan. He mounted a strong argument in favour of Beadman and, ultimately, what the owner says goes. Cassidy's partnership with Redoute's Choice would be no more.

The racing public were looking forward to the resumption of hostilities between Redoute's Choice and Testa Rossa. However, the Futurity Stakes turned out to be an anti-climax; Testa Rossa did his job with a good win, but Redoute's Choice finished third behind the winner and Miss Pennymoney. After the race he pulled up sore, the vet diagnosing a damaged shoulder.

Despite the loss, I still had in mind taking the horse to Sydney to run in the two big middle-distance races there, the Doncaster Handicap and the Epsom. I thought that as the distances got longer Redoute's Choice would really shine. But Messara didn't share my enthusiasm — his thinking was that with every loss Redoute's Choice's value as a stallion was being reduced.

Messara put the question to me bluntly. 'Can you guarantee that if we take him to Sydney he'll win?'

Well, of course, I couldn't guarantee that. He'd be running in the opposite direction for the first time, under handicap conditions, against big fields. We didn't know how well he'd travel and we didn't know how the shoulder would hold up.

'There are no guarantees in racing, John. You know that as well as anyone.'

'Exactly. So that's that then. We're retiring him.'

And that *was* that. Redoute's Choice finished a career that spanned just twelve and a half months with four Group 1 wins and almost $1.6 million in prize money. And with some better luck he would have doubled that amount. Six months later he was serving his first mare on Messara's Arrowfield Stud for a $30,000 stud fee, making him one of the most expensive sires in the world. But Messara had priced him well — he was soon topping the sire's charts in winners produced, and has been Australia's leading sire over the past decade.

I was disappointed to lose the horse of course — I would have loved to have seen him blossom into the champion middle-distance galloper I was sure he'd have become. However, I fully accepted John Messara's decision — there was no dispute between us there. The dispute with Messara, and several other leading breeders for that matter, was to come just a short time later.

* * *

One racing journalist in an article on me, called me a 'visionary.' I've copped a lot of criticism as a trainer, so I'll take the plaudits when they come too! But it's true that I did give a lot of thought to this great industry I was privileged to work in. There are always ways to make it greater and it would be myopic to believe it doesn't have its problems. And I've never been afraid to put forward those views, no matter how many boats of self-interest might get rocked.

I was one of the first to put forward the case for night racing far, Moonee Valley has been the only major track to embrace the concept, but with great success. I also called for the introduction of synthetic tracks, and lobbied long and hard for the establishment of a state-of-the-art training complex out at Cranbourne, to take the burden off the inner-city training establishments at Caulfield and Flemington.

As far back as the mid-eighties I was arguing that Australian racing needed a good dose of rationalisation if it were to prosper — specifically the closing down of many of the uneconomical country racetracks and the merging of the three racing clubs in Melbourne (the Victorian Racing Club, the Moonee Valley Racing Club and the Melbourne Racing Club) into a single, streamlined body. Both ideas required tough decisions by the racing authorities and government of the day and a few people would have their noses out of joint. Unfortunately, we are yet to get the right people in power who are courageous enough to make those hard decisions.

Proponents of small town racetracks will argue the romantic notion that country race meetings are a rich thread in the tapestry of Australian racing. The truth however is that they are an anachronism. Apart from the annual town cup day, these race meetings are attended by just a handful of diehard punters, and horse owners compete for meagre prize money that barely covers costs. Country racetracks should be consigned to the same dustbin of history that the old small-town movie houses find themselves in. They should be closed down and instead the number of meetings at metropolitan tracks (preferably on synthetic surfaces) should be increased. I would keep just a few of the major regional tracks like Geelong, Ballarat and Bendigo. However even these major regional centres are struggling. Last time I was at Ballarat I sat in the grandstand, and had the whole upper deck to myself. Perfect for quiet contemplation, a great spot for a spiritual retreat...but less than ideal for a race meeting!

The chances of a major rationalisation of country racing in my lifetime, however, are zero. Local politicians fight tooth and nail against any push to close them down, no doubt convinced they are properly representing the wishes of their electorate. I think they're only representing the handful of people employed by the local racetrack — apart from those jobs, racing brings no economic benefit to the community. The last thing racing needs in these tough economic times is financial waste, yet that's exactly what country racing is — and that wasted money could be better diverted to the bigger racing centres.

I've also been engaged in a decades-long running battle with the bookmaking industry and its cannibalisation of Tabcorp and the tote — again at the expense of Victorian racing. For years Victorian racing and the government-owned TAB had a mutually beneficial arrangement. The TAB had the monopoly on off-course betting, there was healthy competition at the track between bookies and the tote, and a healthy percentage of TAB profits were returned straight back to racing for prize money. When the TAB was privatised and became Tabcorp, a very favourable agreement was negotiated where racing would receive approximately 25% from Tabcorp's wagering revenue, as well as 25% of its revenue from gaming products.

The eighties and nineties, however, saw the emergence of a serious threat to Tabcorp's off-course monopoly. Corporate bookmakers lobbied long, hard and successfully, for the right to offer off-course phone betting. Initially these bookies would serve only the bigger punters with the government setting a high minimum bet that would deter most regular punters. But give a bookie an inch and it's only a matter of time before it becomes a mile; the minimum bet was progressively reduced so that soon everyone but the smallest punter could access the corporate bookies and their phone bets.

As Tabcorp began to lose market share, racing, too, began to suffer. Bookmakers were required to return some of their earnings to the racing clubs but it was only a fraction of the amount that the TAB gave back. As an example, one of the biggest bookmakers of the nineties, Anthony Doughty, had an annual turnover of millions of dollars. And each year he was giving back just $15,000 of those millions to racing — not even enough to cover the prize money for a maiden at Kyneton!

The threat to racing has become even greater with the rise of the 'super' betting agencies, some of them based offshore. Despite the huge profits these corporations make, they begrudgingly return just a pittance to racing. They are the proverbial parasites that feed off the racing industry but give little back in return.

The principal racing authority in Victoria, Racing Victoria Limited (RVL), compounded the problem when they decided to replace a tax on bookmakers' turnover with a profits tax. This was the brainchild of the then CEO of RVL, Rob Hines, a former boss at Jupiters Casino who had been a surprise appointment to head Victorian racing. The problem with a profits tax is that bookies are no different to most people — they like to minimise their tax by under-reporting profits. Unlike most people, however, bookies have far more profit-concealing avenues available to them. Some of the ridiculously low profits bookies were declaring would have been laughable if it hadn't been bleeding Victorian racing dry.

I lobbied politicians and wrote letters to the newspapers on this issue. Not all those letters were published however. In fact, RVL 'suggested' to the newspapers that they discontinue publishing my views, and the newspapers obliged. So much for freedom of speech, eh!

In 2012 the racing authorities finally reversed the decision and restored a turnover tax. By that time other trainers had joined me in my protest. Some, including Peter Moody, had threatened to abandon Victorian racing altogether and move interstate. Despite the authority's backdown the damage had been done. Victoria had always led the country in racing prize money, thereby attracting the better horses. But while Victoria laboured under a profits tax, New South Wales — which instead had a turnover tax — overtook us to become the most lucrative place to race your horses.

The profits tax was arguably the single biggest detriment to Victorian racing that I've seen in my 40-odd years in the business. And the architect of this folly, Rob Hines, at the end of his controversial reign then ended up in a highly-paid role as head media consultant for RVL. Someone needs to sit down and explain to me how these excessively paid CEOs can oversee disastrous investments, financial meltdowns and incompetent decision-making, then exit with their golden parachute and land in some other excessively paid position as if nothing had happened!

* * *

My biggest off-course battle, however, was with another powerful sector of the industry, the breeders and bloodstock agents. In early 2000, I purchased a yearling at one of the Sydney Yearling Sales for the not inconsiderable sum of $200,000. But when it came time to break the horse in, the breaker was perplexed.

'It feels like it has a flat tyre.' he told me when he provided his first report. 'It's just not right.'

The vets couldn't find anything wrong with it apart from some back pain, which we had a chiropractor treat. I gave the horse a gentle gallop; the right hind fetlock blew up and the horse went lame. When we x-rayed the horse, we discovered it had an OCD lesion in the fetlock, which it had developed as a foal. (An OCD is a malformation of the osteochondral joint in a horse's joint).

The horse was unlikely to ever be able to race, so naturally I wanted to return the horse and get my money back. I contacted the stud who prepared the sale.

'Oh, it's got nothing to do with us. You'll need to chase it up with the breeder,' was the hand-ball response.

The breeder, Gary Chittick, a New Zealander, flatly refused to cancel the sale, and I had no legal recourse. After all, the sales catalogue sets it out in no uncertain terms: the purchaser buys the yearling with 'all faults.' It may have been the policy, but that clearly doesn't make it right. Can you imagine, say, a department store trying to get away with that? Imagine buying an expensive home stereo system, getting it home and taking it out of the box, only to find it doesn't play, and then the department store refusing to take it back! At a yearling sale there was no warranty, no guarantee that the yearlings were without medical issues that might prevent them from doing what they were purchased to do (i.e race) and no return policy...basically 'caveat emptor,' I had done my dough.

I was absolutely furious, livid with anger. I was in no position financially to calmly watch $200,000 flush down the proverbial toilet! What made me even angrier was that the colt I had bought had originally been put up for sale in New Zealand, but then withdrawn before the sales took place. It doesn't take a great deal of imagination to surmise that the breeder knew full well that the colt was unsound, but had decided to then offload it on some unsuspecting buyer/sucker at the Australian sales.

This wasn't an isolated incident either. At the January sales in 2002, I purchased a $100,000 yearling. We got it home and couldn't even put it on the treadmill. An x-ray showed it had a broken sesamoid. Soon after I attended the Magic Million Sales. Emirates Park, the racing operations set up by Dubai businessman Nasser Lootah, had commissioned me to look for suitable yearlings to purchase on their behalf. I recommended an Octagonal colt and Emirates Park paid $400,000 for it. But, again, when we broke in the horse there was clearly something seriously wrong with it. The colt could barely break into a gallop and x-rays revealed a large cyst on the stifle that would need to be surgically removed. Even then the likelihood was that the colt would never be sound enough to race. Emirates Park tried to return the colt to the vendor, Ramsey Pastoral Company, but they, too, were refused their money back.

I knew that other trainers had had issues with yearling purchases, and when I asked a leading vet he told me his research on OCDs in young horses showed that around six to seven per cent of all foals develop them. Though most OCDs either disappear or can be successfully removed, there were still a large number of yearlings who become effectively useless as racehorses.

The problem of unsound yearlings being sold to unsuspecting buyers could be solved with the introduction of x-raying of joints pre-sale. These x-rays would then be made available to prospective buyers — as was the practice already in place in many other countries. Although I knew it was going to cause an outcry in the breeding industry, I decided to take a stand on the matter. In May 2001, I wrote a long letter to The Australian newspaper outlining my bad experiences and my proposed solution.

The letter created an uproar from breeders, stud-owners and auction houses, who all vehemently opposed my proposal for pre-sale x-raying. And why wouldn't they? X-raying would be an additional cost (though I had proposed that it be paid for by a small levy on the purchase price), and it would also mean that they would sell less yearlings.

John Messara, for whom I had recently been trainer with Redoute's Choice, was one of the loudest critics. Messara said it would 'create a hornet's nest.' And I agreed. My question was, who should buy the protective clothing, the breeder or the purchaser?

Reg Inglis, who had only a few years earlier bailed me out of financial difficulties with a generous line of credit, instantly became a sworn enemy. I will never forget a confrontation with him at the Sydney Easter Sales immediately after the publication of my letter. Inglis, who was an imposing man in both manner and physique — he was over six feet tall and solidly built — got me up against the wall and bellowed in my face, 'No x-rays!' And then, as if I hadn't heard the first time, he repeated it, slowly and more loudly. 'NO…x-rays!' jabbing his finger in my chest for emphasis. For a moment, there I thought I was about to experience some physical harm. Thankfully though he regained control of his temper and stormed off.

The reaction as a result of my letter wasn't just on the breeders' side. At those Easter Sales, literally dozens of buyers were x-raying their yearlings straight after purchase, and trying to return their purchases when the x-rays revealed problems. In most cases the vendors refused. However, and this was something that further angered me, that all depended on how big a customer the buyer was.

The Hong Kong Jockey Club, which overseas horse-racing in Hong Kong, were traditionally big-spenders at our yearling sales. With no significant breeding industry in Hong Kong, they used the Australasian sales as a substantial source of racing stock. When they announced in 2001 that they would boycott future sales if they weren't allowed to x-ray pre-sales, the breeders — frightened of losing a major client — acquiesced to the Hong Kong buyers' demands. Clearly there was going to be one policy for the big end of town, and another for the battlers.

That letter to The Australian newspaper had made me a lot of powerful enemies in the racing industry, but I refused to back down. I followed up with more letters to the newspapers, in particular pointing out the injustice of bigger spenders getting more favourable treatment. I had never been one for media attention, but now I was actively courting them, voicing my concerns in every media interview. I was determined not to let this issue go away. Privately I received letters of support from other owners and trainers, plenty of words of encouragement, though tellingly no other trainer was prepared to publicly support my stand. I was the lone cry in the wilderness it seemed.

Eventually, however, the breeders had to cave in. I had advice from highly regarded lawyers that in a court of law if it was proven that a yearling had been sold with a pre-existing condition the court would almost certainly find in favour of the purchaser. Despite vendors claims to the contrary, purchasers were protected under the Commonwealth Trade Practices Act and sections of each State and Territory's Fair-Trading Acts.

The Inglis Premier Yearling sales at Easter in 2002 were to prove to be the watershed moment in the whole x-ray debate. The hornet's nest that John Messara so feared had been well and truly stirred! The sales descended into farce. Some buyers announced they would join the Hong Kong Jockey Club's boycott. Other buyers were busy negotiating private arrangements with sellers that would allow them to return any yearlings where post-sale x-rays revealed faults. This got Reg Inglis's temper boiling again; he was running around everywhere as if the sky had fallen in, threatening vendors with expulsion from the sales if they provided x-rays to buyers. And apparently the x-ray machines at Randwick almost went into meltdown while the sales were on; buyer after buyer wanted to get x-rays as a kind of insurance policy.

There was uproar when the second highest priced yearling at that sale, a $1.4 million Danehill colt bought by billionaire owner Eduardo Cojuangco, was returned to the vendor when x-rays revealed problems. In total, about 10% of the yearlings were returned after x-rays unearthed faults.

The industry needed to sort out the issue as soon as possible as the whole sales process had turned into a chaotic, unworkable mess. Not long after, reason finally prevailed and x-rays were routinely made available to would-be purchasers and pre-sales.

I had won a major victory, not just for myself, but for all owners and trainers. With victory, however, there can come a cost. For a long time, I was persona non-grata with the breeding industry who, individually and collectively, were some of the most powerful men in racing. There were plenty of uncomfortable moments in the years that followed — I'd show up at auction sales and immediately feel like a leper. I'd get glares and stony looks, vendors would turn and walk the other way when I approached. And I think it's safe to say that I wouldn't be getting a line of credit from Reg Inglis again for a long time.

CHAPTER 12

After Redoute's Choice was retired to stud I didn't have to wait long until I had another potential champion in my care. I had picked up a striking grey colt by Secret Savings at the Magic Millions sales at the start of 2000. Secret Savings was a first season sire, an unknown quantity, but that has never been a concern for me. He was a US horse that enjoyed some racing success there in the mid-1990s and had then been brought to Australia by Gai Waterhouse. The horse raced just four times on Australian soil, but won three of those races including the Doncaster Handicap.

What struck me most about this grey yearling as he paraded about the Magic Millions sales ring was his walk. I just liked the way he moved, so nicely balanced. It's almost something intangible that we can sense when assessing yearlings. He also had a good head and shoulder and intelligent eyes. Sometimes assessing a yearling is a bit like judging a person from an initial meeting, and this colt struck me as relaxed and sensible.

As the offspring of an unfettered first-season sire I expected the colt to go for around $40,000. That amount, however, almost doubled on the back of some confident bidding and I almost dropped out. My instincts though told me to take a gamble and, eventually, for $75,000 I got my horse. We named him Dash For Cash and he ended up being one of my favourite horses to train.

His two-year-old season was virtually doomed by shin

soreness. However, despite never being quite right and running with a good deal of discomfort, he won his first start, a two-year-old maiden at Sandown, by over three lengths. I had always seen him as a Golden Slipper prospect, but acceptances for the Slipper are determined by how much prize-money a horse has won. Obviously, a solitary win in a Sandown maiden wasn't going to cut it. As the Slipper loomed closer, the only way we could make the prize money threshold was to win the last remaining lead-up race to the Slipper, the Pago Pago Stakes in Sydney.

In the Pago Pago, Dash For Cash got into trouble early on, missed a couple of runs, then flew home at the end to be just beaten at the post. It was one of the best runs I'd seen by one of my horses, and even better considering the shin problems that he had to endure. Second place failed to get him into the Slipper, but with the level of discomfort he was in after the Pago Pago, we wouldn't have raced him in it anyway.

Dash For Cash returned as a three-year-old in the spring of 2001, a frustrating campaign of minor placings in a succession of group races. Frustrating in that he put in some great runs, but just couldn't break through for his next win.

2002 started much the same way as 2001 ended. I took him up to the Gold Coast for the Magic Millions Trophy against fellow three-year-olds over 1400 metres. It was a trying lead-up for my colt: an 18-hour road trip in high thirties temperatures would have sapped the strength out of most horses. The day of the race I remember as one of the hottest days I've ever had to suffer, the Queensland sub-tropical humidity only making it worse. And Dash For Cash was again bridesmaid — after a tough, honest effort he finished third to the previous year's Golden Slipper winner, Ha Ha, after being knocked down by a horse being ridden by D Oliver.

Then, suddenly, the drought of near misses broke. Dash For

Cash became unbeatable for the rest of the autumn season. He won the Group 3 Australia Day Vase at Caulfield over 1400 metres, then a fortnight later another Group 3 race, The VRC Debonair over 1400 metres at Flemington.

He next lined up in the Group 1 Australian Guineas over 1600 metres. On board was Scott Seamer, a thirty-three year-old jockey who in the space of a remarkable nine-month period had gone from journeyman jockey to winner of an amazing nine Group 1 winners. Seamer had been on board Dash For Cash's third place run that searing hot day on the Gold Coast at the start of the year. He thought the run had been a courageous one and was keen to ride the colt again. And I was keen for some of Seamer's Group1 winning success to rub off on me.

In the Guineas, Seamer immediately showed his magic touch was still working well. He gave Dash For Cash a beautiful run, positioning him just behind the leaders, then took the horse to the lead with 250 metres to go. His main rival, Royal Code, came flying home down the straight. The challenger's jockey, Glenn Boss, dropped his whip as they sped towards the finish line, but it wouldn't have made any difference (Boss himself later agreed that the dropped whip wasn't a factor in Royal Code's defeat). In any case, the record books now show that Dash For Cash won the 2002 Australian Guineas by just under a length.

I was hoping that Seamer would stay with the horse for his next race, the Group 1 Futurity Stakes at Flemington. Seamer instead opted to ride another horse, Barkada, so I gave the ride to Kerrin McEvoy. Some might have thought that Seamer's decision to switch rides was a strong tip for Barkada, but I've been in the game long enough to know that jockeys are notoriously poor judges when it comes to choosing mounts. I reckon you could write a good-sized, entertaining book just about those occasions when jockeys have made the wrong riding choice.

The Futurity is over 1400 metres, but I wasn't particularly concerned that Dash For Cash was dropping back in distance. The colt was training beautifully and thriving on the beach work we were giving him. The weather was my biggest concern: a constant drizzle in the lead-up to the race had left the Flemington surface soft. Any more rain and the track would become one for the mudlarks — something Dash For Cash was not.

In the run of the race McEvoy positioned Dash For Cash nicely behind the leaders, including Seamer on Barkada who had taken the front-running role. At the top of the straight McEvoy got the run he was looking for and challenged Barkada. The two fought it out down the straight before Barkada gave in and started to fall away. Seconds later Dash For Cash, too, had had enough, just as noted mud-runner Chattanooga came rushing home. But Dash For Cash got his second wind, just held off Chattanooga's lunge at the finish line to win by a short half-head. Meanwhile Scott Seamer added another chapter to that yet-to-be-written *I Chose the Wrong Horse to Ride* book — Barkada trailed off to finish fifth.

One of Dash For Cash's greatest races was to come the following spring in his four-year-old season. Typically for Dash For Cash that great run was not a famous victory, but yet another honourable defeat. Although Dash For Cash had shown he was one of the best sprinter-milers going around, I took a gamble and instead targeted him towards the Caulfield Cup. No one else could see his potential over 2400 metres; bookies were offering 100-1 on his winning the Cup, which I was happy to take with a couple of hundred dollars each-way.

The main lead-up race was the Turnbull Stakes, a weight-for-age event over 2000 metres. Dash For Cash, with Noel Callow riding this time, would be up against one of the best distance runners of the modern era, the Western Australian star, Northerly. Northerly's weight-for-age record was an imposing one, and he went into the race a short-priced favourite. Dash For Cash in contrast was a rank outsider. The punters didn't account for Dash For Cash's relaxed racing style (ideal for distance running) plus his sheer dogged courage and grit.

Dash For Cash was certainly looking relaxed throughout the race. As I watched on from the stand I remember turning to one of my staff and saying, 'He's going to give Northerly a real shake.'

Barely had I said those words and Dash For Cash lost a couple of lengths when he struck interference in the straight. Maybe I should keep my thoughts to myself next time and not jinx my runners. But Dash For Cash had shrugged off his set-back, put his head down and started chasing Northerly again. Closer and closer he drew to his superstar rival; Northerly, who had been cruising to victory, suddenly realised he had a fight on his hands. Dash For Cash pushed him all the way; by this time our group in the crowd had shouted themselves hoarse. Northerly, however, was to prove his champion status and prevail, winning by half a neck which, in a distance race, is about the barest of margins.

After that Turnbull Stakes run, Dash For Cash's Caulfield Cup odds tumbled to 10-1. A day before the big race Dash For Cash was in the wash-bay at Caulfield getting a hose down. A horse in the next bay leaned over and had a sniff of Dash For Cash's rump. Being a four-year-old stallion Dash For Cash didn't particularly take to that intrusion of his privacy, gave a squeal and lashed out with his hind legs, badly gashing one of them. We stitched him up and he ran in the Cup anyway, but was soundly beaten. I would have dearly loved to win the Caulfield Cup. It was my home track, there is the rich history of the race itself, and it is also one of the hardest races to win. Unfortunately, it was not to be that year; in fact, I'm still waiting for my first Caulfield Cup win.

Dash For Cash's final campaign was the Autumn Carnival of 2003. It was a memorable campaign, though for all the wrong reasons. His schedule comprised of four Group One events; the Australia Stakes at Moonee Valley in March, the Darley Stakes over 1500 metres at Rosehill, the $2.5 million Doncaster Handicap (1600 metres), and finishing with the All-Aged Stakes at Randwick, also over 1600 metres. You couldn't have chosen a tougher campaign, but I was supremely confident that my horse would pick up at least one victory.

In the Australia Stakes Dash For Cash got trapped in the field, then came rattling home down the short Valley straight to finish a close second to the John Hawkes-trained Yell. In the Darley Stakes, Dash For Cash was up against Yell's superstar stablemate, Lohnro. Danny Nikolic was on board Dash for Cash, and took him to the lead early on. He held on to that lead into the straight, with Lohnro sitting just behind him. With 600 metres to go Lohnro started to accelerate, Dash For Cash accelerated too, then suddenly Lohnro just went boom! And took off, breaking a couple of sectional records in the process. Lohnro won by two lengths, and we had to be content with second prize-money again.

In the Doncaster Handicap, Australia's most prestigious mile race, Dash For Cash would be up against Lohnro again, but this time meeting him three kilos better off in the weights. My plan was to let someone else lead this time, but a wide draw meant he had to again set the pace. For 1585 metres it looked like Dash for Cash would land the Doncaster, only for Grand Armee to inch ahead of him in the final stretch. I've rarely felt so frustrated after a race — we had finally licked the champion Lohnro despite running in a style that didn't suit, only to be pipped by another horse.

In the All Aged Stakes, we finally got an inside barrier draw. Dash For Cash got caught a little behind the front-runners but broke free to challenge the leader, the Gai Waterhouse-trained Arlington Road. Just as it looked like Dash For Cash would grab the lead, the winning post arrived... and Arlington Road had held on by a short half head. That made four Group 1 seconds in four starts this campaign — surely some kind of unwanted record!

It was a heart-wrenching end to a great career for Dash For Cash. However, despite the string of second-placings the courageous grey provided a lot of joy and thrills for myself and his co-owners, the majority of whom were first-time racehorse owners. Dash For Cash won just short of $2 million in prizemoney from his thirty starts and did a wonderful job. He won two Group One's, and finished runner-up a further four times. We sold him to the premier stud in Victoria, which at that time was called Collingrove Stud and was co-owned by David Hayes and members of the Sangster family.

* * *

When Dash For Cash departed the stables there then followed another prolonged drought in terms of big race wins. Rinky Dink was the notable exception. She won an Australasian Oaks at Morphetville in May 2004 in a gripping four-horse finish, in the process giving me my 18th Group One victory. She was probably the best filly I have trained after Canny Lass. Her breeder, Peter Liston, had offered her to five trainers who all knocked him back. Then I saw her when I was out visiting his stud and pointed her out. I bought her for $40,000 with Peter keeping a share in her. She went on to win about $600,000 in prize money.

Apart from Rinky Dink, winners were hard to come by. I was well down in the trainer's championship — I think by the 04-05 season I had dropped to fifteenth and was in danger of becoming yesterday's man. There's nothing more frustrating than those long barren streaks that trainers go through. The early morning rises, the hard work both in the stables and at the office that are the trainer's lot, all for zero reward. It's like jogging on the spot

— a lot of effort spent but getting nowhere. Frustration can make you do stupid things...and, unfortunately, I went and did two very stupid things.

I had had barren runs of luck with racing before, but this time felt different. I guess it started with Dash For Cash and his series of hard-luck stories. But was it all bad luck, I found myself wondering. Dash For Cash was as talented as any horse I've trained, and more than that, he was genuine, a courageous fighter who always gave his all. And yet there always seemed to be a horse or two who was just a little bit better. Were there some of those famed one-percenters that I wasn't performing while my rivals were, and this was costing me victories?

This nagging suspicion continued even after Dash For Cash had gone. It wasn't as if I had a team of duds and hacks. There were a few that looked like genuine stars in the making. And yet they kept getting beaten. Meanwhile other trainers went from success to success.

I was tearing my hair out in frustration as I tried different things to get us back to our winning ways. I experimented with feed, with the track work I was giving the horses. I abandoned some methods that I'd used for decades and introduced new ones. Blinkers went on, then off, I mucked around with riding tactics, all to no avail.

Then one morning I had my vet down at the stable to give the horses a thorough going over. Dr Gordon Duncan had been my vet for several years. Highly respected in his field he also served as stable vet for several other trainers at Caulfield. My frustration brimming over, I said to him, 'I'm getting desperate here, doc. I just can't train a winner. Tell me, are you doing anything for the other trainer that you're not doing for me?'

'Well Rick, a lot of them are drenching their horses.'

Drenching is the practice of using a stomach tube to clean the horse's insides with a bicarbonate solution. The bicarb can reduce the build-up of lactic acid in a horse, effectively giving it greater stamina. It's perfectly legal, but because it can improve a horse's performance, it isn't allowed to be done less than twenty-four hours before a race.

'You do the same then,' I instructed Duncan. 'We'll see if that makes a difference.'

I ordered drenching equipment and after it arrived I told Duncan to start drenching four of my horses currently in work. Two of them, Oddball and Polaire, would be running at Sandown that Saturday.

I hadn't drenched a horse in years and so must admit to some ignorance about the twenty-four-hour rule. The result was that Dr Duncan drenched Oddball and Polaire at around seven o'clock on the morning of the race. Before the race both horses went through the normal testing processes. Polaire's bicarb level was slightly above the prescribed level and he was able to take his place in the field (the stewards allow a small margin of leeway) and he finished second. However, Oddball's bicarb level was well over the limit; he was immediately scratched and myself and Dr Duncan were hauled before the stewards.

The matter then went before the Racing Appeals and Disciplinary Board which had only been introduced a few months earlier. We were the first to appear before the Board for a doping infraction. Explaining oneself to the stewards is nerve-racking enough, but going before the Board was almost like being on trial.

I had my own counsel to assist me, a lawyer called Tony Chay. Because I had studied law at university all those years ago, I considered myself if not an expert on the law, at least better informed than the average person. Tony Chay probably didn't appreciate my opinions during the hearing. At one point, after I had interjected once too often for his liking, he announced in a loud enough voice for all and sundry to hear, 'Would you like me to stand down, Rick, and you can take over?'

It was amusing because I've often felt like saying the exact same thing to interfering owners.

I put it down to the stress of the situation because I was in real danger of having my licence suspended, not to mention my good reputation dragged through the mud. Dr Duncan, too, was feeling the stress, initially telling the Board he had tubed the horses the evening before the race, before admitting it had happened on race day.

In the end, both Duncan and I were fortunate; each of us received a fine and a tongue-lashing. I was fined $13,000, which is a lot of money when you don't have any! I tried to negotiate a partial payment arrangement, but the Board seemed dubious regarding my claims of poverty.

'I seem to recall that you have a lifetime service nomination to Redoute's Choice, currently the most valuable stallion in Australia. But now you're telling us that you're broke?'

I felt a bit sheepish that my financial incompetence would get an airing in the court room. 'Actually, I had to sell that nomination a few years ago.'

'And what happened to the proceeds of the sale?'

I looked down at my feet and replied, 'I'm afraid it's all gone.'

Money, in fact, was a key component of the second big mistake I made in that period, or more accurately, spending money I didn't have and couldn't afford.

The Magic Million Yearling sales are held every January on the Gold Coast. In 2006, I had resolved not to spend any money at that year's sale. In the first instance, I thought the Magic Millions — which are massively promoted affairs — were also very expensive. The first big yearling sales of the year, they create an atmosphere that often results in buyers getting over-enthusiastic and paying too much. And in the second instance, I had no money to spend.

Nevertheless, I thought I'd travel up to the Gold Coast around that time for a holiday. I might stick my head in — it's always a good idea to keep abreast of the current market — but I would mainly be spending my time on a deck-chair at the side of the hotel swimming pool, enjoying the sunshine.

That was my first error of judgement. The second was to take a call from one of the Magic Millions sales staff. I'm probably the greatest gift a salesman can receive. Even in my immediate post-university days when I was mismanaging the family farm down in Tasmania, I was in the black book of every agricultural equipment sales representative in the state, a reliable sucker for all the latest farming gadgets and tools. I mistakenly believed that if a new machine could plough a paddock in one day, instead of three, it was better to buy the new machine then continue using the old one.

'Rick, haven't seen your face in the crowds. We're missing you,' the sales rep said, oozing charm. 'Did you decide to stay down in Melbourne?'

'Actually, I am up here, but purely for holiday-making purposes. I was due for some rest and relaxation. So I won't be a buyer this year.'

'We've got some really nice yearlings this year. Probably the best line-up in terms of quality that I can remember. Some beautiful looking animals on parade...'

And so on, I'm sure you get the drift. I cut the call short, thanking the salesman for keeping me in mind and told him I had to get back to my sunbathing.

I lay in the sun thinking, daydreaming really. Then started daydreaming about the next great racehorse that would come my way. Maybe it's just up the road, waiting to go under the hammer at the Magic Millions sales.

I quickly reminded myself that I had no money to spend. Then I was daydreaming again, but this time it was a hard-luck daydream. In it I watched a champion colt go around, winning black-type race after black-type race. It had been picked up at a bargain price at the Magic Millions by one of my rival trainers, while I was lazing around by a hotel pool just a few minutes down the road. Every trainer and owner has a story about the champion that got away; twenty-five years on and I'm still stewing over being Rubiton's underbidder. It's a horrible feeling, and before I knew it I was out of the deckchair, grabbing some clothes and heading off to the Sales.

Two days later the Sales were over and I had spent around $1 million. I felt sick to the stomach the next day, waking up and realising what I had done. It was like a bout of madness that takes me over. Needless to say, none of those purchases turned out to be champions, in fact, most of them I couldn't on-sell, and I was facing financial ruin again.

* * *

After that financial disaster, I was forced to be much more conservative in my horse-dealing. 'Forced' being the operative word, as the major yearling sales companies began refusing en masse to give me credit. And I didn't blame them — I wouldn't have given me credit if I were in their shoes. After all, I had to be one of Australian racing's best-known brokes at the time.

Without good horses, my Group-winning drought stretched on and on. By the start of 2009 the drought was approaching five years and I had to do something quick. I headed up to the Gold Coast Magic Millions sales and made some discrete financial inquiries.

'Any chance of getting a line of credit — '

'No, Rick, none' was the swift response. 'If you bid, you'll only embarrass us and yourself. Pay off your purchases from previous years, and we might let you.'

I would have loved to pay off my debts, but it just wasn't possible at that moment. To do so, I needed good horses bringing in the prize money. But — classic Catch 22 situation — with no money to spend I wasn't likely to get my hands on a good horse.

But I could still look, even if I didn't buy. I think it was the second day of the sales, and this chestnut colt was brought out and it was a magnificent specimen of a racehorse. If it had had two legs, long blond hair and breasts, you'd be holding up an 11 out of 10 sign! Instantly I felt the madness take over me; I was convinced that this colt could be The One, the next champion in my stable.

The previous evening I had run into a friend of mine called Bill van Rooy. He was up on the Gold Coast on holiday. I had trained horses for him before and immediately phoned him up.

'Billy, I've just seen a great yearling at the Sales, a lovely looking colt. And I wonder if you wouldn't mind bidding on it.'

And Bill van Rooy, bless his heart, said, 'Sure Rick, no worries.' Billy came down to the Sales; I told him I thought the colt might go for $100,000, maybe even $120,000. Billy started bidding, the price got past $100,000. When the bidding price reached $120,000 he glanced around at me. What to do? It's more than I wanted to pay but I was determined to get the colt. I nodded my head, 'Let's keep going.'

We eventually got it for $135,000. The broodmare was called Orong, which reminded me of a nice young girl I had once dated who had had a flat in Orrong Road, Toorak. So I called the colt Toorak Toff.

Bill took a 60% stake in the horse, but that still left me $55,000 short. Fortunately, I was able to come up with another co-owner from what at that time seemed the most unlikely of places.

I had been estranged from my brother, Dyson, for a long time; in fact, we hadn't even spoken for thirty years. It's hard to explain why. We'd been very different boys growing up, and were constantly at each other's throats, fighting like tigers over the smallest things. Then my parents divorced, I stayed with Mum and Dyson went off with my father, and for three decades we lived completely separate lives.

Dyson had never been given the same opportunities that I — the eldest and mother's favourite — had been given. And I have no doubt he carried a resentment towards me for years. Yet he more than made up for the lack of opportunities, becoming the successful lawyer that I was meant to be. Dyson, too, had a public profile, the last Chairman of the hapless, doomed Fitzroy Football Club, and forever earning the wrath of diehard Lions fans when he presided over the relocation to Brisbane.

It wasn't until about twelve years ago that I finally got in touch with Dyson again. We will never be close-knit, but at least now in our ripe old years we're no longer in constant warfare with each other.

It was around the time that I bought Toorak Toff that Dyson was in the news again, this time as victor in a high-profile defamation case involving the former VFL star and anti-domestic violence campaigner, Phil Cleary. Cleary had made some insinuations about Dyson's handling of a case, Dyson took him to court for defamation, and the court ruled in Dyson's favour. More importantly they awarded him $600,000 in damages. Now Dyson would never be known for his extravagant lifestyle, so when I read about the pay-out in the newspapers, I remember thinking, 'What on earth is he going to do with all that money?'

And so I offered to help him out of his dilemma by offering him a share in Toorak Toff. And that's how my estranged brother came to be on my owners' books, not just with Toorak Toff but a couple of other horses as well.

I never really saw Toorak Toff as a two-year-old type, yet the first time we raced him he was an impressive winner. It's always the sign of a handy horse when they win easily on debut.

I then took him to Adelaide for the Magic Millions Stakes there. He again won comfortably, and the $165,000 prize money immediately put all the owners ahead on their original investment. Still in Adelaide, he won a Group Three race, The Jantz, before we took him to Sydney. I had set him for the Group One AJC Sires Produce Stakes, run over 1400 metres at Randwick in April. It had been six long years since my last Group 1 success, but I went into the race feeling confident. I felt even more confident as they came down the Randwick straight, with jockey Blake Shinn nicely placed to make a winning run.

In racing, timing is everything, and perhaps the timing was a little bit out when Shinn dashed Toorak Toff to the lead 200 metres from the winning post. If it had been a race over 1200 metres it would have been the perfectly timed ride. As it was Toorak Toff wasn't able to hang on after that surge and was swamped on the line by three other horses to finish fourth. Unlike some irate punters — Toorak Toff had been the subject of a big betting plunge — I didn't blame Shinn at all. I had always considered Toorak Toff a miler so it was reasonable to expect him to be able to run out those final two hundred metres.

Toorak Toff returned in Spring 2010. With Damien Oliver on board, he stunned everyone when he came from last to beat a crack field of sprinters in the Vain Stakes at Caulfield over 1100 metres. His next start was in Sydney, in the Golden Rose at Rosehill over 1400 metres. Prize money: one million dollars. It was the first time I'd been back to Rosehill since that ill-fated day when Redoute's Choice was scratched on the morning of the Golden Slipper.

Toorak Toff had been plagued by wide barrier draws throughout his short career, and the Golden Rose was no different. In the Golden Rose, he was forced to travel wide the whole way, although one advantage of this was that he avoided a lot of the interference other horses suffered in the roughly run race. Oliver was again on board, and he had to go early in the straight, but the leader, the Gai Waterhouse-trained Squamosa, was beginning to tire and racing erratically. That Rosehill straight seemed to stretch an eternity, which was just as well because Toorak Toff reached Squamosa almost on the line and got his head in front. And then the line reached Toorak Toff just before a fast-finishing Ilovethiscity could reel him in.

That win was my nineteenth Group 1 success. And it had been a bloody long wait, as I reminded the Rosehill crowd in my acceptance speech. Yet it wasn't my major target that Spring. The race I really wanted to win was the Caulfield Guineas.

First there was the Caulfield Guineas Prelude, over 1400 metres. Again, Toorak Toff drew a wide barrier, but went into the race an even-money favourite. The Prelude was not to be one of Damien Oliver's better rides; he got caught several horses wide for most of the running of the race. Then Oliver, perhaps remembering the Golden Rose run, took off way too early, rushing Toorak Toff to the lead at the turn. It left him easy pickings for the Peter Moody-trained Anacheeva storming home.

However, I had the utmost faith in Oliver who, despite his well-documented flaws, was arguably the most talented jockey going around at the time. Hindsight is a wonderful thing, but perhaps I was too trusting of the rogue jockey.

Although Toorak Toff was favourite for the Caulfield Guineas, bookies had him at 3-1, and there were at least half a dozen other good chances, including Ilovethiscity and Anacheeva. Toorak Toff drew barrier eight in the sixteen-horse field — not a disaster, but it did mean there were seven horses better drawn than him.

The morning of the Guineas started out as normal. Although

at my home track, in fact, literally in my backyard, I made my usual early morning start and gave some horses light track work. Toorak Toff looked in tip-top shape, was eating well, normal temperature and blood readings. And from then on, the morning and normality parted ways.

I got a call on my mobile. As I went to answer it I checked the call display, but no number was displayed.

'Rick Hore-Lacy,' I answered.

There was a voice I didn't recognise on the other end. He had just one message for me. 'Your horse is off.'

'Beg yours?'

'Your horse is off.'

'What do you mean?'

'Look, you don't know me, but I can tell you, your horse is off; he won't win today.'

'Who is this? Hello?' But the line had gone dead, the anonymous tipster had hung up.

A prank call? Someone trying to be funny? Possibly, but I wasn't taking any chances. Immediately I rang the other owners, then Chief Steward Terry Bailey to report the disturbing phone call.

Bailey took the threat seriously enough to send the vets to check Toorak Toff's health. But the vets could find nothing wrong with the horse, and Bailey made the decision to allow the horse to race.

By race start Toorak Toff had lost his race favouritism. Perhaps I hadn't been the only one to receive the anonymous phone call. As we approached race start I gave my riding instructions to Damien Oliver, keeping them simple.

'Try to get in to about one or two off the rails and keep the horse just off the pace. And don't go too early on him. The mile distance will suit, so just allow him to relax and save him for a strong finish.'

What happened next was one was one of the worst rides I've ever witnessed by a topline jockey. I've certainly seen a few momentary brain-fades from jockeys, careless mistakes that have cost a victory, but never such a sustained display of inept riding. If you knew nothing about Australian racing and had been watching that race, you would've thought, Oh, they've got some kid from the provincial circuit to ride, or some hack track work rider...not the number one jockey in Australia.

At they jumped, Toorak Toff's head got pulled slightly to the side, as if Oliver had given the rein a tug. It caused Toorak Toff to miss the start by a length. Then they got to the Caulfield Hill, an incline about five furlongs from home. If there's one thing you never do as a rider, it is try to make ground up the Hill, because it takes all the steam out of the horse. Oliver had a beautiful sit, but then suddenly decided to pull the horse to the outside and catch up with the leaders. From then on he was four wide all the way, except at the turn when he was about ten wide. Even then, Toorak Toff was going fine, still had victory in his grasp. However, Oliver decided to take him back to the inside again, where he hit the slower going, and that was his challenge snuffed out. The race was won by Peter Moody's Anacheeva, with Toorak Toff finishing out of the placings in fourth.

With the benefit of hindsight, I blame myself for Dash For Cash's defeat in 3YO Magic Millions and with Toorak Toff, I made the mistake of not 'slinging' Oliver for his winning ride on Toorak Toff in the million dollar Roses Stakes on Sydney. I was to pay dearly for it.

A few years later, in 2012, the Stewards partially caught up with Oliver when they gave him a year's suspension for having a $10,000 bet on another horse in a race in which he was riding. If someone were to ask me who is the best rider to have ridden in my forty years in the game, I would have answered without hesitation, Damien Oliver. There is a huge gap, however, between Oliver as a rider and Oliver as a man.

Normally after a race, trainer and jockey confer, a quick post-mortem on what went right or wrong. But I was absolutely livid with Oliver, I couldn't even trust myself to speak to him, instead I pointedly ignored him. I would leave that to the Stewards. Oliver, of course, had an explanation for every wrong-headed move he'd made in the race — the slow tempo didn't suit, the horse was pulling and wouldn't relax so I had to let him go, I was blocked for a run here, suffered a check there, took him wide where the going was better, blah blah blah. The Stewards listened, gave Oliver a stern warning about his riding 'misjudgements.' and that was the end of the matter.

The Caulfield Guineas is one of the handful of top races in Australia that are regarded as 'stallion-defining' events, a victory in which adds millions to the horse's value. One bloodstock agent said before the race that Toorak Toff's value was around $4 million, but if victorious he could be worth as much as $15 million. That's how much victory in the Caulfield Guineas was worth to the owners — $10 million. That's how much Damien Oliver cost us. And I wouldn't let him on one of my horses again if he were the last jockey on earth.

CHAPTER 13

After the Caulfield Guineas travesty, Toorak Toff was given a short spell, then returned to racing in December 2010 in a Flemington handicap. It was the beginning of a campaign that I hoped would climax with a victory in the Australian Guineas in the early autumn. Instead, the horse flopped badly in that first start back, finishing fifth. When he returned to scale he was in a lot of stress, breathing loudly and heavily. His condition failed to improve so I immediately brought top horse vet, Dr Alistair McLean in to have a look. The doc did a throat scope and diagnosed him as a 'roarer.' 'Roarers' suffer a blockage in the throat passage that disrupts their breathing, with heavy breathing noises ('roaring') the most obvious symptom.

We had two options: have him undergo surgery in which there was only a fifty per cent success rate, or retire him to stud. I conferred with the other owners and we agreed on the latter, and soon after I made the announcement of Toorak Toff's retirement, effective immediately.

I had told my co-owners that we could get as much as $10 million for Toorak Toff, but when the offers did come in, they were way under that. The best offer we received was just $3 million, which was almost insulting. Once we divvied up that money amongst the owners, and the taxman took his cut, my share would have been less than what I would normally spend on replacement yearlings at the upcoming sales. In other words, I would have no star horse *and* no money.

I got back on the phone, this time to Sydney veterinarian, Dr Jonathan Lumsden. Six months earlier, Lumsden had performed surgery to cure the 'roaring' of another champion three-year-old whose career had seemed prematurely over. After Lumsden's surgery, that horse, So You Think, returned for the spring campaign, seemingly better than ever, and continued the good form in Europe.

Toorak Toff went under the knife. There followed an anxious recovery period but Toorak Toff showed his typical resilience. In September 2011, he returned to racing in the Group 1 Sir Rupert Clarke Stakes at Caulfield. The horse's deeds the previous spring were now a distant memory in punters' minds, with Toorak Toff rated an 11-1 chance. I had another runner in the race, the eight-year-old but evergreen Pinnacles, an outsider at 25-1. The morning of the race I joked to my staff, 'It'd be funny if we quinellaed it! Imagine what that would pay!' But instead I had a conservative each-way bet on Toorak Toff.

Craig Williams was on board Toorak Toff and quickly got the horse in the box seat just tucked in behind the leaders. The Toff cruised to the front in the straight and never seemed troubled to win by one and a half lengths. The second placegetter was honest and hard-working, but just not in Toorak Toff's class — good ol' Pinnacles. The quinella incidentally paid 125-1!

The Sir Rupert Clarke was the last of Toorak Toff's wins. We retired him for a second time, with a racing record of 18 starts for six wins and just under $1.3 million in prize money.

Pinnacles' career was also about to come to an end, but not in the way we hoped he would go out. Pinnacles was no champion, but he was honest, gutsy and always gave 100 per cent. There was a time, however, when I thought he would end up being one of my biggest duds. I paid $100,000 for him at the Inglis Easter Sales of 2005, thinking I'd got a bargain. Having spent that out of my own pocket I then had problems finding someone who'd buy him. Pinnacles had flat feet that put off potential clients. Compounding this, the horse never showed much interest in racing.

I sent him off to the paddock and then more or less forgot about him, until I needed a new lead pony for track work. Pinnacles was given the task of leading off one of my proven runners in an early morning gallop. He led off alright; took off on his rider and the other horse couldn't catch him. It was then that I thought he might be worth trying again.

When I couldn't find a buyer for Pinnacles, my two daughters Kate and Emma bought part-shares in him, as did my brother-in-law, Maria's brother, Bill. So the horse became almost like a family pet.

Pinnacles' best run was in the Group 1 Doncaster Handicap in Sydney. Against the best milers in the country, Pinnacles was at rough odds of 60 to 1, but almost caused a boil over to finish third. He raced over sixty times, and when he won the Sale Cup at eight years old, it took his earnings to over $1 million. And being the biggest stakeholder in the horse, there were plenty of times he had eased my financial troubles.

The Sale Cup win earned him a spot in the $1 million Emirates Stakes at Flemington which takes place on the final day of the Melbourne Spring Carnival. It's a great day, big crowds, fashions in the field, one Group race after another, a real festive occasion. That year, 2011, I was enjoying myself, pleased to have ended the Carnival with a Group 1 win under my belt. But then the day went horribly wrong. During the running of the Emirates, Pinnacles got the staggers and pulled up lame, unable to finish. Watching from the grandstand, my concern suddenly ratcheted up several levels when the vet arrived, did a quick examination, then called for the screen. The screen, of course, to shield the crowd from the distress of watching a horse euthanised.

As soon as I saw that screen, I took off as fast as I could. I had been a handy sprinter in my Geelong Grammar days, and had probably never run as fast since then until that Emirates Stakes day. I must have looked an odd sight, this seventy-two year-old geezer in his suit and dress shoes, sprinting the wrong way down the Flemington straight!

I got to the screen literally just as they were about to shoot him. 'What the hell are you doing?' I shouted at the veterinarian.

Everyone there stopped, the doctor looked up with a slightly peeved expression. 'The horse has torn the ligaments away from his sesamoids. We're going to have to put him down.'

I'm not a veterinarian, but I knew this was hardly a life-threatening injury. Sure, he would never race again, but he could still enjoy a happy life after racing.

'Like hell you'll put him down,' I told the doctor. I stood there, hands on hips, trying to look as much like an irresistible force or immovable object as I could. The veterinarian saw the fierce defiance in my eyes, shrugged his shoulders, and raised himself with a heavy sigh from his crouched position beside Pinnacles.

'Suit yourself. He's your responsibility now,' the vet replied as he put the gun back in his medical bag.

'That's right, my responsibility.' There were many times when Pinnacles had looked after me with a well-timed win, and now I was going to look after him.

Pinnacles never did race again; the accident has left him with a slight but permanent limp. He now spends his days in a paddock near Pakenham, enjoying his retirement. He's still as frisky and cheeky as ever, and every time I go out to see him he even gives me a demonstration gallop, as if trying to convince me to let him race one more time again.

* * *

One of the best recommendations for a career in horse training is the healthy lifestyle it offers. Early to bed and early to rise, out in the fresh air all day. Apart from a period in the late 80s when I suffered badly from the tension and pressure that training at the top brings, I've enjoyed good health. I reckon I'd be a damn sight fitter than most men my age.

I've managed to avoid doctors and hospitals most of my life, apart from my annual check-up with the local family doctor. It was at one of those routine check-ups, in 2008, that the doctor greeted me with a slight frown.

'Rick, we've got all your blood tests in. Cholesterol levels are fine, no indication of diabetes. But the PSA test is showing an abnormally high reading.'

PSA? I had no idea what that was.

'The PSA test shows if there are any irregularities in your prostate. Specifically, a high reading can be an indicator of cancer in the prostate.'

When you hear the word 'cancer' in a doctor's office, the word hits you almost like a physical blow.

'You're telling me I have cancer?'

'Not necessarily. It could be just an irregularity. But there is a definite risk there, so I suggest we book you in with a urologist.'

I took the doctor's advice, went along to the urologist and another PSA test, which confirmed the first reading wasn't an anomaly. I had a biopsy performed where they scraped a sample of cells from my prostrate and sent them off to a lab, and returned a week or two later for the verdict.

I'm pretty good at reading faces, and the moment I met the eyes of the urologist I knew the news was grim.

'Well, Rick, the biopsy shows that there are a small number of cancer cells.' He took out a sheet of paper from his manila folder, with a diagram of what I assumed was the prostrate. Pointing to the diagram he told me, 'The cancer is fairly evenly spread with signs of here and here and here.'

There was a short silence between us.

'So…what happens now?'

'You've got two options. At the moment, the cancer levels are low, so you can just leave it — what we call the 'wait and see' approach. These levels might very well remain low. Many elderly men take this approach, the cancer doesn't spread, and when they do die it's of natural causes.' In other words, old men die with prostate cancer but not 'of it.'

'And the other option?' I asked.

The other option is that we remove the prostate completely, a radical prostatectomy. If we do that early enough, it means we get it before it can spread.'

'Well maybe that's the way to go.'

'There are, however, some possible side-effects from the surgery. Some men, after a prostatectomy, have ongoing problems with bladder control, perhaps ten per cent of men. Another possible consequence is impotence. After a prostatectomy, some men are no longer able to have an erection. In your age group, there's about a sixty to seventy per cent chance of impotency.'

I might have gulped at that point, and my complexion gone a couple of shades whiter, because he quickly added, 'We have found that sometimes drugs like Viagra can help, or erectile implants, or even surgery.'

But my mind was still wrestling with the idea of permanent

impotency. At that moment, it seemed even more distressing than the cancer itself.

'Well doctor, I'd be more inclined towards the wait and see approach. I don't particularly like the idea of never having sex again.'

'That's your choice, Rick. But let me put it this way: there aren't too many people having sex in the cemetery!'

I'd never really thought too deeply about my own mortality up until that point. Now, for the first time I was facing the reality that, eventually, inevitably, I was going to die...and possibly a lot sooner than I had originally planned! It's an unsettling experience, and maybe that explains what I did next, one of the biggest mistakes of my life.

* * *

The new girl had only been with us a short while, but I knew it wasn't going to work. She was young, about twenty years old, and this was her first time working as a stable-hand. Her inexperience was obvious, she seemed very uncertain of herself, but that wasn't what concerned me. A lot of people in a new job feel tentative and unsure, it's only natural.

With all my new employees, I stress the importance of being disciplined and conscientious of keeping the place clean. I also impress on them how important correct feeding is to the health and condition of my horses. In both areas, cleanliness and good feeding processes, there is absolutely no room for cutting corners.

And so I was ropeable when I discovered that some of the horses' feed had been contaminated. This young girl had been sweeping up the horse droppings, and for reasons only she could fathom, had mixed the droppings up with feed. It was either laziness or extreme carelessness or possibly both.

I immediately called her into my office and gave her a dressing down. And as I did I had this feeling that she hadn't really understood how much of a stuff-up she had made. I felt certain that his would just be the first of a series of careless oversights and mistakes. Nobody likes sacking an employee, but sometimes it seems like the only choice.

'I'm sorry, but I'm going to have to let you go.' Now the waterworks started, so I quickly added, 'I really think it's best for you, that you don't waste too much time pursuing a career that probably doesn't suit you.'

My words had no effect. She became even more distraught, started blubbering something unintelligible. I'm a softy at heart, and I don't like seeing a girl cry. To console her, I put my arm around her. I could feel her sobbing starting to subside as I held her close to me, her breathing now becoming more regular.

She had made a stupid mistake, but it was nothing compared to what I did next. I drew back a little, lifted her chin until she was looking in my eyes, then kissed her on the mouth.

The kiss lasted just a few seconds. She had opened her mouth, but quickly she drew back. I was suddenly drawn between two opposing but powerful forces. My mind was telling me that I had made a misjudgement, that I needed to back away now, but my dick was telling me the opposite. Not for the first time in my life the dick was starting to win this battle of wills.

During my hesitation, the girl had freed herself from my embrace and backed away. There were two things I could have then done. I could have apologised profusely and backed away. Or I could have made things worse. Unfortunately, I chose the latter. Seeing the girl's lack of romantic interest in me, I took another tack. Perhaps if I offered her money then she would have sex with me. Of course, now these thoughts seem ludicrous, even outrageous. But, unfortunately, that's how some men's minds behave when we're aroused — it makes us stupid. And there is no fool like an old fool!

The moment the words came out of my mouth, I could see the hurt look in her eyes as she backed even further away from me. There followed an awkward few moments, neither of us knowing what to do or say, and the girl made a hurried exit.

It wasn't until a few days later that I was hit with the ramifications of my rash moment of weakness. I received a visit from the police.

'We've received a complaint, from a girl who was working for you.'

I had a sinking feeling in my stomach. I knew I had been wrong, but I instantly feared that the girl might have exaggerated the incident out of spite. Fortunately, that wasn't the case, but I was still summoned to appear in court, accused of sexual harassment. My lawyer made no effort to defend me, asked no questions of my accuser. Perhaps he thought what I had done was indefensible, but I would have been better off representing myself.

The magistrate found me guilty, as I had pleaded, and I was ordered to pay $500 to charity and write a letter of apology to the girl and her parents. But if I thought that would be the end of the matter I was badly mistaken.

Apparently, the girl had joined the Australian Workers Union, which represents a number of occupations in the racing industry. The Union got into her ear that my sentence was plainly inadequate and she should try to have another shot at me. I had always thought that once a court had found you guilty and meted out its punishment that was that. But, apparently it seems that now, if the one bringing a charge doesn't like the original punishment, they can have another crack at it.

The second time the young woman and her Union took the matter to the Racing Appeals and Disciplinary Board. The RADB panel took a much harsher view of the matter. They declared my actions 'disgusting and reprehensible.' one panellist said they were 'grubby' — which made a great headline for the Herald Sun the next day. And this time I was fined $20,000.

I'm not going to use this book to defend my actions with the young woman, even if I don't believe the media or the courts told the full story. I have no doubt that the woman was upset, even distressed by my actions, so it would be unfair to offer new evidence in my defence when I've already had two forums in which to provide it. I guess I'm a bit of a dinosaur; I come from a generation of men who, if they were interested in a girl, made their interest clear. Sometimes it paid off and the girl showed her interest in return, and sometimes they told you to go jump. Taking you to court over it, though, is very much a modern development.

There are some people who still think I got off lightly, even the second time. The Australian Workers Union were one, some in the media as well. They think the incident cost me only $20,000, but how much lost business has it cost me? How many potential owners read about my trial and thought, 'That's hardly the sort of person we want training our horses?' Reputation counts for a lot in racing, and my reputation was badly tarnished.

Google is a great source for researching material — I've used it myself a few times while writing this book. But if you do a Google News search for newspaper articles on the trainer, Rick Hore-Lacy, the first few pages are almost entirely about the court case. That's my legacy now: not the trainer of Golden Slipper winner Canny Lad, or champion sire Redoute's Choice, or the person responsible for the pre-sale x-raying of yearlings. Once breeder John Messara had lauded me as 'the Stallion Maker.' Now I am better known under the Herald Sun's notorious headline, 'Grubby Trainer.' So I think I've paid quite a heavy price for that incident with the young woman, certainly a lot more than $20,000.

* * *

What also disappointed me about my actions was that is gave racing's opponents more ammunition to attack the industry. If Rick Hore-Lacy kissed a stable hand, well then, that must be just the tip of an iceberg of sexual harassment and worker exploitation (their logic, not mine). Racing does have its regulation handful of bad apples, just like any other industry you could think of, but it's also full of some of the most generous and honest people you could hope to meet.

That's why I get furious when outsiders take a swipe at the industry and the people in it. Just last year, a County Court judge named Gordon Lewis decided to have his fifteen minutes of fame and made various scandalous accusations about racing. Most ludicrous of all was his claim that 'criminal activity in the industry was rampant.'

What absolute bullshit! I've been a trainer for almost forty years and only once can I recall a request not to let a horse of mine run on its merits. That was over thirty years ago, the request came from one of my owners, and we quickly parted company after that. Forty years of training and that's the only time that sort of thing has happened.

For the record, I've also never been asked to launder money (Judge Lewis seemed to think that this was an everyday occurrence for horse trainers) or even suspect that I might have been used for that purpose. There were one or two times when I suspected a jockey might not have been doing his utmost to win. (Sadly, now that Racing Victoria has allowed Betfair and other corporate bookmakers to introduce so-called exotic betting, this is likely to happen more often). Sure, there are some trainers who bend the rules, trying to get an edge over the competition. Like I said, there are always a couple of bad apples. But Judge Lewis tried to make out that every race meeting was like a casting call for *Underbelly*, with a rogue's gallery of criminals filling the grandstands and betting rings.

The reality, however, is far different. For every Tony Mokbel in the industry there are literally thousands of law-abiding, tax-paying citizens. Racing's practitioners run the full socio-economic spectrum; captains of industry rub shoulders with university students, the fashionistas with knockabouts from the bush, celebrities from the sport and entertainment world with suburban tradies and housewives. And that's half its appeal, part of its magic. Racing is a great leveller; I've seen the most unassuming Joe and Josephine Average enjoy unbelievable success through horse ownership. And I've seen some of Australia's wealthiest individuals humbled, reduced to mug punters by racing's fickle fortunes.

* * *

Someone asked me why I stopped training as abruptly as I did and it was because I could see the writing on the wall. My clients were getting old with me and were either falling off the perch or had stopped buying yearlings. Some of the clients I did still have were struggling to pay their training fees, and when the fees don't get paid, it becomes an impossible feat to keep a stable going. Unlike most of the other old trainers, I didn't have a son or daughter to pass the baton to. I never encouraged my kids to follow in my footsteps — there's too much instability, and no money in it anyway.

When I look back on my life, I would have to say that the journey has been interesting and eventful. I have met a hell of a lot of nice people along the way and I like to think I have done a bit for the Racing Industry. I was responsible for the introduction of pre-sale x-rays of yearlings' joints and knees, was one of the first advocates for Night and Sunday Racing, and was one of the first to offer the chance to 'race horses with nice people' back in 1987, that is, racing partnerships.

My biggest regret is that I didn't spend more time with my son in his formative years and he ended up committing suicide at the age of twenty-four. I think about it nearly every day. I also wonder what might have been if I had finished my law degree and gone into politics. But there is no point in having regrets — it doesn't change anything.

I have been lucky enough to have trained some champions, many of which I chose myself at yearling sales over the years. These horses will forever be woven in to the rich tapestry of the racing industry, and the legacy of some (like Redoute's Choice and now Toorak Toff) will live on for many years to come through their careers as Sires. Over my years in racing I've felt the exhilaration of the highest highs, and the despair of the lowest lows, and it's all added up to what has been a *colourful* career to say the least!

If I could offer one piece of advice to anyone reading this book — it would be 'DON'T GET OLD.'

Unfortunately, that is exactly what happened to me. Nothing works as well as it used to, but in particular, my memory. I can remember what happened fifty years ago, but can't remember what happened yesterday, which does have some redeeming features in that I can watch the same movie I saw a few weeks ago and enjoy it even more the second or third time around because I've forgotten most of it!

In 2014, I noticed that my once confident stride that was infamously fast was becoming more of a shuffle. I also noticed that my short-term memory was getting even worse — though I have always been forgetful. For years my least favourite expression has been 'don't you remember Rick?' because in most cases I didn't.

Upon going to the doctor and having a multitude of tests I was diagnosed with Normal Pressure Hydrocephalus. It is essentially when the valve that regulates spinal fluid in the brain is damaged and no longer flushes out the correct amount, the consequences of which result in problems with balance and short-term memory.

This condition, according to the doctors, may have been caused or exacerbated by a kick to the head by a mad horse twenty years earlier. I can no longer remember which horse (there have been a few), but I like to think that it was a good horse — it makes it a little easier to justify the condition.

I have just turned seventy-eight and in the last year or so both my memory and my balance when walking has gotten much worse. My long-term memory is still good, but I struggle to remember inconsequential events from yesterday. I'm hoping this book will be a lasting legacy, and that, for the most part, the racing industry pundits, the punters and the race-going public remember my contribution to racing as a positive one. I like to think that over the years, I've managed to give back a little to the industry that gave me — a thirty-seven-year old punter with no racing blood at all — nearly forty years in this great game.

I had a wild ride, with triumphant highs and crushing lows but through the foul luck and outrageous fortune I stayed true to who I am — unapologetically opinionated, politically incorrect and honest to a fault.

And as the great Frank Sinatra said, I did it my way!